Praise for
The Long Grief Journey

"*The Long Grief Journey* offers co[...] meaningful life after a great loss, [...] feel. Because it is written by ther[...] this book helps disentangle feelings that may currently be overwhelming and addresses so many questions that grieving people have."

—Mary-Frances O'Connor, PhD, author of *The Grieving Brain: The Surprising Science of How We Learn from Love and Loss*

"When I picked up my copy of *The Long Grief Journey* I didn't even need to put on my reading glasses to see that they were stating in large print so many questions I always have about grief, along with exercises to do and shared stories from fellow grievers. *The Long Grief Journey* is a book that should be in the library of everyone who deals with grief, either as someone who is bereaved or as a professional."

—Jan Warner, author of *Grief Day by Day: Simple Practices and Daily Guidance for Living with Loss*

"For those whose grief is long and unrelenting, this book offers validation and normalization of the pervasive sense of loss and the depression that may accompany it. Pamela and Bradie's comprehensive study of the grieving process explores the many ways long-term grief can holistically impact one's life, deplete emotional resources, and contribute to serious mental health issues. The authors present concrete, practical advice in a loving, compassionate, and constructive manner, encouraging the bereaved to live a life with meaning and purpose while honoring their loved ones. What a beautiful gift of hope to those grieving and a valuable resource for those seeking to support them."

—Claire Aagaard, grief counselor and
author of *When a Child Dies: A Hopeful Healing
Guide for Surviving the Loss of a Child*

"A compassionate and comprehensive look at long term grief, with practical, everyday examples of self-help exercises to aid in coping. Blair and Hansen bring clarity to the complicated processes involved in grieving, especially for those for whom grieving is unresolved and prolonged. A warm balm for those in pain."

—Elizabeth Seward MD

"This book accomplishes a rare feat—addressing from its title page to its final chapter the often overlooked but pervasive experience of prolonged unresolved grief that is inherent in the human condition. It draws upon the authors own personal journeys confronting loss and prolonged grief and integrates the work of highly regarded authors in the humanities, psychology, psychiatry, as well as the views of mental health practitioners and educators.

In so doing, it provides critical insights and guidance on how to cope with the greatest challenge a human being can ever face— the unexpected loss of a person we deeply love."

—Ronald B. Miller PhD, author of *Facing Human Suffering: Psychology and Psychotherapy as Moral Engagement*

"*The Long Grief Journey* tackles many topics that are often difficult to talk about and face when it comes to grief. This book's treatment of the theme of regret stands out as a profound contribution to the field."

—Michael Conforti PhD, author and founder and director of The Assisi Institute

THE
LONG
GRIEF
JOURNEY

How Long-Term Unresolved
Grief Can Affect Your Mental Health
and What to Do about It

PAMELA D. BLAIR, PHD,
and BRADIE MCCABE HANSEN, MA

Published by Sourcebooks
P.O. Box 4410, Naperville, Illinois 60567–4410
(630) 961-3900
sourcebooks.com

Library of Congress Cataloging-in-Publication Data
Names: Blair, Pamela D, author. | McCabe Hansen, Bradie, author.
Title: The long grief journey : how long-term unresolved grief can affect
your mental health and what to do about it / Pamela D. Blair and Bradie
McCabe Hansen, M.A.
Description: Naperville, Illinois : Sourcebooks, [2023] | Includes
bibliographical references and index. | Summary: "There is an idea in
Western society that grieving for a loved one should only last six
months to a year. But those who have felt this loss know that the
grieving process continues silently for much longer. This book is for
the people who have experienced loss and who by all appearances seem to
have "moved on"-but internally they bear the sometimes-crippling weight
of sadness and longing for their loved one. Written by grief experts,
The Long Grief Journey is a much-needed resource that includes
exercises, journal prompts, and introduces rituals that aid the bereaved
as they learn to live with loss"-- Provided by publisher.
Identifiers: LCCN 2022026556 (print) | LCCN 2022026557
(ebook) | (trade paperback) | (adobe pdf) | (epub)
Subjects: LCSH: Grief. | Bereavement. | Loss (Psychology)
Classification: LCC BF575.G7 B528 2023 (print) | LCC BF575.G7 (ebook) |
DDC 155.9/37--dc23/eng/20220628
LC record available at https://lccn.loc.gov/2022026556
LC ebook record available at https://lccn.loc.gov/2022026557

Printed and bound in Canada.
MBP 10 9 8 7 6 5 4 3 2 1

Contents

Authors' Note on Confidentiality

Throughout *The Long Grief Journey* you will read excerpts, quotes, and stories that were gleaned from interviews conducted solely for the purpose of writing this book, and clinical material taken from the decades of therapeutic practice from both Pam's and Bradie's careers. Some people allowed us to use their first names while others wished to use an alternate name. This was always honored. In the case of clinical material, some people gave permission to use their stories and read the content before it was published. Some vignettes are a combination of several people's stories that reflect similar themes, and details are changed enough that specific people are not recognizable.

Introduction

WHY DID WE WRITE THIS BOOK?

Does the world need another book about grief and loss? The answer is a wholehearted "Yes!" This is based on a combined forty years of experience in our therapy practices where we often heard our clients say "I thought I'd feel better by now" after the loss of a loved one.

We wrote *The Long Grief Journey* because there are few non-clinical books that address those who are experiencing the continued challenges of grieving that go beyond the usual expectations for recovery—and what exactly is recovery? Although many grievers want a quick fix to their pain, our position is that healing from grief has no specific timeline, and that the challenging effects of grief can extend far into one's life to varying degrees.

Redefining a meaningful life years after the loss of a loved one can create ongoing physical, social, psychological, and spiritual challenges. The international best-selling classic on sudden loss and coping with grief, *I Wasn't Ready to Say Goodbye* (coauthored by Brook Noel and Pamela D. Blair), was written because the authors identified a desperate need for a book on the *sudden loss* of a loved one. *I Wasn't Ready to Say Goodbye* deals very effectively with the challenges and difficulties of the first and second years of grieving but only briefly touches upon what happens when you're further down the road.

The Long Grief Journey is for those caught in the grip of ongoing grief and its long-term effects. This has been called many things, including but not limited to: complicated grief, traumatic grief, complex bereavement, prolonged grief, extended grief, abnormal grief, exaggerated grief, and pervasive grief disorder. Throughout this book we will primarily use the term *long-term grief* to envelop a greater number of those experiencing the ongoing pain of grief without having to necessarily stay within the borders of the diagnostic categories.

How long is too long for you to grieve? What does "moving on" look like for you? These are the big questions, aren't they? Basically, it depends on who you ask.

WHO IS THIS BOOK FOR?

This book is for the person who is careful not to open up to people again because the pain of loss has all but cauterized the delicate veins carrying love to their heart. It is for those who have found a new partner and enjoy love and companionship but have tucked away the pain of still loving their deceased beloved who they feel they cannot talk about anymore for fear of making others uncomfortable. We are reaching out to those who feel as though they are in an alien landscape walking among strangers, alone in the continued oppression of grief, having maybe given up on the idea of climbing out from under it or are unsure of the value of doing so.

This book is also for those who, by all appearances, seem to have "moved on." They're going to work, carrying out their responsibilities, showing up for important life events, yet they quietly bear the weight of their sadness and longing for their loved one. Maybe holidays are especially difficult, and while they might do their best to "make it nice" for others, internally they experience little joy or peace. We're talking to the person whose creative energies have all but dried up since the passing of their loved one, their urge to create suppressed by the loss of their beloved audience or muse.

WHAT DO WE MEAN BY LONG-TERM GRIEF AND THE LONG JOURNEY?

It is our view that recovery from grief does not often occur within the two months, six months, or twelve months following the loss of a loved one. For many people we've spoken to, the second year is often described as surprisingly difficult because the beginning of year two somehow projects an invisible line that marks the expectation of: "You should feel better by now. You went through all the firsts and it's time to move on, get back to life."

Close to three million people die in the United States every year. Imagine that with each death there is at least one person, but likely up to nine people, who are directly and significantly impacted by the death, leading to acute grief symptoms for an extended period of time. Statistics indicate between 10 and 20 percent of those grieving go on to experience complications with grief. No age group is immune from long-term grief, although data suggests the elderly suffer from long-term grief at higher rates given the likelihood of the loss of a life partner.

HOW DO I USE THIS BOOK?

The Long Grief Journey is designed to be a companion for you on your passage through grief and promises to help educate, support, and coach you to rekindle a desire to live a productive, meaning-filled life and to relate to grief in a different way.

The Long Grief Journey will illustrate that you are not alone, and that there are common bonds tying us all together as we walk on the road toward healing. There is no right or wrong way to read this book, but we suggest you keep a journal nearby to write down your thoughts and feelings about what you're reading. There are prompts at the end of each chapter that ask you to engage with the material directly and make a plan to utilize the suggestions that resonate with you.

The Long Grief Journey begins with our own stories and describes where we are now, from four years to almost thirty years after the loss of our loved ones. We then go on to address the effects of long-term grief on a life, particularly in areas to do with emotions, behaviors, relationships, and health. We also talk about some of the overlap between long-term grief and other mental health conditions, like post-traumatic stress disorder (PTSD), depression, and anxiety. Many people either worry about themselves or choose to respond to others' worries for them, and some wonder if there's something wrong with them. We talk about these concerns and when it makes sense to get help. We also speak to many of the difficult obstacles that appear on the long journey of healing and the potential effects of those obstacles.

We then go on to address specific themes that are related to long-term grief. You will find examples that likely resonate with your own story, and you will see how some have traversed their own long journey and how some are navigating the rough terrain now. Specific routines, rituals, and exercises are offered in each chapter with the hope that you will find something of use, no matter where you are on the grief journey.

The Appendix (page 358) addresses pragmatic issues like when to see a doctor and how to select a style of therapy. We also share a list of websites that can be great resources should you choose to pursue therapy, peer support, or simply want to engage in more ways with your grief and healing.

ARE THERE ANY BENEFITS TO ENVISIONING A LESS PAINFUL FUTURE?

Yes, but only when you're ready. Moving forward into a life filled with meaning and wisdom gained is possible no matter how far into the grieving process you are. We believe this deeply, or we would not have written this book. We know it's hard. It may even feel impossible at times. But like the hero in any hero's journey tale, if you can access even the smallest degree of bravery still lingering in your tired soul, it *is* possible to reclaim your birthright to live life fully. In *The Long Grief Journey*, you will find support to face the challenges lurking around corners, and you will learn ways to integrate and make meaning from the loss of your loved one. A first step is letting go of the shoulds that you've accumulated around what you thought long-term grief entails. You're on what might feel like a long trek up a mountain of shoulds. When you crest Mount Should and release the shame and burden associated with getting "back to normal," you have an opportunity to look back from where you've come and gaze forward toward the horizon, with its new possibilities for living.

Our Stories

Some kinds of sea stars can regenerate an entire body
from a lost arm, this because they're able to house
most of their vital organs in their arms. I want to
believe that something whole and new can come from
a broken thing.

Sheryl St. Germain, author of *50 Miles*

It would be near impossible to write a book about long-term grief without having experienced it. We offer our stories to let you know that we are on the journey with you, learning, growing, and stretching as we go.

PAM'S STORY

My personal story of grief begins with my father's and grandmother's deaths, followed by other significant family members, including my mother, and later on my sister and my nephew. But the one that triggered a lingering and painful grief recovery was the sudden death of my son's father, and my daughter Aimee's stepfather, almost thirty years ago.

Have I "moved on" from George's death? In many ways I have. I married again in 1984 to my husband, Steve. I continued my education; was ordained an interfaith minister; published a newsletter; helped to create valuable spiritual and psychological programs for Wainwright House, an alternative educational institute in Rye, New York; lectured nationwide; appeared on TV and radio; dabbled more in theater; became the coauthor of *I Wasn't Ready to Say Goodbye* and two other books; was awarded a PhD; and opened a successful private psychotherapy practice. On paper, as they say, it looked like I had moved on. But had I?

Taking action and resuming life as I did meant putting one foot in front of the other—much of the taking action part was inspired by the loss of George. I marched through each day using busyness to keep from looking too deeply into the wounded eyes of my young son, mindful of how much my daughter was also struggling. Work and dedication to what I loved helped me. I gave what support I could to the children—some days. And with all that the grief continued, a sharp thread weaving its way into the fabric of my life for years.

One of the most difficult things is not having Ian's father sitting beside me, watching our son become a musical theater actor and director much like his father. The experience of seeing him on stage continues to be a combination of pride and longing. If only George were here to see how successful his son is and bask in Ian's achievements with me. The list of if-onlys is a long one and continues to this day. If only he had seen Ian graduate, marry the woman he loves, become a father for the first time, grow into a man his father would be proud of. How his stepdaughter, Aimee, grew into a strong woman and brought a child into her life even if these events only created another experience of grief.

Am I still triggered by life events I can only wish we shared? Yes. Am I different than you? Yes and no. Am I profoundly sad from time to time? Yes and no. Have I created a life with a wonderful new man who shares in some of my son's and daughter's life events? Yes. Do I still see the sadness in my son's eyes and how much he looks like his father? Of course. Would Aimee have had a different life with George in it? Yes, but that's her story to tell.

Creating a future after profound loss has different definitions for each of us. As I look back, I've realized that loss has been a catalyst for creating meaning in my life. It's meant putting feet to the ground and making meaning wherever I can. Perhaps my story and the excerpts from the stories you'll read about in this book will inspire you to author your own definition of grief recovery within a context that works for you as you discover as I did...what can I do now?

BRADIE'S STORY

The first time I experienced grief of my own and consciously witnessed it in others was when I was nine years old and my paternal grandfather died. Since then, I've lost my maternal grandparents, my paternal grandmother, my stepmother's father, and a dear friend. None of these were easy losses to bear, but it was the loss of my mother that knocked me down for a long time, and in many ways, I am still recovering.

On Easter in 2017, I found out my mom was dead. The medical examiner said she'd been dead for several days by the time she was found, but without an autopsy the exact time is anyone's guess.

Her death had followed nights of dreams and signs I received that I couldn't decipher. What good are symbolic communications from your psyche or from God if we can't figure them out, or if the only thing we do with them is say, "Something is happening, but I don't know what?" Why didn't I know my mom was alone, waiting to be found and cared for?

I feel certain I could write a whole book just about the experience leading up to and following my mother's death. It has shaped, and will continue to shape my life. Not a day goes by that I don't think about her at the very least, but usually it's more than that. Usually, it's something I see in the mirror. My mother's death and the circumstances surrounding her death, they left a mark. Certainly on my face. I look different now than I did before. I can see it in my own eyes. As much as certain physical experiences of grief have subsided, what remains is an imprint. When I look at myself I see someone who has seen something, many things, that can't be unseen. My mother's death made me grow up and into a person who cannot deny or minimize the crippling power of emotional pain and grief. It burst my heart open. I've noticed my compassion for people has grown exponentially. I've also noticed a closer tie to heartache.

My mother's death has also left what seems to be a permanent mark on my nervous system. There are some things I could do, but struggled through before she died, that I simply cannot do now. It feels as though certain nerves were cauterized. The nerves that allowed me to engage in small talk and go to social gatherings where you have to chitchat—they're totally gone. I've noticed an increased need to be alone. Since my mother's death, I've also noticed some physical effects I consider to be part of an inflammatory response, especially to do with arthritis. I've been learning about many ways to manage and metabolize stress so it doesn't wreak havoc on my body, a body that needs to move and work to feel okay.

In the year following my mother's death, I, like Pam, put one foot in front of the other and made myself live. But at times it was very difficult because I could not sleep. And I mean I really couldn't sleep. I don't remember what I thought about or what I did, but I remember realizing it wasn't safe to drive, and I wondered if I was going to have to seek out medical intervention. Around the same time, I bought a floor loom a friend was selling. I'd wanted to learn to weave on a loom and this was my chance. My tank full of coffee, my weaving teacher came over one day to show me how to set up my loom. I was exhausted but was motivated by a deep urge to learn an old craft. That night, I had to begin the process of threading all 738 heddles. I had to draw an individual thread through one tiny hole, over and over and over again. I got about half done that first night, and you know what? I slept the whole night through. The next night I threaded the remaining heddles, and the same thing happened. I slept. Ever since then, I've not had a bout of insomnia that even comes close to what I experienced then.

From there I regained some strength and my bearings, and I started the long process of moving through my grief. I worked more in my clinical practice. I taught children fiber art and craft at our local elementary school. I parented, partnering with my husband in the hard work of running a house. I did all the stuff. And in retrospect, that helped. I willed myself forward, and when I struggled, I relied on my therapist, my acupuncturist, close family and friends, and nature to help me through. I still ache from the loss of my mother. Certain holidays and anniversaries remain difficult, but I am learning new ways to make meaning in those moments. I hope throughout this book you will find ideas and ways to make meaning for yourself after the momentous experience of losing someone you love.

2

Understanding the Emotional and Physical Effects of Long-Term Grief

Your absence has gone through me
Like thread through a needle.
Everything I do is stitched with its color.

W. S. Merwin, poet, "Separation"

You've survived the early pain, the initial grief, and the required life-changing readjustments of the first two years or so since you lost your loved one. As you've already experienced, the first year is generally an emotional journey: coping with the initial impact of loss, gaining your footing after the shock, and all the firsts without your loved one, including birthdays, anniversaries, and holidays. A lot is packed into that first roller-coaster year where experiencing the pain of grief is an everyday reality and simple or normal life things can seem like herculean tasks.

Now perhaps you're wondering where you are on the long journey of grief. In general, reorganizing and reexamining one's life characterizes the second year. This is when the reality of the loss hits particularly hard and you realize you've been forever changed. You can no longer pretend life is normal or deny your loved one is gone. Unfortunately, you may be feeling pressure from others (or yourself) to return to some semblance of your past self. If you've been grieving a spouse some may ask, "When are you going to move from that house? Isn't it too much for you now?" and "When are you going to start dating?" Maybe you've already donated their clothes, given things away to family and friends, repainted and repurposed rooms, or relocated. Yet, you still feel the need to get on with life in a bigger way. You might have made some plans to move forward, but something doesn't feel right.

Thus begins the long journey that has no expected arrival time. Your luggage is heavy and carrying its weight is a challenge. When your recovery timeline doesn't match societal expectations, it can make readjustment and assimilation of grief even more difficult. When you're still aching and unsure of how to move forward, it can feel like you have to put on armor every morning, just to face the world. Maybe you're feeling worried about some of the ways grief still has you in its clutches. You know, or loved ones have told you, that some of the things you're doing (or not doing) are not what is typical so long after a loved one has died. Shame and the desire to hide creeps in, which can exacerbate your pain.

WHAT IS ASSIMILATED GRIEF?

The first thing I want you to know about beginning the process of full assimilation of grief into your being, is that you can't "speed" it up. To assimilate, and integrate grief it needs to be: #1: digested; #2: metabolized; #3: distributed throughout your life.

Tim VanDerKamp, life coach

Grief is part of the human experience. Responses to grief and ideas of how people "should" recover from it have changed over time. There isn't a culture on the planet that doesn't have its own rituals, rites, and expectations surrounding mourning, bereavement, grief, and recovery. But how do we know when there's a problem? This is a tricky conversation and is tied to a much bigger cultural theme—trying to capture human emotion in a one-size-fits-all mold. However, there are steps to take that can help you live your life with openness, fullness, and freedom, while holding on to the memory and influence of your loved one.

Assimilation means that following the death of your loved one, you're able to carry on with your life to some degree while holding space for your love and loss. You're able to engage in things that bring you enjoyment, and you can think of your loved one without those thoughts taking over your mood. You're able to talk about the person with others and move through important dates or anniversaries with less distress. You're able to work, care for yourself, care for others, and participate in life. You've been able to make necessary changes to your home and lifestyle. Your life has stretched and adjusted to reflect your experience of loss while you continue to live and share your gifts with yourself and those around you. You do not force your feelings down or forget the life you shared with your loved one and have begun to open up to the full power of the life experience.

David Kessler, renowned writer and speaker on grief and loss, refers to the sixth stage of grief: making meaning. Kessler writes,

People often think there is no way to heal from severe loss. I believe that is not true. You heal when you can remember those who have died with more love than pain, when you find a way to create meaning in your own life in a way that will honor theirs. It requires a decision and a desire to do this, but finding meaning is not extraordinary, it's ordinary. It happens all the time, all over the world.

The call to meaning and to fully living your life is where the river wants to flow on this long journey. Discovering where your blocks are will help you discover what paths you will need to take.

THE EFFECTS AND EXPRESSION OF LONG-TERM GRIEF

Grief, when not allowed to run its course, turns into dissatisfaction with all that life presents. It prevents us from living and embracing life.

Genevieve King, psychotherapist

Everyone is different when it comes to how long-term grief is felt and expressed. The experience can be fluid or rigid, frequent or episodic, quiet or disruptive. The effects of long-term grief over time can seem like mood changes or hide in fatigue and chronic stress. Perhaps you've noticed (or others have said) that you become much more irritable at certain times of the year. Maybe these times correspond with something related to your deceased loved one, and your irritation is actually a signal that you need something or some kind of support to help you get through it.

Generally, the effects of long-term grief fall into four categories: emotional, behavioral, relational, and physical. Getting clear on where you feel stuck can help you make use of this book and identify specific things you can do to achieve some relief. Here is a checklist to help you quickly identify where you might be struggling emotionally:

The Emotional Effects

The emotional effects of long-term grief are the challenges people contend with when trying to live their lives after loss. This ongoing emotional pain often prompts people to consult with a therapist or their doctor.

- Persistent and ongoing yearning for your loved one
- Continued intense sorrow and emotional pain
- Overwhelming guilt
- Ongoing review or reliving of the details surrounding your loved one's death
- Preoccupation with your deceased loved one
- Difficulty with acceptance of their death

- Elevated anger and irritation
- A wish to die in order to be with deceased loved one
- Loss of personal identity
- Difficulty achieving any positive mood

The Behavioral Effects

The behavioral expressions of many of these emotions are often what family members, friends, and coworkers mention when they express concern for your well-being. This could be described as going through the motions of life without really being *in* life.

- Difficulty or refusal to give away items that belonged to your loved one
- Excessive alcohol or drug use
- Reckless behaviors that may put your own life in danger
- Difficulty pursuing interests or pleasurable experiences
- Adherence to rigid routine with little to no flexibility
- Distractibility and lack of focus
- Loss of temper or frequent and intense frustration

The Relational Effects

Relationally, you may feel guilty for approaching opportunities for new love. Or maybe you continue to dread or avoid the holidays or anniversaries that remind you of your loved one.

- Avoidance of people connected to your deceased loved one
- Avoidance or aversion to being with other people socially
- Difficulty trusting other people
- Chronic feelings of aloneness and isolation
- Bitterness toward others who seem happy
- Jealousy
- Resentment that interferes with connection

The Physical Effects

It is difficult to feel okay in the mind and heart when the body is aching, and health conditions interfere with movement and activity, which can further exacerbate the problem of withdrawing from activities and people that were once enjoyed. Here are some typical, problematic physical effects present in long-term grief:

- Troubles with sleep—either sleeplessness or overwhelming urge to sleep
- Significant weight gain or loss
- Heart conditions
- Inflammation
- Body aches
- Blood pressure problems
- Headaches
- Side effects of alcohol and drug abuse

POST-TRAUMATIC STRESS DISORDER AND LONG-LASTING GRIEF

One morning, I woke up very early. I felt an urgency to call her and wondered if it was her reaching out to me. I called and called, but there was no answer, so I went over there. When I opened the door to her apartment, I could see into her bedroom—it looked like she was going to get up for the day, but she just went back down. I experienced a lot of trauma in regard to finding her that way on her bed. I knew she was not going to survive cancer, but whatever took her was sudden. It took intense therapy to get a handle on my feelings of panic.

Amanda

The sudden, unexpected death of a loved one is one of the most common causes of grief complicated by post-traumatic stress disorder. People who suffer with PTSD have been exposed to things considered to be outside the realm of typical human experience. While death is a completely normal and natural part of life, there are many examples of deaths that crack open the way *things are supposed to go.* And there are so many ways people are exposed to situations for which they are wholly unprepared and have no inner map showing how to get from Point A: initial impact, to Point Z: metabolize the impact.

PTSD is marked by reliving a traumatic event, avoiding reminders of the event, and changes in how you experience yourself and other people. That sentence alone captures the emotional tearing of post-traumatic stress; it's a virtual tug of war between reliving and avoidance. The feeling of being in a constant state of hyperarousal is also very common and is expressed though anxiety, fear, apprehension, and panic. The pendulum swings between avoidance and yearning, a disruption in living relationships while wishing for your deceased loved one to be back, and frequently feeling unsafe while bracing for impact.

Consider these typical symptoms often seen at school in children and adolescents: time-management challenges, issues to do with concentration and organization, emotional and behavioral outbursts, irritability, fidgetiness, and regressive behaviors. Sound like attention deficit disorder to you? Or these: anxieties, phobias, separation fears, emotional overload, hypersensitivity, and avoidance. Children who have experienced grief complicated by trauma may show one or more of these symptoms, even years after their loss. Can you see how a child could be diagnosed with anxiety or depression or attention deficit disorder if an evaluator, doctor, or therapist didn't do the digging required to find out what a child might be responding to?

For adults, unaddressed traumatic grief can evolve over time into a life that looks extremely busy. Can you relate to this? In a culture that worships at the feet of productivity and individualism, it's easy to create a life where you avoid thinking and feeling. But, maybe you've seen that grief demands attention and if your mind refuses to process it, your body will pick up the slack.

Struggling with visual flashbacks or the experience of being triggered by smells, sounds, and images is commonly reported by those with PTSD. Intense startle responses and hypervigilance over time can take on a life of their own, creating spoken and unspoken rules of engagement in life and at home.

Susan found her husband in their home after he had died by suicide. Brokenhearted and thrown into parenting grieving children by herself, she went on to simply manage. Managing for Susan looked like taking precautions to minimize any possibility of being overstimulated, startled, or overcome by her visual senses. She was very careful with what she viewed on television and in theaters, what she read, and what she listened to in order to avoid being flooded with overwhelming imagery. The goal: never to relive the moment she opened the door to find her husband. For those she loved, being with her felt like walking on eggshells. At the same time, she was incredibly strong and immensely fragile. All who loved her knew they had to stay within the boundaries of quietude that kept her feeling safe in the world. Jon Kabat-Zinn writes,

> *Chronic anxiety can also fuel severe patterns of what is called experiential avoidance, in which people attempt to avoid at all cost any thoughts, feelings, memories, or physical sensations that might cause distress. This is tantamount to holding themselves back from life itself, out of fear of their own inner experience.*

Many with PTSD struggle with nightmares and intrusive

thoughts. They may want to isolate and have no interest in connecting with others. The emotional energy cost of tending to relationships can feel like too much, resulting in isolation that looks like depression, avoidance that looks like anxiety. It all turns in on itself, creating a scenario where one is potentially left on their own, either physically or emotionally, to manage themselves as best they can. It becomes a matter of protecting the nerves and the senses, but the broken heart continues bleeding.

MAGICAL THINKING

> *I got so mad at my cat for scratching me I told him I*
> *hated him. He didn't come home that night and never*
> *came back. My parents think another animal killed him.*
> *I hate myself because it's my fault something happened*
> *to him.*
>
> Jason, age nine

How many of us can remember moments like this from our childhood where our feelings were so strong, and so overwhelming, it felt as though they'd burst out of our little bodies? Sometimes these feelings are wrapped around excitement and anticipation. Sometimes love. Sometimes fear. Often when children have powerful feelings of anger, they wish for things to happen, or have thoughts that describe their anger in stark detail. Kids might think things like, "I hate you." "I never want to see you again," or "I'll do what I want because you don't know anything!"

It's natural for children to have these feelings and to feel a lot of turmoil about them, because the feelings themselves are experienced as powerful entities that can control the physical world and *make things happen*. This is the definition of magical thinking, which generally occurs between the ages of two and eight. Children are, over the span of these years, figuring out many things, including gaining independence, sorting out initiative and guilt, and over time, developing competency and self-esteem. This is a lot to do, all the while learning how to make sense of cause and effect and of tolerating being separated from loved ones and caregivers.

Enter the loss of a significant loved one. In general, children don't have enough life experience, or the capacity for abstract thought, to understand they are in fact not responsible for things that happen. The reality that life is unfair, unpredictable, and devastating at times is difficult to accept. This can lead to overwhelming guilt and a sense of burden that is too much to bear. In the minds of children, guilt can become an overwhelming burden that is hard to describe to the people who love them. Unfortunately, they often wrestle with these thought beasts on their own, making their way out of the weeds as best they can.

This developmentally predictable way of thinking also causes children to believe that if they wish hard enough or behave in certain ways, they might be able to bring back their loved one, feel close to them somehow, or be released from the pain they are feeling. Imagine the child who will only wear their father's shirt for fear that if she takes it off, he won't be able to find her when he comes back.

Children aren't the only ones who have magical thoughts about death. Imagine a person who never utters a negative word about their deceased loved one, fearful they will be overheard from the grave and will devastate their spirit. The ability to process the death of a whole person is therefore stunted because it is not possible to tell the truth. People as a rule try to make sense out of the world and therefore connect cause-and-effect events that actually have nothing to do with one another. We see this in superstitions and ritualized behaviors before certain events or times of day.

At times when what life throws at us is overwhelming, we might feel stuck replaying the what-if record. "What if I left five minutes later and was home when my husband had a heart attack?" "What if I hadn't fallen asleep and heard the phone ring and picked up my son before he drove home on icy roads?" "What if I intervened sooner and gotten my mom into the hospital before she was overcome by disease?" What if? Our thinking goes round and round, getting stuck on the same bump in the road every time, which is why we must, at some point, tolerate and face the pain and reality of our loved one's death.

QUESTIONS YOU MAY ASK YOURSELF

Depression or grief? How can I tell?

For many years, researchers have been trying to sort out whether complicated grieving is distinguishable from other mental health diagnoses, especially depression, and is responsive to unique and diagnosis-specific treatment options. While this question and others like it were being examined, authors of the *DSM-V* (*Diagnostic and Statistical Manual of Mental Disorders-Fifth Edition*) identified a working diagnosis called persistent complex bereavement disorder. In discussion about the difference between depression and complicated grieving, authors point to a key distinction and it is in how people view themselves. When depression is the primary condition, people tend to be much more self-critical or struggle with self-loathing. Complex grief is marked by self-critical thoughts that are more tied to the deceased and might be due to their evaluation of the relationship itself. Regret and guilt are emotions that color self-evaluation in long-term grief. Also, while both depression and long-term grief might be marked by a preoccupation with death, with grief the longing for death is a result of a deep wish to be with their loved one. With depression, people struggle with day-to-day emotional pain and want relief. This pain is not limited to the loss of a loved one but rather is experienced daily as a persistent state affecting most areas of life. Researchers found that the differences between those suffering from complications of grief as opposed to depression and other mental health conditions are distinct and specific enough that a new diagnosis was added to the revised edition of the *DSM-V*; it is called Prolonged Grief Disorder.

Keeping those distinguishing factors in mind, if you struggled with depression before the loss of your loved one, it is likely your loss only made your personal experience of depression worse. The opposite is also true. As author Alan Wolfelt puts it, "Depression overlaid on top of grief can take normal and necessary symptoms of grief and make them more severe and debilitating. Also, clinical depression can make grief last longer than it might otherwise and even worsen. Sometimes clinical depression inhibits your ability to actively mourn."

It is also possible that the impact of your loss has brought into view an underlying depression you were otherwise managing on your own, and for which you now need help. As much as the mental health community wants to pinpoint exactly what is going on so practitioners can efficiently and properly help people feel better, there is no denying the lines here are murky. (You will find resources in the Appendix on page 358 that speak to ways to get support and help for depression complicated by grief.)

Why am I so anxious?

Anxiety shows up in various ways and can render you incapable of doing what needs to be done in your life in relation to your healing. Many people we've talked to describe a lingering, powerful surge of anxiety for years following the death of a loved one. As Wolfelt shares, "Anxiety and depression often go hand in hand. In fact, surveys show 60 to 70 percent of people with depression also have anxiety, and half of people with anxiety also have significant depression. They are now thought by many psychologists to be two faces of one condition."

When you think about it, this makes a lot of sense. Even the most flexible of us can struggle if we have to consistently pivot, readjust, and reorient to a new situation. Our biological systems crave safety and regularity. Our nervous systems are wired to get us back to a place of equilibrium, which is why chronic and prolonged stress wreaks such havoc on the body.

The death of a loved one throws equilibrium up in the air and our bodies are left to deal with the consequences. When something terrible happens, our systems naturally react with a fight, flight or freeze response. The loss of a loved one is disorienting, painful and is felt as an impact. For many, shock is involved. For others, ongoing stress and anticipation mark the experience leading up to the loss of someone who may have been struggling with chronic disease or a life-threatening injury. These experiences take people out of a felt sense of stability and can be very overstimulating to the nervous system. Anxiety is the flight response. "Get me out of here!" the body and mind scream in unison.

Your body is doing what it can to regulate itself and feel safe again. Later in this book we provide concrete suggestions for what you can do to help calm your nervous system so you can feel grounded in the here and now.

Another kind of anxiety intimately connected to long-term grief has to do with attachment and is referred to as *separation anxiety*. The pain and fear born from highly stressful and often traumatic separations from caregivers during a person's infancy and childhood can play a large role in how a person grieves in the future. Research has shown separation anxiety is significantly higher in those struggling with complicated, long-term grief than in those with PTSD unrelated to loss. Panic, sensitivity to stress, and anxiety about things to come are also more prevalent in the long-term griever. The heartache of loss and separation in childhood can pave the way for long-term grief to take hold. Is it any wonder that someone who experienced such emotional pain in their young years would struggle with grief in the future?

Tom, a man in his sixties who lost his mother at age five, struggled all his life with issues of abandonment, making relationships with women extremely challenging. He'd had two previous marriages that ended primarily due to his over-possessive tendencies. As he reported, each time his wife left to do errands or even went to other rooms in the house, his anxiety became unbearable and would often result in an abusive tirade. His frantic response to her when she returned would often be, "Where have you been?" or "I couldn't find you. Where did you go?"

When should I seek professional help?

Some may ask: If grief is so normal, and death is just a part of life, why do I have to see a therapist or attend a support group to move on? I should be strong enough to do it myself.

Stop shaming yourself. You don't have to walk this journey alone. Consider this—since humans have been drawing on walls in caves and writing stories on stone, animal skins, and papyrus, there have been stories and images dealing with death and the rituals surrounding it. Humans have always sought out other humans such as tribal elders, sages, shamans, rabbis, imams, healers, priests, medicine workers, therapists, and doctors to help navigate the twists and turns of the road of life. Why would now be any different?

Sometimes people seek out help because others encourage

them to do so after years of not knowing how to help the aggrieved feel better. So, people show up to therapy reluctantly, with the idea they're doing this for other people rather than for themselves. This can have mixed results, but in our experience, people who decide to pursue help on their own get the most out of therapy.

If you've arrived at a place where you know you want to feel better than you do now, perhaps you're ready to pursue help. Maybe you want to feel open to new experiences, to have more hope. Maybe you don't want to feel scared all the time, perhaps you want to enjoy some parts of your life, or you want to recollect your loved one without feeling crushed by memory. You likely have had thoughts about wanting something to be different, but don't know where to start.

Start with hope. Start there—wherever you are on the long journey. That's enough. You don't need to be more specific. Imagine taking one step toward a life that feels better, more comfortable—a life with space for making meaning and gathering the gifts of wisdom earned from all you have been through.

3

Regaining Your Bearings

The Search for Purpose and Meaning

*You do eventually have to withdraw energy from
the deceased and channel it back into something
meaningful.*

Ashley Davis Bush, LICSW, *Transcending Loss*

Have you ever fallen down and checked yourself to see if all of your
limbs are okay? To make sure you're all in one piece? Sometimes
after a fall you realize, "Okay, I need to go to the hospital," while
other times you think, "Wow, that was close; I'd better focus on
what I'm doing." This is in some ways like the grief journey. For
many of us, it takes a long time to figure out that we're still hurting, feeling stuck, and off track, or even completely lost. It makes
sense to take stock, to get some perspective on where you are now.
The following is an exercise created to assist you in evaluating
where you are on the journey to regain your bearings. There are
no wrong answers.

Where Am I on My Grief Journey and in My Life?

- I am _____

  (insert age)

- I am a _____

  (e.g., mother, artist, carpenter, surgeon)

- My _____

  (insert relationship and how many months/years ago they died)

- I think of them each _____

  (minute/day/week/year, etc.)

- I have an especially difficult time on _____

  (holidays, birthdays, anniversaries etc.)

- I am saying yes/no to more things like _____

  (people/activities, etc.)

- I have difficulty with _____

  (e.g., social gatherings, small talk, joy/laughter)

When you're done answering these questions, take the time to write a paragraph or two stating honestly where you are on your grief journey. Everyone's answers will be different—some will write a lot, others just a few sentences. For example, this is how one person responded when asked to complete the exercise: "My mother died six years ago. I talk to her all the time. I feel like sometimes I get very sad and resentful or jealous of others who get to hang out with their parents whenever they want. I wish I had my mom here to be a part of my kids' lives. I feel jealous when I see grandmothers out with their kids and get help and support from them. This jealousy makes me feel bad, so I'm working on that."

WHAT WAS ALL THIS FOR?

People sometimes wonder what the point was when they lose someone precious to them. What was the point of all the love and dedication? The effort, the care and tending to, just to be dealt the incredible blow of loss? The way life goes can feel unbearably unfair, and catastrophically difficult.

Whenever we ask ourselves "What was this is all about?" we are really asking one of the greatest and most perplexing questions ever asked. This question has caused people to raise fists to the sky, wail into pillows, and marvel at the sight of something unbearably beautiful. It's the stuff of philosophy, religion, poetry, art, music, and literature. You may never know what it was all for, but you do know it was about love. Maybe the answer waiting for you is the wisdom you have acquired through your loss and anguish.

> *I believe no matter how much pain we're in, there is something inside of us stronger than the pain. That something allows survivors of the worst tragedies to want to live and tell their stories.*
>
> Pamela D. Blair, *I Wasn't Ready to Say Goodbye*

An acute identity crisis coupled with feelings of relief, yearning, depression, anger, bitterness, regret, and guilt are common visitors to the emotional life of the long-term griever. What you were meant to have with your loved one did not come to pass, or at least not in the way you imagined. Fantasies about retirement with your partner, travel with your friend, hosting your children and grandchildren for holidays, and aging with loved ones were chipped away at over the years. On the walk of life, it might feel as though your path took a sharp left and you were suddenly forced to climb up a long, steep, craggy cliff face only to get to a landing where the pain of loss continued to wait.

The quality and details of the months or years leading up to the loss are varied and nuanced. Some losses occur suddenly and shockingly, while others occur following years of progressive physical and/or mental decline. These stressors on body, mind, spirit, and life make a deep impact and invite grief into the journey before a loved one's death has even occurred.

Healing will involve looking at your story as a whole and a story where you were faced with enormous challenges and decisions, including moments you were proud of and moments you wish you could have done better. Love and guilt, longing and relief, fear and courage, these emotions dance together with you and part of the long journey is the work of making meaning from all of these.

QUESTIONS YOU MAY ASK YOURSELF

I can't relax, ever. My life doesn't come close to what I thought it'd be. How can I trust that it all won't be upended again?

There are different kinds of trust. There's the kind that involves trusting other people and allowing yourself to be vulnerable in the waters of new love and new relationships. This kind of trust is outward focused. It is reliant on how others are and what they do, say, and embody when it comes to their principles and ethics.

There's another kind of trust though, possibly more relevant to this conversation, and that is trusting in the relationship you have with yourself. You've gone through the loss of a loved one and that has likely introduced you to aspects of your heart, your personality, and your constitution you didn't know before. Perhaps, years later, you still marvel at how you've made it through and can pinpoint times when you did things or felt things that were entirely new to you. Stretching into these new aspects adds to the trust you have in yourself to meet whatever happens in the future. Some people say, "I can't love anyone else because I don't trust that the same thing won't happen, and I'll have to go through it all over again." No one can guarantee you won't experience loss and grief again. That's putting the onus of trust in the wrong place. What you're really saying is, "I can't love another person because I don't trust myself and my ability to make it through another loss, so I can't risk it again."

Think back on what you've been through. Maybe you

can identify moments when you could have opened the door, turned the page, floated on a quiet river but forgot that *you* were the person you needed to trust. You were the person to show up for life and to see where your story goes. You were, and still are, a courageous person who can take one step, and then another, into the next chapter of your life, getting to know yourself even more along the way.

It's scary, moving out of the realm of grief into something else. How do I know what's on the other side of it?

After a hard winter, signs of spring start to emerge. It might still be very cold and unpleasant to begin with but the light changes and the air smells different. One might think spring should bring on excitement and hope and relief; it does for many. But for some, there is an intense feeling of being unprepared for the energy required to step back into an active social life after having been cocooned in the warmth of one's home for so many months. The same is often true for emerging from the chrysalis of long-term grieving. It can be scary because the self-made house of protection and soothing must be left behind so a new expression of self can be found. Some wonder if it would be easier to stay in that safe place.

What does this attachment to grieving look like? It could manifest as never expressing an interest in, or wanting, a new partner. It could be reflected in an over-focus on other people and their lives (i.e., a good way to avoid living your own life is to be consumed by someone else's). It could be seen in a tendency to stop or prevent new experiences that might take you out of your comfort zone. And you might be in the habit of succumbing to the pattern of grieving even more when things seem good.

If any of this resonates for you, think of all the ways you have already faced challenges in your life that required bravery and a bit of a "throw caution to the wind" attitude. It's not easy, but like any complicated, amazing creature that emerges from its cocoon, your loss has transformed you. As you opt into active living, you'll be able to see how much you have evolved.

EXERCISES AND RITUALS THAT CAN HELP

WHAT PAGE ARE YOU ON?

It's good to periodically check in with yourself to ask, "How am I?" It's like doing a scan of yourself and taking a moment to reflect on what's coming up. You might take it beyond the rudimentary, "Oh, I'm good" or "I feel like crap all the time." Get specific. It can look something like this:

How Am I Doing?

> I'm really tired a lot.
> I'm doing a lot of things I am so happy about and proud of, but I'm not taking enough time to just be. Everything feels like a job, even the fun stuff.
> I'm eating too many baked goods because they are comforting, but my pants are tight, which is pissing me off.
> Everything is fine in my family, but I was hit with a ball of

sadness yesterday that took me out. I missed my mom so much and this came up because of hearing about how a cousin was with her mom. I felt so much pain, and it made me angry and jealous. I ended up just needing to be by myself most of the day because I couldn't snap out of it. Once I realized that I wasn't actually mad at anyone, and that I was really just sad for what I haven't had in so long, I thought about ways I could take care of that part of me and not judge it. I'm working on that.

> I'm glad winter is coming. I love sitting by the fire and knitting and just hanging around.

You get the idea... Check in, with specifics. It's nice to do this once a month if you can remember to do it. This is so you can keep tabs on the pulse of your own life. We get carried away by all the things of life, and it's easy to get years down the road and wonder, "What happened? How'd I get here?" Taking a periodic pulse of your life keeps you connected with yourself, how you are, and can invite intention when it comes to things that could use some tweaking.

SAYING HELLO AGAIN

Are you ready to let go of some things or ask for help? Make a list of the obligations in your life that you dread doing, such as the yearly staff party, the family reunion, the church market, etc. Often these are activities that used to be enjoyable, but since the death of your loved one they have been overstimulating or too painful. Or maybe these things were always stressful, but you had the extra reserves to do them in the past without too much of a problem.

Next to each item on the list, write the word "hello" if you want to keep this activity in your life or "goodbye" next to those that sap your energy or don't support your journey. Then indicate why they are important to keep doing or why you want to let them go. And finally, if you are going to keep doing them, who can you reach out to for support when you want to participate in them?

This exercise is about building a buttress system to support you as you traverse the bridge into the world of socializing. Maybe you've been doing that already, but one or more of the bridges is made of a wobbly, shredded, unpredictable rope. You are now getting clear with yourself on what you want and what you need. From that sturdier place, you can take the steps you feel ready to take.

ENVISIONING THE FUTURE

You know where you are now, but where you are is not *who* you are. If you'd like to move on but can't envision a way forward, and you're experiencing loss of purpose, this exercise could help. First, try to answer these questions as best you can:

> Where/who would I like to be one year from now?
> Where/who would I like to be two years from now?
> Where/who would I like to be three years from now?

Next, develop a series of incremental steps on paper so you can check things off. It might sound quite simplistic or a little silly; however this step-by-step technique will help you see progress, slowing you down long enough to avoid the anxiety that comes with cognitive overload. For example, let's suppose you would like to be in relationship again after the loss of your spouse or partner:

Step 1

1. Decide if you're going to look for a new relationship in an online dating site or in person.
2. Decision: Online
3. Why: Certain dating sites are safe and secure.

Step 2

1. How will you ascertain which ones are best?
2. Decision: I'll ask a friend who's done it.
3. Why: Because they've had success.

Step 3:

1. Decide what day you want to start the search.
2. Decision: On Saturday night
3. Why: Saturday is when I miss companionship most and I'll wait until the children are asleep so I won't get interrupted.

Step 4:

1. What device will you use to do your search?

2. Decision: My tablet.

3. Why: It's all I have besides my phone.

Step 5:
---

1. How many minutes, hours, days will you search?

2. Decision: Probably one hour each time.

3. Why: So I can be selective and not rush.

Step 6:
---

1. How will you be selective?

2. Decision: I'll take notes and look at them when I'm not tired.

3. Why: Because I don't want to make impulsive decisions when I'm feeling lonely.

Step 7:
---

1. When will you start communicating with the candidates you've selected?

2. Decision: Not sure yet.

3. Why: I need to take it slow, but I do want to move on this.

When you look back on this exercise, you will see that you've taken seven steps toward your goal! Step 8 might be some kind of reward you give yourself. This step-by-step approach can be applied to almost any situation in which you feel stuck or anxious about moving on in your life.

FAITH TRADITIONS AND ACCESSING SUPPORT

If you have a faith tradition you feel connected to and grounded by, this is a great place to start a search for creating your own rituals. The variety and nuanced ways faith traditions differ are so many we cannot touch on them all here. But there are a few things to keep in mind as you approach this process. If your tradition was one of the reasons you were unable to participate in a ceremony following the death of your loved one, you may be experiencing a complicated interlacing of grief experiences. Losing contact with aspects of self and family identity through traditions because they "turn on you" when you need them most due to rules, judgments, ideas about sexuality, or means of death is crushing.

If you are still feeling connected to your faith but alienated from it due to the emotional and relational cutoff that can occur, try reaching out to the more liberal sects of your faith. Unitarian or interfaith ministers are studied in comparative religions and may be a great resource. Hospital chaplains are also able to speak to and honor various faiths. It could be worthwhile to research chaplains in your area to see if there are any who would be willing and able to support you in your process. In that same vein, interfaith chaplains and ministers are steeped in the philosophy that we are all connected through our various spiritual and faith identities and would certainly be able to be a guide on your journey.

HERITAGE CUSTOMS

Many people do not identify much with a faith tradition, but eagerly soak up story, myth, lore, and cultural history from the homes of their ancestors. A great wealth of opportunity exists here to gather ideas, symbols, and images from those areas of your life to infuse your ritual with meaning and relevance tied to your ancestors. Those who feel connected to their ancestors and with their heritage might describe feeling as though there is a link between themselves and those who came before them, a strong river of life and history flowing through their experience now.

If this resonates with you, there are wonderful ways to excavate ritual and ceremonial ideas to incorporate into your process. Your local library, and certainly the internet, will have plenty of resources that speak to the heritage customs relevant to you. And don't limit yourself to one! Some individuals and families share a marvelous intersection of ethnicities, histories, and cultural intricacies that can be combined to support your living process of grief. Inviting any aspects that speak to you into your ceremony will make your process vibrant, grounded, and deeply personal.

CANDLE RITUAL

Candles are used throughout world cultures to symbolize any number of important moments in life. Keeping a light burning in remembrance signifies that the memory of a loved one still lives on and burns bright. It's a ritual that can be comforting, one that promotes reflection and signifies remembrance.

Both religious and nonreligious people burn funeral candles in remembrance of a loved one who has passed away. In fact, for thousands of years, candles have been used at funerals to symbolize the everlasting spirit. When you light your candle, you can offer a meditation, a prayer, or an intention based on your journey, or simply hold a space for the love you have for the one who died. Flameless candles are just as meaningful and are often preferred (and safer), so please feel free to use them if you'd rather.

DAILY JOURNALING

Journaling is a wonderful way to communicate privately with your loved one or with yourself. Ira Progoff is the godfather of the contemporary journal-writing movement and many people have benefited from his discoveries. His best-known classic book, *At a Journal Workshop* (1992), is the basic text and guide to the application of what he called the "intensive journal process," and it is still considered the best, most complete work in the ever-expanding library of journaling guides. Writing in a journal about one's ideas, feelings, and experiences is almost always useful, "but an unstructured journal usually just goes around in circles," Progoff said. "To become a valuable tool of psychological self-care, a journal needs a design that will help a human being answer the question 'What is my life trying to become?'" This is one powerful question to ask on the long journey of grief.

LOGGING YOUR DREAMS

By recording dream experiences, you might gain inspiration for moving on or through a difficult problem—one you normally wouldn't have thought of in waking life. You won't remember every detail, but just start by writing down the bits and pieces you do remember. After a while you can start to analyze what your dreams mean or take your journal to your therapist to discuss.

Take a moment to reflect on what you've just read and ask yourself what you can do now to make meaning out of heartbreak. Do any of these exercises resonate with you? Another question to ask yourself is, "What would my loved one want for me?" Keeping these questions in mind, set an intention for the next important steps on your grief journey.

Where Is Everybody?

My Emotional Support Is Gone

We must seek out other artists of the spirit, new friends
who gradually will help us to find the road to life again,
who will walk the road with us.

Joshua Loth Liebman, author, *Peace of Mind*

On the long journey of grief, infinite pathways exist leading us up the mountain to a different view of life. Depending on who you lost and the implications for your life after that loss, you might feel like you need to continue to process and talk years after their death and occasionally need help with certain pragmatic things. Or, you might not technically need anything, but wish people would simply acknowledge or allow some space for talking about your loved one. Many find aspects of their culture to be stale and depleted when it comes to keeping not just the memory of the deceased alive, but also the continued care of those members of our communities whose lives have been forever changed. Cultures that have strong threads of "pick yourself up by your bootstraps and get on with it" woven into their fabric might miss the mark.

Our view is that this philosophy doesn't have to be so binary. Some have told us that self-pity or wallowing in anything is unacceptable in their family. Perhaps you've been told that you shouldn't complain, that you should stop with the anxiety or depression, as though it's in your control to do so. One woman related to us that her family "had to stay in fight mode to survive and resting or needing anything meant giving up. But this way of growing up made it so that when I lost my best friend, I felt like I had to get through it fast. And society supports that. People don't know how to let grief and life exist at the same time."

THE THING ABOUT CULTURE AND GRIEF

Our culture is just dead enough to not appreciate death. It's deemed to be so upsetting that it's something we can't possibly talk about. So, we operate in clandestine ways. Ultimately, anyone who grieves too long is seen as weak. Oh my god it's been a year! A year is nothing for grief. This essential feeling of loss that human beings are capable of, it's all encompassing when it happens, but we are forced to compartmentalize it.

David O'Leary, psychotherapist

It's important to remember that cultural expressions of how grief and long-term grieving are processed and expressed are fluid, ever evolving—and they are sensitive to the specificities of community. The way things are now are not the way things have always been, no matter where you live or the conditions of your life.

Here is one example: Within the last hundred years, the process of dying was moved from the home to the hospital and hospice facilities. Death went from being a family affair that was supported by community with set forms of ritual to an event housed by outside systems with their own needs and parameters. In addition, over the last several generations, families have become more spread out. It's not uncommon for close family members to see one another once or twice a year, if that. Without a doubt, this has affected the ways in which people collectively grieve and support one another in the years following loss. People do much more on their own, and, as a result, they feel alone in the adaptation to new life circumstances without loved ones. It's possible that someone living among close friends in one state may not have one person connected to their old life. It's easy to see that a vacuum might develop where individuals have to fend for themselves in an effort to rebuild a life after loss.

It would be simple to just call these changes in our social fabric "bad" or "unhealthy," or suggest we have to "go back to how things were." But really, it's not that simple and doesn't do much to address the problem at hand. We need a way to be with grief and talk about grief that is not pathologizing, pressure-inducing, shaming, or inhumane. We need to bring into the light the fact that grief affects a whole life for the remainder of that life. This fact is neither good nor bad. It just is. In all of our evolution we haven't come up with ways to stay deeply tied to our humanity as we grieve and support the griever in a way that is outside the private sector.

QUESTIONS YOU MAY ASK YOURSELF

It continues to be difficult to talk about my feelings or need for help because so much time has passed. How can I verbalize those needs?

What you wish for from others is sometimes hard to name. Age and life circumstances shape where this loss is felt over the long term. For those of you raising children, you might want help in the form of mentorship or guidance, or you might simply need help with a carpool. For those of you with grown children or no children, you might be longing for easy companionship, for an interested, compassionate ear. For anyone, just a simple "How are you doing?" genuinely asked, with the intonation of sincerity goes a long way.

Alaiya, who lost her husband two years ago, tells her story.

In the Jewish tradition, it is very prescribed what happens when someone dies. First, you bury someone within twenty-four hours, and then the family and others take over. The house fills with people, and you don't have to talk if you don't want to. You're not supposed to go out. Every night the rabbi came to offer a service and people told stories about Glen. Then, for thirty days I was not allowed to socialize in any groups. But at the end of that, it dropped away. It got really hard. I suddenly realized, "Oh shit, now it's up to me, and I'm still a mess, but I have to begin to function." The next marker is a year from the death when we put a gravestone on the grave. It felt like an accomplishment. But now, two years later, no one asks how I'm doing.

Holly, a single mother whose partner died five years ago, describes the feeling of guilt in asking for help that many have.

One can start to feel as though they are taking too much from others, needing too much, longing for too much. It's as though there's an invisible line drawn in the sand. Once you cross it, the expectation is you need to be "getting on with it." The problem is, many aren't continuing to talk about the actual death of their loved one. They are talking about the ramifications of their death, which are ongoing and many. I find it hard this far out to talk about the chronic stressors and grief that I continue to deal with. It feels to me as though I'm harping on the loss, focusing on something that is in the past to others, even as it continues to be at the forefront for me. Other people have stressors and grief in their lives as well, and I feel at times that I'm over-burdening them or hogging all the stress. With my adult son gone, I no longer have the one person here that would have been my sounding board for all the grief and stress, as well as all of the achievements and milestones. That is difficult.

All the offers of help dried up. How can I get more comfortable with reaching out?

This is an especially difficult reality for people who suddenly find themselves in the role of single parent. In the first year post loss of a partner, people find that friends and family will offer many ways to help, whether it's to bring food, babysit, carpool, etc. But after a while, those offers dry up. One widow shared that three years after the loss of her husband, she feels awkward asking for help from his family with her children because it's as if they don't remember what they promised in the early days of intense grief.

> *But I remember. I remember what they promised, and I was counting on that. It's why we moved closer to them. It's why I uprooted our whole lives; I thought my kids would benefit by being near family, but it's not panning out that way. And as a single mom, I have to sometimes figure out how to be in three places at once. But guess what? I can't.*

Some of you are surrounded by extended family and friends who step in to help shoulder the burden. Others are not. We live in a time when people often settle far from their families of origin. We also live in a very individualistic world where the door isn't open to people outside the nuclear family. It places a burden on those struggling when their need for help changes with time. Some are fortunate, like Alice, who told us, "There are a few people who I can call upon when I need help and they never make me feel bad. I try to give back when I can, but I struggle with how uneven it is right now."

Michelle, whose husband died about eight years ago offers this advice: "What worked for me was doing those things I was already good at. There's no way I could have done it on my own and fortunately, I'm really good at delegating and asking for what I need."

EXERCISES AND RITUALS THAT CAN HELP

THE H.A. EXERCISE

Having trouble expressing your needs to loved ones? Sometimes it's hard to articulate exactly what we want. It doesn't help anyone to stay silent when we have a need, whether great or small. Try using these two expressions when asking for help:

Here's what I need.

Are you willing...?

DRAW FROM A NEW WELL

Wells dry up. It's that simple. And when they do, we have to find a new place to dig. Sometimes we have to dig deep. Sometimes we have to try a few different spots to find a deep enough pool to sustain us. What we need in the immediate aftermath of loss is so different than what we need years later, and then different again, years after that. It evolves and changes, just like our lives do. In some ways, it's more realistic to see that people can't necessarily be the deep well we need. We have to diversify!

Figuring out what you wish you had or what you need will help you see where you can draw support. Consider this example:

I need help with picking up my daughter from school to get her to
an after-school activity. My mother promised me she would do
this for me after my husband died, and she did, for a while. But
then she became less reliable, and I'd have to scramble to figure
out how to leave work early to get her to where she needs to go
and then be home in time for my son. My mother keeps promis-
ing to do it, and I relax, but then this happens again and I'm just
so tired!

Okay. Time to dig a new well, and you might have to test
out a few areas. This may involve putting yourself out there. Are
there carpools? Are there friends that could help? Can you talk
to someone at your workplace to create a schedule that could
accommodate this need and systematize how it will work? If not,
are there other things that your child can do that are closer to
home or connected to the school that she can also enjoy? What's
happening now isn't working, and it's time to tap a different
energy source.

The same kind of thinking can be done when you need emotional support. Sometimes we need to tap a different well to find
people who can talk with us about our grief. Or sometimes we
need to dig the well we already have a bit deeper to see if there's
a reserve of energy there. Saying to someone, "I know it been
a long time since I lost my child, and it seems like I've carried
on well enough, but sometimes I just want to talk about her."
Remember, giving people a chance to show up for you is a gift
to you and to them. It might not always work, but it's worth a try.

IF ROLES WERE REVERSED

Are there people in your life who might be in a similar place as you? If you are aware of them, what might you do to reach out to them to offer a hand? An ear? If you don't know of anyone personally, are you on any social media groups that talk about long-term grief? Could you create one? Might you participate in the holding of others' experiences? Often, by putting out in the world what we want to receive, we create the fertile ground in which that can grow. It's not selfish. It's not manipulative. It's just true. We can often cultivate what we want. If we want a community of people who can talk grief, we need to participate in it. And you have wisdom in this. Reach out. You might find a hand reaches back.

After considering what you've just read, are there steps you are willing to take to address your own needs for support? Take some time to set an intention as you move forward while asking yourself, "What would my loved one want for me?"

Frustration with Yourself, Anger, and Disappointment with Others

Life is not the way it is supposed to be. It is the way it is.
The way you cope with it is what makes the difference.

Virginia Satir, author and psychotherapist

Anger often shows up in the long-term grief cycle, and it's wise to recognize it for what it is so you can decide how you want to use it. Just reading the word *anger* elicits a feeling. Our unconscious and conscious response to it is the stuff of movies, documentaries, music, and art. Just like love, anger is energy. When used for good, it can change history and make things better. When allowed to run amok and do as it pleases, anger can cause irreparable damage and destruction. It can induce terror, as well as breed ever more anger in its wake. You might be wondering, "What does this have to do with anything?"

Anger raises its head when we feel out of control, wrongly treated, the victim of unfairness, or intensely frustrated or disappointed—feelings we will talk about more in this chapter.

Depending on our relationship with anger and how we've experienced others' anger growing up, we may not know what to do with our own. On the positive side, anger can be the fuel needed to make change. Anger is what gives parents the energy to lobby Congress to change gun laws after a school shooting. Anger is what creates groups like Mothers Against Drunk Driving and Mothers Against Police Brutality. Anger sees injustice where it lays, and when shaped by restraint, good thinking, and passion, roots out problems from the darkness, bringing them into the light. We need anger. Just like we need fire.

But like fire, when anger is out of control and unorganized, it destroys, either a person from the inside out, or their relationships with others, or both. When we lose a loved one, particularly when the death is unexpected, traumatic, or untimely, anger can take root. Sometimes people have a tough time expressing anger or have been conditioned to believe there is no place for it, instead holding it inside with no release and the result can be depression, addiction, or isolation. Anger turned outward in the form of blame, projection, and indignation can make relationships explosive, cause erratic and violent behavior toward others, and result in a slew of consequences that at best is isolation and at worst is harm to others and potential incarceration.

If anger has shown up as part of your grief journey, start here: Know that this is true for many people. You are not alone. You can work with your anger in a more generative way. Take a clear and honest look at your life and ask yourself these questions:

- Do I blame myself for the death of my loved one? If so, is this reasonable?
- Do I blame others for the death of my loved one? If so, is this reasonable?
- Do I feel like I have a place to talk about how angry I am with someone who will listen?
- Do I feel like I need help bringing my anger out of my body and into spoken word?
- Do I drink or use drugs when I am angry?
- Do I feel anger toward people whom I feel didn't help me enough after my loss? How do I express this to them? Directly in conversation or indirectly through angry outbursts?
- Has anger affected my relationships?
- Do I suspect anger has affected my health?

If you answered "yes" to any of these questions, a great next step on your journey would be to talk with someone like a therapist, a person connected to your faith, a doctor, or a trusted friend where you could allow yourself to start giving your anger a place to live in open air, where you can examine it and express it—safely. Rage and irritability are often overwhelming and can feel like it comes out of nowhere. When we can openly talk about strong feelings, no matter how "outlandish" we might feel they sound, we release their hold and give them a space to exist without ruining us, eventually getting us to a place where we can harness their energy and put them to use.

As children, we often succumb to fits of temper and rage when faced with unfair situations. Why wouldn't that also be the case when we're adults, particularly when the unfairness of death is so permanent and profound? As you navigate these strong feelings, take a moment to look underneath your anger to see what else lives there. You might see fear and loneliness or righteous indignation that life is grievously unfair and that you can't do much about it. Those parts make themselves more available to healing, but sometimes it's anger that gets your attention enough to make you see that your heart needs tending to.

FRUSTRATION AND DISAPPOINTMENT ARE UNDERRATED EMOTIONS

Lately, bits of resentment and anger are coming up for me, mostly when I hear people talking about the small problems they're going through.

Holly

Frustration and disappointment are major players when it comes to how people manage long-term grief, creating chronic states of being, and over time, influences how people view the world, others, themselves, and their future. The word *frustrate*, according to the etymology dictionary, means "to make of no avail, bring to nothing, prevent from taking effect or coming to fulfillment." From Latin, it means to "deceive, disappoint, make vain." *Disappoint* has a similar thread—its definition includes to "defeat the realization or fulfillment of." If you think about what death is, one might go as far as to say that death frustrates life. Life cannot continue because of the act of death. The continuation, or the fulfillment of living longer, is *disappointed* by the act of death, and the survivors are left carrying the weight of this affront of nature.

In day-to-day life, we might exclaim, "Agh! I'm so frustrated!" by the myriad things that come up as potential blocks to our flow. The continuing aftermath of losing a loved one can bring all of these frustrations into sharp focus. The overwhelming truth of an ongoing living relationship with a loved one has ended and then all the mundane or existential problems of living that arise as a result can feel like too much.

If you find yourself in a state of chronic, strong frustration or disappointment, know that you're not broken or immature. Disappointment is a feeling that can send a child into a meltdown of epic proportions. Sometimes it can feel as though their little bodies cannot contain the enormity of their feelings, and they must fall to the ground and pound their fists and kick their feet and scream, "This isn't fair! I thought something else was going to happen!" If you are caught in this feeling, it might be time to stop as much as you can, rest, and take a breath. You can even hug yourself tight and tell yourself, "I love you, and we're going to be okay." The young child in you needs that hug and needs to know that, yes, you are overwhelmed and for a good reason. And you're going to do what you can to clear a new path and make your way.

GREAT EXPECTATIONS

Occasionally, we must check in with ourselves to see whether the expectations we have are on par with reality. A good way to do this is to ask yourself these questions (or some variation):

- "If my best friend were going through what I am going through, what would I think they should do?"
- "Would I castigate them for avoiding social situations?"
- "Would I judge them for having a hard time keeping their cool during the holidays?"
- "Would I expect them to stop talking about their deceased loved one so they could just get on with it?"
- "Would I criticize them for crying suddenly when a certain song comes on, or a smell wafts through the air, or they see someone who looks like their loved one?"

If we flip things around like that, we can often see that we are holding ourselves to an internalized standard we would never hold someone else to. We are so much less compassionate with ourselves than we are with others, and so much more impatient, critical, and judgmental. Why?

As you continue to make your way on the road of grief, try to take a step toward treating yourself the way you would treat the people you love. Allow yourself that same respect, kindness, and patience.

THE VARIABILITY OF HEALING

We think that the point is to pass the test or overcome the problem, but the truth is that things don't really get solved. They come together and they fall apart. Then they come together again and fall apart again. It's just like that. The healing comes from letting there be room for all this to happen: room for grief, for relief, for misery, for joy.

Pema Chödrön, author of *When Things Fall Apart*

The thing is, everyone grieves differently. While grief is universal and deeply embedded in the human experience, how people interact with it and experience it varies in the most intricate and broad ways. Sadly, people often have a hard time just being with their own feelings, without judging them, and being with other people's feelings, without judging them. Basically, feelings and raw emotion can make even the nicest person a little nervous or overwhelmed. Think about how hard it is to let others cry. There's almost always an automatic urge to get someone to stop crying, to feel better, or to give the dreaded advice, "calm down" or "stop overreacting." We do a whole lot to truncate and control the expression of feeling and emotion in ourselves and in others, and this can do a lot of damage over time.

Healing from loss and grief is not a race to the finish with a medal awarded at the end. It threads into the whole of life. If you are the person who feels you have been left behind in your pain, you can know that you are not alone. Take your sneakers off and put your watch away. Judgment of yourself does nothing but create shame and isolation. You are not them, and your grief is not more or less significant than theirs.

If you feel upset by a loved one's continued expression of grief when you find yourself in a different place, ask yourself this question: "How much of my loved one's grief am I feeling like I have to fix?" If you feel like you have to fix their feelings, you have a clue as to why you might be feeling judgmental or resentful. You don't have to fix anything. You just have to bear witness as best you can. You won't always be able to be exactly what your loved one wants in terms of support and presence, and that's okay, too.

QUESTIONS YOU MAY ASK YOURSELF

Why am I stuck? Is something wrong with me?

Grief is a mighty emotional and spiritual experience with which to reckon. The word *grief* is thrown around in the casual lexicon of our time, which to some extent has diffused its original power. But in its very essence and in its original Latin form, the word grief is *gravis,* meaning gravity, heaviness, and oppression. Grief weighs upon a soul, adds weight to the luggage we carry on the long journey, and embodies the experiences of suffering and hardship. Grief is a gargantuan emotional entity that, depending on its cause and fertile ground in which it resides for a time, is incredibly difficult to assimilate and get out from under.

Other than the inherent qualities of grief that make it so painful, there are other conditions that can contribute to complications with grieving and therefore extend the time it takes for some to reclaim their lives in a meaning-filled way. Some have already been addressed previously and are:

- A pre-existing mental health condition like depression, anxiety, or post-traumatic stress disorder
- Previous losses
- Thinking style and developmental age

Others include:

- Alcohol and drug abuse and/or addiction
- A complicated relationship with your deceased loved one
- An interdependent relationship with your loved one
- A relationship with your loved one that was marked by very strong emotional intimacy unique to that relationship
- The conditions surrounding your loved one's death, particularly if their death was sudden, unexpected, traumatic, and/or violent and if they were alone at the time
- A perceived or real lack of social support and connection
- A perceived or real experience of your loved one's death not being relevant to you or a "real" loss
- Financial and other life stressors

- Multiple losses at the same time
- Community losses where there were large numbers of people who died or were killed

Every death stirs up grief from previous losses. How am I supposed to heal if there's always something more to grieve?

As we move through life, we collect experiences, lessons, scars, and stories. Life does in fact leave a mark, and in the way arthritis moves into joints injured years before, new loss churns up old wounds, and we are given yet another chance to heal in a different way.

We all carry around within us a younger version of ourselves. As folks who do inner-child work can attest, sometimes at certain crossroads in adulthood, we must soothe the frightened inner child who didn't have the skills, life experience, or support to handle complex and often destabilizing circumstances. When you feel your response to a given situation is beyond what you'd think makes sense, this could be a signal that a younger and more vulnerable part of you needs soothing and tending to.

Sometimes people experience losses at times when they have so much on their shoulders, they cannot succumb to mourning the way the soul craves. Perhaps there are children to care for, careers that can't be ignored, or life circumstances that are not supportive enough to accommodate one's pain. It might not be until much later, when you experience another loss, that you can allow for the whole of your grief to flow out and get some air.

For example, Barbara was in terrific pain related to the tragic sudden death of her pet dog, Marty, that happened several years ago when he was hit by a car. The pain felt fresh and debilitating to her. "I don't know how to explain it, but I woke up in a terribly depressed mood this morning, thinking about Marty. I couldn't stop crying. I couldn't shake the mood," she said. She realized that revisiting her dog's death was connected to the sudden death of her mother about ten years prior—a death she hadn't fully processed. Her mother, too, was struck by a car while crossing the street. After realizing the connection between the two sudden deaths, Barbara finally did some necessary grieving around the loss of her mother.

There is no linear or clear-cut timeline for grieving, as it doesn't have identifiable boundaries—it floats and shape shifts. It catches the breeze to come back for more attention, to be processed and understood even more. When we don't resist the visitation of old pain, we give it a chance to weave into the fabric of our lives. The silver lining is that love and remembrance keeps our loved one alive in our hearts.

I get so angry when people complain about trivial things or have so much of what I want. How can I stop myself from getting mad like that?

Life is unfair, plain and simple. It's a hard truth and one that is so hard to get over, no matter how good we are at keeping temper tantrums at bay. Why do some people get to gather with lots of family and loved ones at important times while others spend significant moments alone? Why do some get to hold a loved one's hand as they pass away while others are informed over the phone? Jealousy and resentment are formidable opponents and what's most important to remember is that the feeling is not wrong or bad or shameful. It just is, and it requires a loving response from yourself.

Your loved one dying was *not* the way the story was supposed to end. There were hopes and dreams bridging the present to the future. When death interferes with that vision, there is a side road that one must take that has to do with reimagining what is to come. It's easy to sink into a feeling of intolerance for what others complain about, when your own life has been turned upside down. And you know what? Some things really are trivial, especially when held in contrast to devastating loss. But, comparing our pains to others' doesn't get us very far on our healing journey. With each loving gesture you offer yourself, you create new ground for opportunities to develop where anger and frustration were growing before.

When you're frustrated, resentful, or jealous, take action. You can either sit in a tangled mess of emotions or take meaningful steps to claim your life as your own and release the idea that other people are living their lives to attack you. Everyone has their story, their struggles, and their triumphs. If you're angry that you don't get to have what others have, work with it. You may not have your loved one with you, but what part of them can you bring into the here and now? You may not be able to relate to another's stress because it is so far from what you've experienced, but you know stress. You know heartbreak. You know fear. From that place, maybe there are waters you share, where you might look to one another and think, "I don't totally get you, and I wish you got me more, but isn't life hard sometimes?"

EXERCISES AND RITUALS THAT CAN HELP

COMPARE AND CONTRAST NO MORE

There's a difference between looking toward people you admire and respect and considering how they've done things in their lives that you'd like to incorporate into your own and comparing yourself to others from a place of judgment and self-attack. You know the drill: "Why can't I be like that person? Why were they able to get back into life so much faster than me? What's wrong with me? With the world?" This isn't helpful because behind every corner of comparing yourself to someone else is some kind of competition, and in any competition, someone wins and someone loses. There's no place for this in areas of the heart. It's hard on the soul for there to be a winner and loser. As the winner, you had to determine you are doing grief better, and the specter of judgment lives there, which has an impact. As the loser, you set yourself up for feeling broken. Who really is the winner there?

This exercise is simple: Every single time you hear yourself think or say out loud anything that has to do with you doing something better or worse than another person when it comes to healing from grief (and most things, for that matter), release it with love and compassion. You can say something like, "I'm letting this thought go because we are all in this together." Notice how you feel each and every time you do this. You may observe that over time, you compare yourself to others less and feel more open to simply what is.

WALKING INTO AWARENESS

In the nineties, Pam developed a popular therapeutic program entitled, "Walking into Awareness."

> Choose a beautiful place to take a walk that could last between twenty and forty minutes. If you have trouble walking, you can sit quietly and visualize this exercise.

> Before you leave, set an intention centered around where you are on your journey. It could be something like, "On my walk, I will tune into my environment and notice the sights, smells, and textures of my world. I won't judge them or myself. I will notice them and be with what is around me."

> You'll notice your thoughts will wander and drift. Gently nudge them back to noticing the world around you.

> When you're home or in a quiet place, write about or reflect on what came up for you on your walk. What did you notice?

Rediscovering nature can offer you nourishing energy. This is an exercise you can do whenever you're feeling stuck or anxious. The results will surprise you. Even a short walk of ten to fifteen minutes can be enough to provide the space for insight to arise around a specific concern.

DIALOGUE WITH THE "BLOCK"

Those who are grieving can easily become paralyzed by spiritual and emotional roadblocks on the long journey. This includes things like fear, anger, resentment, money concerns, judgment from others or yourself, striving for perfection, or lack of emotional support.

We can't move forward efficiently if we don't acknowledge the blocks that are getting in the way. These blocks can dam up the flow of energy in your life and over time and wear down relationships and connections, leading to even more feelings of grief, anger at others, and frustrations with yourself.

Close your eyes. Imagine a road you'd like to take in your life. Now imagine a boulder or other large obstacle blocking your way. Give it a name. Then imagine a dialogue with it.

You: I see you. You're a large brick building with no windows standing in the middle of the road.

Block: Yes. So what? I'm big and I'll be here forever.

You: You're keeping me from getting to the other side of guilt.

Block: Well, over time your guilt created me and put me here.

You: In that case, I can take you apart, brick by brick.

This dialogue with a block ends with you mindfully naming and removing each brick. It can take time, but the result is you can end up releasing the guilt holding you back from a more meaningful life. Identify what's standing in your way and have a dialogue with it. It might be a wall, a person, an institution, a memory, a perceived failure. See if you can't dismantle that block and continue on your way toward healing.

TIMED FEELINGS

Even many years after the loss we sometimes just need to honor our feelings about it. But there are things we have to do, places we need to be, so consider giving yourself the care and respect you deserve in this way:

- Set a five-minute timer and light a small candle if you'd like.
- Place a photo of your loved one in front of you.
- Allow yourself to feel sad (or angry, or whatever emotion surfaces).
- After five minutes, blow out the candle, take a deep breath, and move on with your day.

SHAKE IT OUT

What kind of fast-paced music (classical, rock, country) do you like? MaryAnn loves the band Metallica. When things are getting to her, she tries to remember to take some time, crank up the volume, and dance around the room, shaking off whatever uncomfortable feeling she's having. Take a moment to locate the best music for yourself, and let go of your inhibitions for a bit. You might even invite members of your family to join the fun.

I'M HAPPY WHEN...

We sometimes struggle with expressing happiness while we're grieving. Perhaps we're concerned that friends and family will assume we're not being respectful if we do, and we feel guilty.

No one can be happy all the time, but try noticing when you are. Or notice how you feel after you finish this sentence ten times (noting even the small things; e.g., I'm happy when my coffee is hot): I'm happy when...

TRUST IS A BRIDGE

Trust is an essential part of any relationship that is thought to be close, bonded, and important. It is only in the safety of trust that we can let our guard down and speak freely and honestly. Trust is strong, but fragile. Even the most bonded of people have moments where something was said or not said, done or not done, that resulted in a breach of trust. It takes a long time to heal from these breaks and to rebuild. Why is trust so important in the land of grief? Because grief lays bare our vulnerability and our heartbrokenness. And, to the extent that we can be real with the people in our lives, we can let others know us, be with us. We can be with them in a way that is ultimately so much more bonded and satisfying than when we feel we have to keep all of our deepest feelings contained and locked away.

How do we build trust or tend to it? We allow for it to grow by participating in it. Here are things to consider:

> Make eye contact when you are talking with people; let them see you, and you see them.
> When you're asked a question, answer it honestly, and if you can't, be honest about that, too.

> Let people in by reaching out. Sometimes when we show up for other people, we show them that we can be with them with care and love, creating a bond.

> If you've been hurt by someone's reaction to you or the grief you continue to experience, you can say, "I feel like I can't talk about how I really am because it seems like how I feel is annoying to you." See what happens. It might not go perfectly, but giving people the chance to show up in a better way is one step toward rebuilding broken trust.

> Don't make promises you can't keep. This creates the fertile ground in which words matter, actions matter, and time is not taken for granted.

If you've been hurt by a person or people as you've moved through the long grief process, you may have had a natural reaction to close down and go within. Like the sea anemone, you may have employed a trusty, hard exterior to protect your vulnerable parts. But the anemone has to open up again and feel around and take nourishment from the passing particles and creatures. Are you longing to open up again? Are there people you especially want to do this with? What ideas do you have to start building that bridge?

CURIOSITY IS CONNECTION

An absolute surefire way to combat the terrible effects of comparing and judging is to be curious. Be curious about how other people think about grief, what their process has been, and what their long journey has been like. You might see images on Facebook or Instagram that make it look like someone is doing just great years after loss with not a care in the world! But if you were to ask them, they might say they've embraced certain things with gusto so they wouldn't fall into despair, that they find certain hobbies or the experience of traveling to be comforting and a part of their healing, not because they're not hurting anymore. We make a lot of assumptions about where we think other people are coming from, and we're very often wrong because we don't have the whole story. So, be curious. Read, research, write, ask questions. Get involved in the process. You may find there's a lot more going on than meets the eye, and that can dissolve judgment and comparisons like salt in warm water.

As you reflect on this chapter, can you envision new ways to respond to anger, frustration, or resentment toward others or your life circumstances? Do any suggestions stand out to you as ones you'd like to try? What do you imagine your loved one would want for you as you traverse your grief journey?

Taking your thinking a step further, write an intention for yourself moving forward when it comes to working with your anger, rather than letting it work you.

6

Hidden Longing and the Value of Bringing It Into the Light

It isn't possible to love and part. You will wish that it was. You can transmute love, ignore it, muddle it, but you can never pull it out of you. I know by experience that the poets are right: love is eternal.

E. M. Forster, author of *A Room with a View*

One of the dominant features of complicated grief is the feeling of longing for the loved one who has died. Longing for something we cannot have can take many forms, but when it interferes with our ability to actively live in the life we have, it can become a boulder blocking the way on the long journey of grief. One way to turn this longing into a more manageable and generative emotional experience is to understand that it is normal to feel connected to, and in relationship with, our deceased loved ones—it's just different now. Sonya, who lost her cherished friend Marcus, described it this way:

To me death is a veil that is drawn around us. Sometimes the veil is heavy, and we cannot see through it; at other times, the veil is more transparent, and we are given glimpses to the other side. I know that I cannot pass through this veil at will, but I am grateful for the few opportunities when I can sense the presence on the other side.

MAINTAINING CONNECTION

Dennis Klass's writing on the idea of continuing bonds makes plain the idea that people rather naturally and organically maintain connection with their deceased loved ones. It's not a connection talked about very openly, nor has it been part of a mainstream response to acute or long-term grieving. No matter how much we try to push against it, there exists a persistent, stubborn, and, in our view, abusive messaging about the importance of letting go and getting over the loss of a loved one. When people are suffering and aching from the heartbreak of loss, the last thing they need is to have their longing for their loved one pathologized. It further isolates people in their ongoing despair, ultimately sentencing some to shame, confusion, and loneliness. We also forget that this idea of letting go and breaking ties with our deceased loved ones is rather new in relation to how healing is prescribed, borne from a more medicalized model of overcoming human suffering.

I never got to say a proper goodbye to my father or my uncle, and it hurts to know that we will never physically be together again. Sometimes I feel like I can feel them with me if I'm lonely, through a song that comes on, or through a warm feeling. It makes me feel as though they are encouraging me to keep going because in those moments, I feel weak and need reminders that I can push through these slumps. I still can't help but feel connected to them as if they have not completely gone away.

Brenna

So, what does this mean? How do we maintain a bond with our loved one that is generative, soothing, and helpful?

There are ways of keeping a connection with your deceased loved one that don't prohibit you from enjoying life and relating to other people in the here and now. Psychologist Andrea Kelly said that what she found was "when you're thrown down deep and lose your bearings, you're forced to find new footholds that anchor you to yourself and your loved ones—in ways that are unexpected and need time to be discovered." The idea is to not shove your grief underground. Relaying stories, reflections, and memories can, as appropriate, be a part of your new life and new relationships. It is also quite normal to be emotionally activated during special moments such as anniversaries, weddings, or graduations. If after many years you feel like grief is getting in the way of living your life with peacefulness and enjoyment, it may be wise to seek out support, whether through therapy or faith-based counseling. Other healing modalities can help you understand what you're holding onto and why, and you can learn about how to move forward without hiding from it.

In the meantime, start here: try not to judge yourself because you still have moments of intense grief.

Some of us carry an incredible loyalty to our deceased loved ones, never wanting to sully or diminish their importance in our lives by letting other people in. The truth about the heart is that it is not really measured on an either-or scale. The more we open our hearts, the more we love, and there is so much space for everyone we've loved to take up a bit of real estate. If you have a person in your life who you feel might struggle with your connection to your loved one, you could try explaining to them how maintaining connection is helpful to you because of your shared history. In addition, you might use your journal to communicate privately with your lost loved one. Some find it especially helpful to write to their loved one if there are concerns they want to share. The beautiful part of thoughts, prayers, wishes, and longings is that they can be yours alone and shared as you wish.

Another way to keep your loved one alive in your heart is to prepare food they enjoyed and then share it with others. Sending out love to them if they come into your mind is another. You might feel pulled to do things more at certain times than others. That's okay. You might include them in prayers every night before going to sleep. That's okay. You might enjoy a view of a sunset and invite them to notice the beauty that abounds. That's okay, too. The key is, you are still living your life. You are doing things that are important to you. You are tending to your relationships and those things you value, while actively carrying your love in your heart. They can coexist.

QUESTIONS YOU MAY ASK YOURSELF

How can I keep an active connection with my loved one in a way that doesn't upset the rest of my family?

Just like in life, the way we stay connected to our loved ones who have died is personal and unique to the relationship. While some people might want to maintain connection in a similar way as you, others might not, and this can create tension at times when all anyone needs and wants is calm and peace. Many have been offended that no one wants to accompany them to their weekly, monthly, or yearly cemetery visit. Tears have been shed and family cut off because some don't want to talk about the deceased as much as others do. If you step back and really think on this, isn't it better that each person be in control of how they manage their grief and connection with the deceased?

If you want to make sure your lost loved one is a presence at family functions or on special occasions, you can, but in a way that honors the boundaries of others in attendance. You can light candles with your loved one in mind. You can put out pictures and just let them be there, without much ado. You can make dates with yourself to visit gravesites or places you hold dear, and you can invite those who you know would enjoy and welcome that excursion, being sure not to take offense if they decline the gesture. The key is this: don't expect others to grieve and stay connected in the same way as you, and make sure not to take over someone else's event by insisting on symbolic expressions for your loved one. Own your own process and abide by it in a way that lets others have their own. Then you will be honoring yourself, your deceased loved one, and those who you share your grief with.

My mother talks to my deceased father all the time. Is that okay?

An ongoing relationship with your deceased spouse can be a wonderful comfort. Won't it make matters worse, you ask? Do you have to consult a medium or psychic, hold a séance? Do you have to meditate, change your religious beliefs? No. All you need do is communicate—silently. One way is to journal your communication—ask questions and wait for the internal response your loved one might have given you if they were still alive.

Carrie had this experience.

During a particularly difficult time with our son, I suddenly awoke at exactly 3:33 a.m. As I lay there I felt a silent, heartfelt communication from Mark. Now, I'm not a psychic medium or anything and there was no glowing entity in the room, just the digital display on the clock reading 3:33. The following morning I looked up the spiritual meaning of those numbers and what I discovered is that "someone in the angelic realm is trying to communicate with you." I decided to go with that especially since I'd heard Oprah once say that "if you've lost a loved one, you now have a personal guiding angel." To this day, over thirty years later, I still see a comforting, "Hello, I'm still around" sign like the license plate on the car in front of me yesterday that said 333-MRT (his initials).

Jennifer told us that she still silently communicates with her partner, and it has been eighteen years since her sudden death.

She's my parking angel. It started when our son was taking karate lessons, and I had trouble finding a space anywhere near his classes. One day, this time out loud, I said, "Please, honey, can you help us find a space?" To the amazement of my son and I, a space opened up immediately in front of the karate studio. After that, whenever I had something important to do with my son, I'd ask for her help. Is this communication and help from the other side real? I don't know. But I know I enjoy the possibility and the connection.

How can you make this kind of communication happen? The only advice we can give is to allow yourself to be open to the possibility—to not negate the signs or communications if they happen spontaneously.

EXERCISES AND RITUALS THAT CAN HELP

LET YOURSELF TALK

This is simple. Just talk (out loud or silently). Let yourself commune with the people you love and miss and don't judge yourself for doing it. Sometimes it might be a simple "hi." Other times, you might have a conversation. There's no right or wrong. Just let yourself be and do what comes naturally and know that this is okay, normal, and part of a healing life process for many people.

LEARN MORE ABOUT THEM

If you feel you've been shortchanged and wish you knew more about your lost loved one, it can be most helpful to find information about them through the eyes and experiences of those who knew them. Gordon, for example, lost his dad when he was three. In tracking down two of his father's old friends, he found out that his dad liked to roller skate and sing with his guitar at parties when he was a teenager! Anecdotes and stories can give you insights and information you never had. As a result, your life and memory of your loved one might become filled with added meaning, growing your relationship all the while.

CREATE A MEMORY BOX

Sometimes we may want to "visit" with our loved one in a tangible way but we don't really have a place to go or a thing to do. If you have items that belonged to your loved one or remind you of them, you might consider making a memory box. It can be a shoe box, wooden craft box, antique chest—there is no limit! T'Mia Ross, a psychotherapist who lost her sister when she was eleven years old, made one and recommends it to others. There are myriad ways you can do this, even if you don't have many or any items to put in it. You can gather things that represent your loved one, write poetry, words, or reflections that capture who they were to you. Maybe things from nature remind you of them and can be placed within this box. You can decorate it inside and out and add to it whenever you wish. Memories, images, dreams—there is no limit to what can be put inside. This could be an ever-changing memorial to your loved one that you visit from time to time for solace, connection, and reflection.

SET A MEMORY TABLE

When a beloved member of your family dies, a hole is left in the heart of the home. Not one room is untouched by this impact. The ways in which people deal with this are many and are often organic and cannot be planned. As people reclaim their homes as places in which new life can grow, some might struggle with complicated feelings of guilt and fear. Or, if someone has chosen to repurpose a room that was their loved one's, they might fear they've lost a touchstone, a place where they can go to be with their beloved. Creating a new touchstone can help. A memory table is one way to do this.

To make your own memory table you simply need:

> A place to put pictures or items where they won't be moved about or pushed aside. This can be a table, a mantel, or a shelf.
> Pictures of your loved one(s). Or if you don't have pictures, some item that symbolizes their presence.
> Other items that might speak to you and that you can touch or hold.

The rest is up to you and your style. Some people like to keep fresh flowers on their table. Others light incense or add things to it that are relevant to holidays or religious rites or practices. It can be organic and ever changing, and it can be your new touchstone.

HONOR DAYS

Taking advantage of days that are already in the cultural calendar is a step you can take toward actively working with remembrance and connection with your loved one. All over the world, there are specific days and even months that are devoted to tending to and holding space for memory of and relationship with the dead. You don't have to be of a particular faith to recognize these times or participate in them, although many of them are steeped in religious ritual and tradition. As an example, All Souls' Day is typically observed by Roman Catholics and is a time when prayer is offered to the faithful who have died in an effort to help their souls migrate to heaven. But when looking at the history of the day and how it corresponds to Halloween and to the end of harvest season, we can see that it is tied to a long history of people ritualizing the ebb and flow of life and death and our place in nature. Even those who are not Catholic can participate in this ancient flow.

ANCESTRY RESEARCH

Many find comfort in sorting out where their lived experience fits into the larger landscape of family survival and family loss and is often a tremendous and powerful story. What people have survived over time is remarkable and you—we—are all part of that story.

As you let the ideas from this chapter marinate for a bit, can you think of ways you are already maintaining a connection with your loved one? If this is something you've been longing for, or wanting to make more meaningful, take some time to consider how you might maintain or deepen your connection to your loved one. Also, allow yourself to consider what they would want for you as you traverse the long road of grief. And finally, like anyone must do periodically on any long journey, take a moment to reflect on where you are and where you want to go, and make your intention for moving forward.

7

Your Loved Ones Are
Not Their Stuff

*As with grief, so with the task of deciding when to part
with a loved one's possessions: The timetable needs to
suit only one person. You.*

Jill Smolowe, author and journalist

Your loved one is not their stuff. This is an important concept to reconcile. Their belongings are simply those things that decorated their life. Try to remember that your loved one exists in a special place in your heart that will not be tarnished or impacted by not keeping all or most of their possessions around you. In fact, you might find a more flowing relationship with your internalized love when their love is what you have to refer to, rather than the papers, the lamp, the socks, the robe.

If you don't find joy in an object or have a use for it, consider letting it move on to someone who may need or enjoy it. Most importantly, try not to keep anything, even heirlooms, out of guilt or because it was a gift. If you don't give up the possessions you no longer care about, they have the potential to drain your energy and crowd out the things you truly want in your life. The energy of *things* can have an effect on your sense of well-being. Elise wanted to get rid of a lot of furniture she inherited from her verbally and emotionally abusive parents. She had never liked their furniture but felt she *should* keep it in the family. When she realized that the furniture itself seemed to belittle her, she couldn't let it go fast enough.

If you're at the crossroads marked by the sign: "Keep Everything as It Is ⟵⟶ Keep a Few Precious Things," it is time to start thinking about how you want to approach the process. Only you can make the tangible decisions that help you choose which path to take.

THE HOLD OF OUR LOVED ONE'S BELONGINGS

I have a broken piece of furniture in my house that is stained and basically useless until I invest the money to get it fixed. Until then, it will stay in the basement, taking up a lot of space and reminding me always that I have to fix things my father let fall into disrepair. It breaks my heart because it's symbolic of so much, but I can't get rid of it—it would be getting rid of what he loved and wanted. How could I discard it?

Cynthia

Letting go of the belongings of those we love is one of the harder, more tangible, and pragmatic aspects of long-term grief. You walk into a house, apartment, office, bedroom, closet, and you can see the evidence of what we carry with us. There is a continuum, of course. Many people are fortunate enough to have precious family heirlooms that have been passed down from generation to generation, and they are cherished, well-cared for things. What makes the cabinet full of delicate teacups more special than a drawer full of socks, or a closet full of dresses? It's simply the value we place on them, right? What if the value cannot be measured in dollars, but rather in love and memory? What if the value is simply that it keeps us feeling connected to those we love and miss? In this case, a lamp is *not* just a lamp.

Psychotherapist David O'Leary considers viewing things this way.

When looking at why people are attached to belongings, it's important to look at the heart of the attachment. If it's functional in that it's an item that could be used at some point, it's easier to let go. It's more difficult to do with sentimental attachments.

The problem is holding on to too much and carrying so much with us through our lives can evolve from loving remembrance to an anchor stuck on a rock. Cynthia's father's furniture is taking up space in her house and is creating an atmosphere of being tethered rather than spacious in relation to him. It's clear there's a history there, and it is captured by the fact that a broken piece of furniture is now her problem to fix at her expense. There is no pleasure in it for her. She does not carry a sense of pride or hopefulness, just resentment when considering fixing the piece.

How do we let go? We can let go when we are carrying around the baggage of others. We can let go when the quality and condition of our life is impacted by the holding on to others' belongings. We can let go when we are holding on to things that bring up painful memories. We can let go when the only reason we are holding on is to avoid feeling guilty.

Rachel told us how she finally let go of her mother's things after some time had passed.

Healing and letting go are hard, but as they say, time seems to be your friend. I inherited all my mother's belongings from her four-bedroom house. Many items sat for years in my basement. I started with donating her clothes. I figured they would go to good use, and my mom would have liked that. It was important to me that the items I was getting rid of had a purpose. Giving dishes away I didn't need and random household stuff was the easy part. Some special pieces were given to family. Then came the hard stuff. I have always been a sensitive and sentimental soul. My children wanted very few of my mother's things. My brother only wanted a couple of items. I had to push myself forward. I was drowning in stuff and my house was cluttered. Then I was afraid if I didn't keep things, I wouldn't remember her. My health is not great and I needed to downsize. Something I decided to do that I found helpful was to take a photo of the sentimental item I felt I couldn't live without. This way I still have the memory attached to it which made it easier to let the item go.

WHEN HOLDING ON BECOMES HOARDING

People don't grieve the thing that is willingly given away,
but they do grieve the thing that is taken.

David O'Leary, psychotherapist

Hoarding disorder is recognized in the *DSM-V (Diagnostic and Statistical Manual of Mental Disorders, Fifth Edition)*. Features of it include having great difficulty discarding or getting rid of items to the degree that living space becomes significantly to severely impaired. Often anxiety, depression, and grief are associated mental health concerns. There is significant distress when items are discarded or when one is attempting to discard. Eventually, individuals' living conditions, relationships, employment, and health are impacted. The transition from excessive holding-on to hoarding can be slow moving and incremental. You don't just suddenly have a hoard. It builds over time and without help can literally take over a life.

If you are wondering if you are struggling with hoarding behaviors and need help, there are therapists who are specifically trained to help people identify where they are on the hoarding continuum. We provide resource information in the Appendix (page 358) for your consideration. Until then, know that sometimes holding on to things is simply a signal that you are trying to hold on to something else—something intangible and precious, whether it's love, hope, or memory. And with work and dedication to yourself, you can hold on to all of those things while claiming back for yourself a lifestyle in which you can be free.

FAST VERSUS SLOW APPROACH

Now that you are considering how to traverse this part of your journey's difficult terrain, consider what approach you'd like to take. This is not a one-size-fits-all process. For instance, Marjorie was overwhelmed by the number of belongings she inherited from her parents. She decided to take the slow approach because there were so many decisions to make, and she was feeling fragile. Some of your loved one's belongings might be easier to part with than others. Making a plan for dealing with the different tasks will help you stay on track.

The slow approach involves these steps:

First know this: moving through this process is best approached mindfully, leaving space for feelings and memory. One good idea is, if you are facing the work of dismantling a room, take pictures.

Then:

- Break the task into chunks. If you have a lot of rooms or storage areas to deal with, break it into smaller parts, like a closet, then a dresser, then a desk.

- Have at the ready boxes or bags that are already labeled with the names of where they are going.
- If it would be helpful, have a support person with you.
- Make sure you eat and stay hydrated. Sometimes when we get going on a task like this, we forget to take care of basic needs and we suddenly lose steam and get weary.
- Try to have the goal be to finish a given task in the time allotted, so that there is not that lingering feeling of needing to get back to something.
- Reward yourself with tender loving care, an easeful activity, a good meal.
- Honor the fact that this is difficult. You are doing something hard. Having a box of tissues nearby is a good idea.

The slow approach is one that allows you to move through a process at a pace that feels right to you, but that is still dedicated to the overall effort of keeping a few items that are meaningful and releasing the rest over time.

The slow approach worked for Alex who struggled with letting go of his wife's clothing. Over the years, dust had settled on her clothes and shoes, keeping Alex stuck. He set a goal to fill one box a day to donate until the task was done. He started with three pairs of her shoes. When he got overwhelmed, he invited a compassionate friend to stand with him in the closet as he removed more of her things, which made it easier and less lonely.

The fast approach most often occurs during the immediate

aftermath of the death. But it can also happen when one makes the decision to move quickly one day after years of being stuck.

If, after a long time, you are feeling ready to quickly release a loved one's belongings, the steps are the same as for those moving more slowly. The pace is simply accelerated. You can still be mindful, honor the process you are going through, and give yourself a lot of love as you do it. Ultimately, being mindful will result in experiencing less distress in the long run.

Also know that it's normal to worry that you'll regret releasing certain items of your loved ones. This especially comes up for people who have handmade things from them. But what is regret about in this context? Are you afraid of grieving again? Or that you will diminish a feeling of connection with them, or kill off their memory? Is there part of you that worries you might hurt them, even though they are no longer alive? Let yourself be with these worries, and, if you can, put them into words, very clearly. Articulate for yourself what you are afraid of feeling and then make clear for yourself, and even for your loved one, what your goal is in letting go of certain things. Like when Sera said,

> I love all of your artwork, Mom, but there's so much of it that I can't keep it all. I will share what I can with others and those parts of projects you never finished. I will donate, recycle, or dispose of everything in a respectful way because to carry it all with me will mean I won't enjoy any of it.

QUESTIONS YOU MAY ASK YOURSELF

Their room is like a museum. I go there when I miss them and can't imagine changing one thing in it. What do I do?

Whether you lost a child, a spouse, a sibling, or a parent, this can be a very real dilemma for people as they try to make their way on their grief journey. It speaks to the fact that people need a place where they can be with their loved one who has died. This is natural and is deeply embedded in our ancestral DNA. Sometimes, though, our need of place interferes with the flow of life, and we need to consider alternate ways to connect with and be with our beloved.

Place so often holds the essence of a person. Their mood, style, smell, and specialness. But if you think about it, place tends to evolve with people as they age. Nothing stays static for long. Not really. That's why certain habits of keeping things as they were are not really in line with nature and how things are. Over time, this too can act as that pesky anchor that is stuck on a rock. How might you dislodge it so you can continue moving through life with connection to your loved one held intact?

You do need a place. You need a place to go where you can feel close to your loved one. This can be a place in your home, in your neighborhood, or simply in your heart. It's the place you land when you need connection. And maybe you need part of them to be there, symbolized by a belonging of theirs. Think about what you might keep that is an essential artifact of your loved one. When you hold it, do you feel connected to them? Some ideas to consider are:

- a favorite shirt
- a stuffed animal
- a blanket
- a piece of jewelry
- a perfume or cologne
- a scarf
- a pair of shoes
- a hat
- a pillow

I've been putting it off for years, but now it's time for me to figure out what to do with my loved one's possessions. Where do I begin?

Sue had a very challenging time removing her husband's things from their home of thirty-one years. Four years had passed since he died when she said,

> I feel like I'd be removing him from my heart—like I'd be disrespecting Jim if I sold or donated his favorite shirts, the books he was hoping to read. His college diploma is still hanging in his office! I feel like he'd think I was being unloving.

Finding meaning connected with your loved one's belongings often helps. Bradie helped a man distribute a room full of bags of yarn that the man's wife had at the time of her death. In Bradie's view the yarn itself symbolized hope. His wife made things for other people she knew and loved as well as for people she'd never meet. When Bradie picked up the yarn from his house, it could barely fit in her car, but over the course of several months, she found places to distribute the yarn—a local group that makes things for people who are suffering, retirement communities, local schools, and people who couldn't afford to buy yarn. This made him feel that his wife's hope and love made it into other people's hands and would continue to be expressed in the world.

Alex, a man in his forties, was struggling with a similar issue. Three and a half years prior to seeking help he said,

> I've decided to sell our house and move closer to my daughter. But each time I open what was a shared walk-in closet with my wife, I see her shoes on the floor and her dresses hanging neatly in a row, and a part of me is waiting for her to ask me to step aside so she can grab her favorite outfit to get to work on time. Her clothes make me feel like she's still with me.

Eventually, Alex was able to make some progress in releasing his wife's clothing when he thought about social issues that were important to her. He started donating her clothing to organizations that help refugees resettle and victims of domestic violence who need a fresh start. Doing this in his wife's name, he felt proud of her and of himself.

EXERCISES AND RITUALS THAT CAN HELP

TEN THINGS I DID TODAY

This exercise will help you feel you've created some momentum in moving forward. We sometimes forget to acknowledge all we do in a day, especially when we're feeling stuck in some other area in our lives. Before you go to sleep each night, take the time to list on paper (or in your mind) ten things you accomplished, either big or small—no judgment. The goal here is to stop beating yourself up for not releasing your loved one's belongings, and instead to start harnessing the energy that you do have in other areas of your life. For example, when Manny, who lost his wife two and half years ago, tried this exercise here's what he listed.

> Emptied the dishwasher
> Fed the cats
> Called a friend to ask for help
> Washed and folded one box of her clothes to donate
> Vacuumed the bedroom
> Paid the cell phone bill
> Hung up my clothes
> Shredded some old paperwork
> Checked the tire pressure
> Watched a movie after dinner

It really does help. Try it. It will release you from self-attack and remind you that you do a lot and will be able to do those things that are difficult.

IDENTIFY THE WHY

Ask yourself why you want to move forward with managing the possessions of your loved one's life. Maybe you have a philosophical way of organizing your life where the motto is "less is best," but you have not been able to enact your philosophy because of the more powerful connection you have to your loved one's belongings. Maybe you want to move into a smaller space. Maybe you have a reason to free up space in your home but can't bring yourself to do it. Maybe deep down you know it's time to let go of many of the things that were part of your beloved's every day, especially the things that are not a part of *your* every day. Answering the "why" will help you identify and reclaim the energy to navigate this difficult part of your journey.

IDENTIFY THE ESSENCE OF YOUR LOVED ONE

If you were to describe your loved one in a few sentences, what would you say? What are the first images, sensations, and recollections that come to mind? The age of your loved one and the nature of their death may make this process complicated, so try to recall images from a time when your loved one was most themselves. Consider the essence of your loved one and the belongings most tied to that energy. The essence of a person is intangible and without edges. It is this energy we try so hard to stay connected to after they have died, and we often reach for that by holding onto their belongings even if it means things sit in a box or in the midst of a pile in a storage unit. Can you identify which of those items you'd like to keep or offer to family and friends? Just a few precious belongings that capture this essence?

CHOOSING A SUPPORT PERSON

Whether you decide to take the slow approach or the fast approach, you might consider having someone you trust assist you and who will not judge your pace. If you want someone to help you during the process of sorting, cleaning out, and donating, consider carefully what kind of help you're looking for and make your expectations known. It's great if you want someone to listen to your stories as you go through things that you may or may not want to keep, but if you ask a person who has their PhD in Marie Kondo cleaning (i.e., keep only what sparks joy in you), you are setting yourself and your support person up for a rough ride. They may not be able to sit by and watch you put more and more things into the keep pile without pushing you to pare down. In the same vein, if you want someone to help push you to make bigger and more significant decisions around letting go of things, picking the most sentimental friend you have will likely get you nowhere.

IDENTIFY MEANINGFUL PLACES TO DONATE ITEMS

Part of the issue with letting go of the belongings of our deceased loved ones is the belief that their essence is all tied up in their things. So, it matters where these things go, right? This is where meaning intersects with essence. If you've had trouble with this part of your journey, finding a place that is meaningful to you or your loved one can really help.

Can you identify a place that holds meaning associated with your loved one's belongings? Or people who would benefit from having them? If your loved one was an artist and you have a lot of supplies and materials, is there a local school, senior center, or community resource that would scoop them up happily and put them to good use? You can know that your beloved's things will be used in the way they were intended and feel comfort in knowing their spirit will live on in that way. Often people feel better when they donate items to specific groups of people in the community rather than bringing things to a large donation center. Many communities also have stores where people can bring gently used clothing, household goods, or furniture where all of the profits are donated to local charities.

CREATIVE WAYS TO REPURPOSE CLOTHING

In terms of clothing, many people have found comfort in making quilts and pillows out of shirts and scarves. Certainly, children and adults who lose a parent, spouse, or sibling find great comfort in having one or two items they can touch or wear to feel close to their lost loved one.

MAKING DECISIONS ABOUT PERSONAL JOURNALS

Sometimes, the person who wrote the journals articulated in their will who would inherit them at the time of their death, or specific instructions were given on how to deal with them. Other times, it is up to the person closest to their loved one to make decisions regarding what to do with them. In some cases, this can be such a wonderful treasure trove to have, where the beloved's voice comes through in the writing with stories that will be cherished for generations to come. In other cases, journals can include details of a person's life that challenge the way family members thought things were. Here are some questions to ask yourself as the holder of such personal material:

> Was your loved one a private person who kept things to themselves?

> Did your loved one ever express their thoughts about their journals?

> If you've read the journals, are there things in them that would hurt people in your family?

> If you've read them, do you think the journals hold information or details about your family that people in generations to come would appreciate?

> Do you want people in generations to come to read the journals?

If you lean toward keeping them for future generations, it makes sense to store them in a box made for long-term paper storage in a space that is climate controlled to avoid molding and decay. If they are now technically in your ownership, you should, either in your own will or with the journals themselves, leave directions as to who should receive them and what you hope to be done with them. If you decide the journals are private to your loved one and should not be passed on for further reading, you should destroy them.

Destroy is such a painful word, but if you know your loved one would shudder to think of anyone reading their private and personal thoughts, you are taking exquisite care of them by keeping their journals private. If throwing journals in the trash seems too callous, we suggest a burning ritual. There is spiritual significance to releasing words back into the ether, freeing them from the page and allowing them to reclaim the space they lived before they were uttered into written word. You can set an intention as you begin the process, and you can communicate to your loved one that you are honoring their privacy and that releasing their words is allowing for more spaciousness around them and their memory. You can take great comfort in knowing that this is an incredibly thorough way for you to honor someone's privacy.

How to carry out a burning ritual:

> Ensure you have a safe space to burn paper (e.g., fireplace, fire pit, charcoal grill).
> Ensure that it's legal to burn things outside (monitor fire conditions and risk in your area).
> Make sure that all of what you are placing in the fire is safe to burn; remove any paperclips, staples, plastic, and artifacts that won't burn well or safely in a fireplace.
> Create your intention for carrying out this choice.

If burning is not an option, you might consider shredding the pages or composting them.

RELIGIOUS OR SPIRITUAL ARTIFACTS

This can be a tough one for people, depending on whether they share the same belief system as their loved one or not. It's hard to know what to do with things that carry so much meaning for people, and, in some cases, are held with a certain degree of reverence. Religious texts, statuary, crucifixes, and related art all need to find new homes occasionally, but where? And how?

If you've come to a place where you know you need to pass things on, take time to consider places that would appreciate such meaningful objects. Places of worship, prayer, and meditation are wonderful starting points. Perhaps hospitals, nursing homes, hospice centers, and rehabilitation centers would also be interested. The whole of what you have to share with others might not end up in one place, but you can be sure that if people say yes to your donation, it will be received with the love and care that your loved one would have wanted.

After reading this chapter, it's time to consider writing or thinking about what you can do now. Can you make a plan with incremental steps to reach a goal of releasing a loved one's belongings?

Now consider writing about an intention that deals with letting go of physical things and reclaiming space in your life.

8

You Didn't Get to Grieve the Way You Wanted

Social recognition and support is one of the central needs of mourning, but it is often not available to survivors of relationships that were not recognized or supported in the first place.

Alan Wolfelt, PhD, grief counselor
and author of *When Grief Is Complicated*

As if recovering from grief isn't hard enough, many face the heartbreaking experience of their grief not being perceived as important, valid, or worthy of attention or respect. This is *disenfranchised grief*, and it is a major player contributing to why some have greater difficulty than others moving forward from loss. As personal and private as grieving can be, the support of a person grieving is laden with social and cultural mandates and customs. It is through extensions made by others that people feel buttressed as they try to find their bearings on their grief journey. But what if grief is not recognized or validated?

WHY DISENFRANCHISED GRIEF HURTS SO MUCH

*In grief groups, a big conversation we had was around
how to own, validate, and manage your own grief in a
culture that doesn't want to have these conversations.
It's important to figure out who in your life can tolerate
talking about grief and normalize it with you. It might
not be the people you live with or who are in your family.*

Walter Brownsword, psychologist

Any time we feel pain, and that pain is not recognized, appreciated, or valued by those close to us or by society, we feel alone. And to be blunt, our society is rough. There are some unwritten rules that have created a line of demarcation between grief that is supported and accepted, and grief that is minimized, underappreciated, and disregarded. Certain kinds of loss are known for not being appreciated for their potential power and impact. These are loss of a grandparent, loss of a pet, loss of a sibling, and loss of a friend. In addition to these specific losses, many people who have lost loved ones with whom there was a complicated relationship express feeling alone and lonely in the land of grief. Addiction, abuse of any kind, neglect, adoption situations, mental illness, disability, being elderly, suicide, and death as a result of something that was criminal or considered the fault of the person who died are all fertile ground to breed unimpressive responses from those who might otherwise be considered the go-to support system for those grieving. Also, many people are in relationships that are not valued, understood, or respected by a given group, whether it be family, community, or religious organizations, etc. When someone loses a partner who was not accepted, or when you are the surviving member of a partnership who is left out of funeral rituals and memorial services, you are being denied the human need to participate in active mourning. The pain these experiences cause grievers can be traumatic and can certainly impact the process of healing and figuring out how to live with grief.

Those who are living with long-term grief benefit from feeling part of a community that understands and does not judge or feel impatient with the griever. As soon as someone is given the signal that they or their grief is not valued, they have to do something with all of the emotions. Where do they go? Do they morph into something else? Do they result in loneliness and despair? Or anger? Depending on the circumstances, this can result in someone feeling shame about their pain, and in an effort to protect themselves against judgment, they must go within and go underground with their grief. It's easy to see why this would not work in the long run.

THE IMPORTANCE OF RECLAIMING YOUR RIGHT TO GRIEVE

Grief, like love, is a part of being human. No one can take it away from you or force you not to feel. You can give away that power of yours to feel as you do, but in the realm of grieving, if you've been given the idea that your grief isn't real, doesn't matter, or shouldn't be as powerful as it is, it's time to take your power back. As unique as individuals are from one another, so is your grief. Take a stand now and claim your place on the grief journey. Place a marker signifying the fact that you've been there, you know what grief is, and thank you very much, but you'll be taking over the rest of your journey from here.

QUESTIONS YOU MAY ASK YOURSELF

How do I move on when I never got to grieve in public or in a formal way?

For a variety of reasons, some bereaved people never get the chance to openly acknowledge their grief, receive social and family support, and publicly mourn. Couples who are likely to experience disenfranchised grief are those who were in a partnership not supported by their family or culture or were divorced at the time of death. Other issues that contribute to disenfranchised grief have a moral undertone and again have to do with judgments and values from the larger social or family context. Losing a loved one to suicide, drug or alcohol addiction, or who surrendered a child at birth might find themselves facing less societal support as there are still persecutory aspects to these behaviors.

At the heart of it, the person you lost is not who family and culture approved of or wanted you to love. Perhaps a quiet decision has been made that your deceased beloved did not deserve the kind of send-off that another person might. Therefore, even as years pass, your continued emotional pain may not be taken seriously, supported, or shared.

Susan came out later in life to her friends and family. Although she lived with Jennifer for about ten years before she died of cancer, some in Susan's family were reluctant to acknowledge her partner. Coming out was a herculean task given their communities and religious upbringings. Susan had no say in how the funeral services were planned, was not asked to speak, and was treated like "just a friend." If it were not for the community they developed as a couple, Susan thinks she wouldn't have survived her grief. Going to other people's services now brings back very painful memories, because every time she sees her family respond to the bereaved with more love, compassion, and support than she ever received.

Death due to addiction or mental health struggles can also create situations that breed disenfranchised grief. Shari shared this experience that describes so well the strange way many people try to simplify grief when it's complicated.

My husband died because of his addiction, but certain family members refer to him as a "drunk" no matter how often I tell them I'm offended by it. The judgment is constant. When we talk about who's sick, who's dying, and who died, I always hear stories about what a good person he or she was. My grandmother likes to say how loved they must have been because of how many people attended the funeral. You know how many people were at my husband's services? None, because we didn't have one. I seem to be the only one who can remember what he was like before he became addicted.

Death by suicide can impact support in a similar way. Rick described it this way:

Jodie was the love of my life. We weren't married but lived together for almost twelve years. When she took her life, it was a surprise to all who knew her, including me. Friends thought I should have known that Jodie was at risk of hurting herself, but I had no idea her depression was so severe. What I find most surprising all these years later is how people react when I bring her name up. Nobody can talk about her with me and listen. People say I should move on. I'll move on when I'm ready, but it's hard when I can't talk about her with them.

When no one can talk about or reference the way someone died because of the taboo nature of their death, there is an undercurrent of silence, of suppressing truth, that leaves the hard work of grieving to the partner left behind.

For some, ritual and tradition are very important. For now, know that you can say goodbye to your beloved in a meaningful and symbolic way, in the way you would have liked to do in the immediate aftermath of your loss. Imagine taking control back from judgment and stigma and giving your loved one the send-off you know they would have liked. No matter how much time has passed, this can help.

The family culture I am a part of does not welcome outward expression of emotion. I feel traumatized by how much I had to hold in my feelings and white-knuckle my way through the weeks and months following my loved one's death. Am I right to consider this traumatic?

Anyone who has had to sit through a funeral or memorial service and felt the need to contort, constrain, shove, and hide their deep and true emotions so that they don't cry, lose it, fall apart, look bad, make others uncomfortable, scare people, or seem dramatic, and on and on, knows just this trauma. And reflecting on those moments, even many years later, can bring a person to their knees with grief and sadness for what they had to endure during a most painful time in their lives. Plenty of people have written about the toxic way our supposedly evolved culture deals with the most human and truthful of pains. It touches every person of every group, color, creed, religion, and faith if they do not have people in their lives who are open and welcoming of sincere and true expressed feeling.

Something has been stolen from those of us who have been trained to feel that expressions of grief and sorrow are too much, too overwhelming, and too private. Many things have been stolen, in fact. First our feeling of trust in our own people and community is damaged. If we can't be our realest and rawest with those we are closest to, where can we? Next, we lose out on an organic and fluid expression of grief in the moment. All that contorting does only one thing: it pushes grief into the corners of our minds and hearts and bodies where, if it's not allowed expression and air, it gets stuck, redirected, and becomes stale, causing other ailments and pains in a life and in a body.

If you can relate to this form of emotional trauma you are not alone, and you are encouraged to take back your rightful place at the table of real and authentic grieving.

My family didn't let me go to funerals or services for those who died in our family when I was a child. How do I address this issue now that I'm an adult?

Sadly, this is a very common story. Death in western culture has become something outside of us, managed by hospitals, doctors, morticians, and funeral directors. We've gone from a species intimately connected to death, with requisite rituals, to one that, through its own collective anxiety, places a tremendous number of assumptions on children, namely, that they can't handle knowing about death or managing grief. Some families are of the opinion that funerals are not a place for children, and grieving rituals are too much for them to witness. What folks forget though, is that children are going through loss, too, and when they are left on their own to sort out what's going on, isolated from the collective grieving of the family, they are often re-traumatized by their own fears and confusions, coupled with intense and unprocessed grief that can extend into later years.

Frank's sister Ella died when they were ten and eight years old, respectively. He shared,

The sudden impact of this tragedy was beyond anything I had experienced before, and it was scary. What I remember most is terrible loneliness. Not only was my little sister dead, but no one was talking to or explaining to me what was going on.

Frank has carried a gaping wound that, well into adulthood, has not healed.

The goal here is to reclaim grief for yourself, and not just the grief of your loved one's death. There was likely a lot of collateral damage from the decisions made by others when you were a child. It's never too late to create a grieving practice or ritual that was woefully missing at another time. See suggestions for creating a ritual for yourself in the exercises at the end of this chapter.

I feel as though nobody understands where I'm coming from. How can I find people who get it?

Not everyone will understand where another person's grief is coming from, or why it is as powerful as it is. As painful as it is, it's important to accept that sometimes we just don't get each other, and sometimes the capacity for empathy in a person is woefully lacking. Brian, who lost his mother, compares the experience of people wanting him to move on from his grief to expecting someone with a leg injury to just put down their crutches and walk like they normally do, before their leg is healed. We'd never expect that, yet we do from people with broken hearts because their injury is invisible, and it's hard to sit with. What's important to remember is, your healing doesn't stop where someone else's patience, empathy, and compassion do. Think of it this way: your love has nothing to do with other people. So why should your ability to grieve hinge on others' understanding of you? It's wonderful to be held in the caring embrace of empathy from others, but sometimes it's just not there.

That's when it's important to get your needs met elsewhere. There are people who do understand disenfranchised grief and its impact on the long journey of grief, and they are islands of sanctuary for those who continue to suffer. We do better when we talk to people who get where we are coming from. It's grounding; it creates a sense of acceptance and understanding, and it allows for the survivor to fully rest in what they are experiencing without censoring themselves and their feelings.

So how do you go about finding those people? Disenfranchised grief has significant side effects, including loneliness. When we don't feel understood or heard, we feel alone. So it's time to allow yourself to try something new, to try to find others who might help you, and who you might help in return. There are groups online that are specifically geared toward attending to disenfranchised grief, and some are listed in the Appendix of this book on page 371. And, if there's anything to cull from social media that is useful, accessing groups on Facebook, Instagram, and other platforms can help, not just in finding people with shared experiences, but also in the way of finding out about other resources. Checking in with therapists who specialize in grief work is also a good option.

The first step is to believe and trust that your grief means something and deserves respect and a place at the table of your life experience.

EXERCISES AND RITUALS THAT CAN HELP

START WITH SELF COMPASSION

Let's assume the reason you're stuck in the pain of long-term grief is because you're not quite sure how to be kinder or more compassionate to yourself. Ask yourself: How is your inner child being treated by you? Yes, you're an adult and you function in the adult world. But the feeling side of you may be complicated by an uncaring relationship with the child within. We often get a glimpse of this "child" when we're in pain. The first question is: When you were a child (pick an age), how did your parental figures respond to you when you were in pain? Is it possible that the adult you is continuing to treat yourself in a similar, unhelpful fashion? A useful inner dialogue with the child within might start with, "I'm sorry I haven't been kinder to you. When you're (trying to date again, cleaning out your loved one's closet, feeling like you can't trust, experiencing days of pain, etc.), I promise to give you what you need." And like with any child, the goal is to keep your promises.

We hesitate to go too deeply into the inner-child process unless you have a competent therapist to support you, as reliving certain aspects of childhood can become painful at times. However, there are some useful insights you can glean with simple dialogue. Find a quiet place and begin by writing a question with your dominant hand (maybe it's your right hand) asking your inner self (or inner child) the following: "What do you need today?"

Now shift your pen to the nondominant hand and respond. In the beginning, it may feel unnatural to write this way, but in fact it becomes childlike as you struggle to respond. After the child-like, scribbled, or printed response, make sure you respond in an honest, loving way. Here's an example:

Adult: "What do you need today?"

Child: "I want a hug."

Adult: "You want a hug. I'll try to get you one today."

Child: "I don't like tight hugs."

Adult: "Okay, I'll find someone to give us a safe, kind hug. Is there anything else I can do for you?"

Child: "I'm scared to go into that room."

Adult: "The room where Peter died?"

Child: "Yeah."

Adult: "I understand. I'll go in there with you for a short while and comfort you while we're in there. Afterward we'll do something fun. Okay?"

Child: "Okay, I guess."

After practicing this dialogue for a while (or one that fits your particular situation), you may find you don't need to write down the exchange and that it will become more internalized.

WATER RITUAL

Water is a powerful element as it relates to death, grief, and immortality. Whatever your personal views on such things as life after death, what happens to the spirit of a person after they die, or religious ideas about heaven and hell, there is no question that for many thousands of years water has played an integral part in humans' rites and rituals when it comes to death. Water is also deeply symbolic of and connected to images of life, rebirth, and cleansing. Incorporating water into your ritual is a wonderful way to unite through the journey of life and death, rebirth and reunion, power and peace.

What you will need:

> seeds, small pieces of bread, or a handful of dirt or sand that is by the water
> a blanket to sit on or a portable chair

Find a place with moving water such as the ocean, a stream, lake, river, reservoir, brook, or pond. There needs to be some movement in the water. If you can, choose a meaningful site, one where you feel comfortable, safe, and calm.

Sit down and center yourself in whatever way you know how. This can simply mean finding a comfortable position and taking some steadying breaths.

Think of the intention you would like to pass to your loved one.

Sit for a while and experience the environment around you. Notice the temperature of the air, the sound of the trees or plants rustling in the breeze, if there is one. Listen to the birds, the insects, the water itself.

Say a prayer or make a wish or an express hope for yourself and for your loved one.

Make a cup with your hand and dip it into the water, allowing it to fill up. With your other hand add the seeds (these are a symbol of sustenance; if you don't have seeds, use anything that is biodegradable, safe for the environment, and might be enjoyed by the animals that live in and near the water). Then lower your hand into the water, palm up, letting the seeds float away with the movement of the water.

Offer your gift to your ancestors.

Offer your gift to your loved one.

SEASONAL OR YEARLY ACKNOWLEDGMENTS

Many people enjoy and have found great comfort in acknowledging special days. Some choose to memorialize birthdays while others choose the day the death occurred. Some choose both. There are many ways to do this. In faith traditions there is often a way to have your loved one mentioned during a service to have the congregation pray for them. In local papers, people can take out a bit of space to remember their loved one with a birthday or anniversary announcement.

Others prefer to make their yearly acknowledgments more private. Going to a loved one's favorite restaurant and getting a meal on their birthday or lighting a candle or incense on the day of their death are some simple things we can do to stay connected and acknowledge them. There is really no limit to what people can do to honor their loved ones, and anniversaries are a perfect time to anchor in ritual.

RELEASING THE SPECTER OF RESENTMENT

Part of what can keep people tethered to the complicated pain of long-term grieving is resentment. Resentment toward the person who died. Resentment toward the people who didn't understand their pain. Resentment at having not been given a proper chance to say goodbye. Resentment is like a cavity. If you don't get it dealt with, it will grow and grow and eventually your tooth will decay and there's no saving it. So, what do we do with resentment? If it were as easy as deciding to simply let it go, the feeling wouldn't be that big of a deal, but we know it is! It's the bitter pill we swallow again and again when we are just so hurt we can't get over it.

If resentment toward those who did not respond to your grieving the way you would have wanted is part of what is keeping you anchored to your pain, know that you need to work it. You need to work over the feeling the way a dentist deals with a cavity, and the way a potter works with clay. Try this exercise:

Take out a piece of paper and from the top, write in order:

My Resentments

Example: I resent the fact that people kept saying to me that my sister is in a better place now because she was in so much pain, and therefore made me feel selfish for being so crushed by her death.

The Person/People I Resent

Example: My partner, my grandmother, my boss

What I Wish They Did

Example: Just listened. I wish they didn't try to reason me

out of my grief. Of course I didn't want my sister to be in pain, but she was my best friend and I know she didn't want to die. I just needed them to support me instead of making me feel guilty.

Do I Still Need What I Needed Then?

Example: I'm over it with my boss because I don't really care what they think. But I carry a lot of anger toward my partner who, in my view, just didn't want to deal with my grief. I am still angry at him, and it's been over five years. I feel like he cut himself off from a part of me.

How Can I Tend to That Need?

Example: I can communicate with him and share with him how I feel so that I don't feel like a part of me is dead to him. But also, I feel like I need to get clear on the fact that my grief and depression did not mean I wanted my sister to suffer. I think I will write her a letter and tell her how much I love her and miss her. I won't apologize for my grief anymore. I will also start to acknowledge more openly her birthday and do something special on it.

SHEDDING JUDGMENTS: A VISUALIZATION

Throughout our lives, many of us absorb the weight of what others put on us. Sometimes these judgments are direct, like, "You are so oversensitive." Sometimes they are judgments we fear others have of us, like, "I'm afraid they'll think I'm being dramatic." Sometimes they are projections from other people, like, "You're always so focused on the negative" from a person who complains constantly but doesn't realize it. If we are not careful, over time these ideas that are put on us can get heavy. So heavy that our posture changes. Our walk. Our openness to our life and to the world. We forget what we look like, what we like, what we love.

Picture yourself sitting or standing in the center of a dressing room. There are mirrors all around you and you are wearing many coats. So many, that it's hard to lay your arms flat against your body. You are bogged down. Each coat represents a judgment. The judgment might be in relation to grief but could be about anything.

Now, name the judgment—that is the first coat—and take it off, slowly. In your mind's eye, move toward the side of the dressing room and hang the coat up on the hook, and say, "I am no longer wearing you" and go back to the center of the dressing room. Look at yourself in the mirror and notice the next coat. Consider it for a while, its texture and weight, and open your mind to which judgment this coat is. Once you've determined that, move toward another hook on the wall and hang the coat on that hook. Again, return to the center of the dressing room.

Each time you remove a coat of judgment, take some time to notice any changes in how you are standing and whether your limbs might more easily move about. Continue in this way until you are wearing no more coats.

When you are through, take some time to write about the judgments you released. Are you scared that if you don't carry them, that somehow you won't become a better person? Know this: judgments don't help us to grow. They are persecutory when they remain only judgments. Here is an example: I am removing the Coat of Drama. I am not going to wear what others say to me when they don't like to sit with my emotions. I will learn how to tend to and take care of my strong emotions in a way that is loving and supportive to me. I will not shame myself anymore by using the word 'drama' to describe my powerful feelings.

THERE'S A CLUB FOR THIS

It is never too late to find people to talk to about grief. So many are tending to their pain in privacy, out of sight from anyone who might think they are indulging in pain or bringing down the mood of a gathering. But guess what? If you are grieving in private, so are others. Start looking around your community for grief support groups. They are often found in hospitals, hospice organizations, or churches. If you don't find anything, bump out the radius of your search. Writing groups, knitting clubs, and walking troupes are all good places to start. This might seem random, but what often happens is that when people gather, particularly to create things in company, conversation inevitably lands on loss. Because loss is part of life, and we all need to talk about it.

If you've been dealing with disenfranchised grief, did anything in this chapter speak to you? Can you create an intention for yourself for moving forward? Would it help you to reexamine and reclaim your grieving process through ritual or ceremony? How might you do that?

Loneliness

The ache of loneliness fills our hearts, and the mind covers it with fear. Loneliness, that deep isolation, is the dark shadow of our life.

Jiddu Krishnamurti, philosopher

and author of *Commentaries on Living 2*

Lonely, according to the *Merriam-Webster* dictionary, means "being without company and being cut off from others." Loneliness produces "a feeling of bleakness desolation." Desolation means "grief or sadness" and carries with it a heavy emotional meaning that surrounds depression, despondency, heartsickness, and so on. Desolation is a word evolved from the Latin word *desolate,* meaning "to leave all alone, forsake, empty of inhabitants." Here we touch the core of the pain. Loneliness in its most powerful form is desolating, and for many people, death of a loved one is what brings them to this barren place.

THE TROUBLE WITH LONELINESS

I'm so desperately lonely. I feel it in my skin and in my
body. It hurts and I don't know how I can go on like this.
It's just too painful, and nothing is changing. No one can
do anything.

J.

Being alone is different than being lonely. Someone can be exquisitely lonely amid many people, while another can be very comfortable, and, in fact, delighted to be alone and in their own company. Loneliness is a subjective state of emotion, and it imparts a great deal of pain on a life. It is associated with grief, depression, addiction, mental health conditions, sleep issues, family disruptions, and even Alzheimer's disease. Loneliness is also known to cause physical problems such as inflammation, autoimmune conditions, and certain cancers. Why might this be?

Humans are meant to be in community. We are a deeply social species, and we rely on others to keep us alive from the moment we are born until we can take over the reins of our lives. Physical dependency is connected to the emotional and psychological way we bond. In fact, it's the emotional comfort we derive from others, primarily our earliest caregivers at first, that wins when it comes to who we attach to more.

Harry Harlow was a researcher in the 1950s. He specifically looked at attachment and had the idea—different than other behavioral psychologists at the time—that attachment was formed via physical connection and tactile comforts, not the need for food. In fact, he was correct as evidenced by the research he did with rhesus monkeys. Sometimes it takes a little research to prove what to many seems terribly obvious. We need contact, physical affection, and the feeling of safety derived from being cared for by another.

As we age, this need turns into something else. We need people in our corner we can turn to for support, love, help, and company. Individual needs as they relate to this are wildly varied, and many factors play into how people meet their longing for affection. Bottom line: when a loved one who met those needs dies, it can hit people at their core.

QUESTIONS YOU MAY ASK YOURSELF

Can one live fully while staying connected to a deceased loved one?

Yes. The idea of maintaining connection is a thread through this book because it is so clearly a part of finding balance as we move forward on the long journey of grief. Dennis Klass's work really gave voice to the reality that people quite naturally do this, but don't talk about it for fear of seeming unwell or troubled. The idea here is that we can maintain connection to our deceased loved ones while we live in the physical world with other people, who also meet our relational needs and whose needs we meet. Both can happen simultaneously. These bonds can include having dreams of your loved one, remembering birthdays, and marking anniversaries of significant events, talking with them, and honoring them in some way.

I'm having a difficult time letting new people in. Should I never love, befriend, or trust again?

Of course not. But it's probably wise to move slowly. Hence the general advice to make no major decision in the first year after a death—don't buy or sell a house, start a relationship, or change jobs, etc. We might add don't try to quickly replace your deceased loved one with someone who may have some of the same attributes.

Occasionally we will find ourselves leaning on someone *too much*. Even in the face of absence or loneliness we must learn that we, ourselves, need to be there for *ourselves*. Many people report not having much experience with learning to enjoy their own company. As you continue to walk the road of grief without your loved one physically by your side, notice if you are being a friend to yourself. Allow for those things your loved one saw in you to shine. As you gather more strength and resolve, you'll ultimately make good choices about who you let into your life based upon desire rather than need.

Give yourself plenty of time to fill the hole of your loss, keeping in mind that you will not find an exact clone. You will eventually find someone you can trust and have good times with, but it will take time to build a deep connection.

In the meantime, make a conscious effort to connect to the love you felt and continue to feel for your loved one. Gratitude is an expression of love that draws the curtains and opens the windows. It allows the sun and air to wrap around your story together.

EXERCISES AND RITUALS THAT CAN HELP

WHO AM I WITHOUT YOU?

We don't often examine just how unique we are or celebrate our innate positive qualities. Perhaps you're left with questions about who you are now because you defined yourself through your loved one's eyes. Try this exercise to gain some insight by finishing the following sentence ten times, making sure to concentrate on the positive:

I am a person who_____

Now read your answers back to yourself. Or, to make the exercise even more powerful, try reading it out loud.

YOU ARE SOMEONE WORTH GETTING TO KNOW

The idea of having a relationship with yourself can seem a bit foreign to some, but really, who do you spend the most time with out of all the people in your life? You! This is not so much an exercise as it is an invitation to open up the lines of curiosity and communication with yourself. Here's one way to do it: Consider something you like to do. Maybe it's poking through antique stores. Or going for a walk. Or watching movies. Then, make a date with yourself to do that thing. Let's say you choose to drive to a nearby town to check out their antique shops. As you take yourself on this date, just be with yourself. Don't double book your time by making phone calls in the car on your way there or spending the whole time on your phone texting or on social media. Treat this time as you would if you were seeing someone you love being with. Devote all of your attention to you and what you are experiencing. As you walk through a shop, notice what you are drawn to, and be curious about it. Curiosity about yourself is one of the greatest gifts you can give yourself. You might notice you are always drawn to certain textures or trinkets or pieces of furniture. Enjoy that detail as if you were learning this about a new love. Maybe you'll buy yourself something. Maybe not. But relish this time with yourself and let it feed you. There is more of you where that came from and the more you enjoy your own company, the more discerning you will be when it comes to making choices about the people you welcome into your life.

As you practice this you can translate this line of curiosity to harder moments. You can be curious and interested in what grief feels like to you. You can experience those moments when it wells up out of nowhere as an invitation to more intimately know yourself and your feelings. You can do this with any feeling; noticing a feeling doesn't mean acting on a feeling. Take the feelings you have when you are driving, and someone cuts you off. Maybe you notice a sharp rise in anger, like red hot fire. You do not have to do anything about that anger. You can just let it come and go and be interested in what that was about. We can literally do this with everything our minds throw at us. Give it a try.

TENDERNESS SCAVENGER HUNT

When we feel lonely, it's tempting to feel as though no one in the world gets it, understands, wants to understand, or cares. People can start to feel like enemies, or at least like strangers. It can help to spot the tenderness and kindness that is happening all around us. This doesn't have to be dramatic and newsworthy kindness, even though that's nice, too. It can be as simple as noticing the food in the donation basket at your local grocery, or a person holding the door for someone. It can be witnessing an embrace at the airport between people who haven't seen one another in a while, or warm greetings shared between patrons and people working in a store, post office, or library. It can also be taking notice of those things you do that add warmth to this world that can feel so lonely and cold sometimes.

On any given day, you can decide to notice tenderness. Write it down like this:

The Tenderness	The Outcome	Insight
Someone at the store let another person go ahead of them in line because they had less in their cart.	Gratitude Smiles Conversation	It's nice to notice what is going on with other people. Little things make a big difference.
I offered to help someone carry multiple packages into the post office.	The person declined, which was confusing given how much they were struggling, but another person there smiled at me and shrugged. I didn't feel invisible.	Just because I offer something, it doesn't mean it will be accepted in the way I meant, but it won't go unrecognized, even if I am the only one who knows my intention.
I saw a wall of mittens that were handmade by people and donated to folks who need warm clothes.	People will have warm mittens. I will make a pair and add them to the wall. The town has a spot that has evidence of love and care.	There are generous and caring people all over the place. But they might be sitting at home knitting! I need to trust that they are there.

EYE TO EYE

Making eye contact is another organic way we can bridge the gap between feeling alone and feeling connected with people. Cultures have different etiquette around eye contact, so this is not a one-size-fits-all suggestion. However, eye contact is a building block of human connection and is integral to how we communicate. Following a devastating loss, it makes sense that we might want to close the "windows to our soul" for a time. It's just too intense to be seen in our pain, and maybe we can only tolerate it with certain people for a certain amount of time. As we begin to unfurl again, or think about unfurling into our broader lives, it might make sense to pay attention to how much you are connecting with people in the simplest of ways.

It's possible to go through entire days without actually looking at someone while they are talking, including people we live with! Over time, this chips away at how connected we feel and how connected others feel to us. Are you really listening when other people talk? Can you minimize distractions and devote your full attention to someone? What does that feel like?

Out in the world, whether it's the places you run errands, or where you work, or where your kids go to school, there are humans. Pay attention to whether you make eye contact with them, even in the briefest of moments. When we connect with others, we are having an experience—we are seeing someone, and they are seeing us. It can be as simple as looking at someone when you say, "Thank you, have a nice day" and then walking away. In that briefest of moments, what happened was simple, human connection. And you know what? It can help. It can help you if you're having a rough day, and it can help another person who might feel grief, pain, or like they are invisible. When people look at one another, one soul says to another, "I see you." And sometimes, that can be the best medicine.

Loneliness is a heavy emotional weight. It can feel as though it will never release its hold, never become a healed wound. It's hard to know what to do about it, so powerful are its effects. But here we've talked about some ideas on how to work with this most powerful of human emotional experiences. Do any resonate with you? Or did any other ideas come to mind as you read? If so, make a plan on how to work them into your life. Get back in the driver's seat of your experience and see what you can do, even if it's the smallest of steps, to move more toward connection. Creating an intention for yourself can help with this. Make clear for yourself what you want to bring into your life and see what happens.

10

Every Loss Changes Your Life, Physically and Emotionally

We bereaved are not alone. We belong to the largest company in all the world—the company of those who have known suffering.

Helen Keller, activist and author of *We Bereaved*

The process of weaving fabric consists of interlacing threads, over and under, over and under. Pull out one of those threads, and the pattern changes, creating an open space, and the fabric is different. Like a missing thread, any loss can change your life, and part of what causes so much pain in the long term is this idea that we have to get back to "normal." But, like that woven material with the thread pulled out, normal is different now and the fabric of life reflects this. For some, the new reality might include having to make significantly different choices to do with money. For others, it might mean that where holidays are spent and how they are celebrated is entirely different. Some may have to navigate a completely new rhythm to life, where the day-to-day functions change. Many have to reckon with an entirely different image of how life is going to be moving forward. This is not easy, and it takes a lot of time to adjust.

There are some themes that come up for people when it comes to the ongoing changes impacting a life after loss. Many of them are connected to the support that falls off in relation to the stress itself. For example, in the first year or so, it makes sense that friends and family will check on how you're faring after losing a spouse. But as time goes on, it's harder to say, "Hey, I've been thinking about the fact that you've had to move out of your house and downsize since your partner died. How's that going?" or, "Now that you're the sole financial supporter of you and your four kids it must be so intense having to go back to school to get further training so you can earn more income." These are the collateral losses that those left behind often face but are not afforded the chance to openly process.

STRESS AND OTHER WORRIES

> *Though many things didn't change on the outside*
> *following my husband's death (I had the same job, kept*
> *our house, drove the same car, my daughter attended*
> *the same pre-school), internally everything changed.*
> *Five years out, I still find myself overwhelmed by the*
> *responsibility while simultaneously missing and grieving*
> *for what my husband would have brought to the table*
> *and all the experiences he missed.*
>
> Holly

Stress is a prime contributor to long-term grief and many of its associated complications, not the least of which are health issues, relational struggles, mental health concerns like depression and anxiety, and addictive behavior. Metabolizing stress and reducing its impact on a life is very important when it comes to healing. The immediate impact of loss is wrought with its own stressors, some of them acute. How this plays out in the long term is variable from person to person. Some struggle with accepting their loved one's death and this causes ongoing and turbulent stress responses. It's as though the wound can never heal enough to stabilize, and, instead, there are waves of ongoing agony. Ben shared,

> My mother was my best friend. I called her all the time to talk about what I was doing and all the decisions I was trying to make. She was always happy to hear from me and helped me so much. Now I'm on my own and I still can't believe it.

For others, acceptance of their loss is not the primary contributor to their stress, but lifestyle and responsibilities are significantly impacted, and this carries its own weight. Alaiya describes holding all the weight of what once were shared decisions.

> I'm a single mom now. I lost someone to talk to about parenting. Someone to do half the stuff of life. I want people to know that you don't just lose that person. You lose so many other things and some of those losses are harder because there is no

help for them. No one asks about how I'm doing as a single mother or the huge financial shifts that have occurred. I'm on my own.

When surviving spouses are still raising children, they find themselves thrust into a world not of their choosing. Everything that comes up is now the responsibility of the surviving parent.

These stressors don't just go away after a year. Every decision now falls to you. As the immediate shock that comes from loss subsides, what lasts are the ramifications of this loss. The passage of time may not cure the feeling of being overwhelmed by how life has changed and the challenges that emerge with each passing year.

Financial strain wreaks havoc on stress and the nervous system. Whether you've lost a partner who was an earner for the family, a parent who supported the household, a sibling whose death has initiated a cascade of events that have impacted family stability, it all hits at a basic core need, which is to feel safe and secure. Jeffrey describes the chronic discomfort from this kind of stress this way:

I can't believe how different life feels now that our family is living on one income. We've been able to stay in our house, but our lives have changed significantly. Sometimes when I can't sleep, I make the mistake of thinking too far out in the future. It's been a discipline, learning how to take one step at a time and trust that I'll be able to make it.

Just as it is with learning, we heal best when we can relax, rest, and trust. Do you have that? If not, what are the factors contributing to a sense of instability or vulnerability?

HEALING FROM THE EXHAUSTION OF IT ALL

We all know the airplane instructions: put your oxygen mask on first before helping others. No better analogy exists when it comes to how we must care for ourselves before we can care for others. One of the things that can add to exhaustion is trying to maintain things as they were or trying to minimize the impact of the loss on your life. The truth is: your life *has* been altered. Part of healing from exhaustion is looking clearly at what your priorities are and what you can let go of.

Sometimes we take on the role of the strong one and show up time and again for others who are aching, but we don't ask for what we need, or take time to tend to ourselves. This can be an act of love for others who are in pain, but it can also be an act of avoidance. It's easier to focus on others sometimes than to tend to what is going on with ourselves. This can happen when someone loses a sibling and feels like they must help their parents, or a parent loses a child and feels like they need to help their partner or their other children. Sometimes people lose a parent and then have to help their surviving parent cope and adjust. What can happen is that people lose contact with their own grief over the years and become the poster child of the Energizer Bunny, always doing and helping, never just being.

Are you exhausted? Are you aware of what is making you

exhausted? Is it time to sort out how to create more space for you, and just you? Even tending to yourself for a little bit each day can make a difference.

TRUSTING YOUR DECISIONS

In a partnership, so many decisions are made jointly. After her husband's death three years ago, Heather continues to feel the full, weighty responsibility of raising their son and worries about the consequences of her decisions.

> I used to love working a decision out with Matt. Now it's just me in my head and it's stressful. I can't reach out to my friends every time I have to sort something out. I know I have to trust myself and let go a little bit of control. Plus, if I make a decision that disappoints my son, I feel the full brunt of his disappointment, which is so hard. He's already lost his dad, and I struggle with trying to keep him happy.

When you've lost someone who offered a perspective you appreciated and relied upon as you moved through life, it is destabilizing. A major road to walk on the journey of grief is finding your true north. Learning to listen to your own reason, to trust yourself, and to expand your support system are all part of it.

QUESTIONS YOU MAY ASK YOURSELF

Where do I even start when I'm stressed, tired, burned out, and don't feel well?

Just asking the question is the start, believe it or not. We have to start somewhere, and your job is to begin addressing issues by determining what they are. Given the many and varied details of people's lives, it is not possible to lay out all of the if-then scenarios, but here are some key things to check into and steps to take to deal with them.

- **How are you sleeping? Are you getting enough? Too little? Too much? Is it interrupted? Do you struggle with insomnia? Bad dreams?**

  However you answer this question will dictate how you might want to move forward, but it's important to take sleep seriously. When we are sleep deprived, we are much more likely to suffer from mood issues, including depression, anxiety, frustration tolerance, chronic stress, and emotional reactivity. We are also more likely to overeat and struggle with issues to do with inflammation and other chronic health conditions. Forgetfulness and lack of organization are also side effects of not enough sleep, and these are obviously contributors to increased stress, which then keeps people awake at night!

If you are struggling with this, seek out support either through research or talking with a sleep specialist. Decide to pursue good "sleep hygiene." Make nighttime routines a priority. Avoid alcohol, caffeine, or too much food in the hours leading up to sleep. Break the habit of looking at screens before sleep—pick up that good book! Declutter your sleeping area, and get anything out of your sleeping space that you don't like. If you can, make your sleeping space your haven.

- **How are you eating?**
What we feed our bodies affects how we feel. No doubt about it. Some foods contribute to ill feelings, inflammation, mood disturbances, and sleep issues. Other foods nourish us and provide us with the fuel we need to live the life we have. It's very important to think about this honestly. Too much sugar, alcohol, processed foods, and unhealthy fats do not help us. At all. If you want to feel better in your body, it makes perfect sense that you give it what it needs. If this is something that you don't know how to do or even know where to begin, a great first step is to do some research or consult with a nutritionist. Many general practitioners have nutritionists on staff who can help you pursue better health goals.

- **Are you exercising?**
Be honest. Again, if this is something you don't know how to initiate, or if it's been so long that you want to make

sure you don't hurt yourself, check in with your doctor to get a sense of where to begin, and make a plan. The research cannot be clearer: exercise helps us feel better, physically and emotionally. What's more, when we are in a good flow with exercise, eating, and sleep, they all reinforce each other. We rest better when we're exercised and fed well. We eat better when we're not sleep deprived and when our bodies are stronger. We exercise more happily when we are well rested and well fed.

- **Are there responsibilities you can let go of, at least for a while?**
  Do that. Ask for help, take a break, say no. Allow yourself to do those things that are priorities and deeply important to you. When you are feeling better, there will be time enough to do all the extras.

- **How's your heart?**
  We mean your spiritual heart. Check in with yourself. Are you tending to your soul work in any way? Do you want to? This does not require having a religious or spiritual path, although if you do, reorienting to that in a way that feels good can be very useful. If you don't, learning to meditate for even just fifteen minutes a day can help tremendously. There are wonderful resources both in books and online. Initiating a meditation practice is a surefire way to give your nervous system a chance to regulate and calm.

Should I leave our family home?

Moving from your home is a big decision very often not easily made. There are so many reasons people move, but it can become complicated when home is tied to the memory of a loved one who has died. Sometimes moving feels like the right idea because the memories are so painful that it's proving difficult to move forward. Other times, life circumstances mandate a move, but leaving all of the memories and a place tied to a loved one is re-traumatizing. Making decisions such as these can be extremely stressful and it's important to get clear on the why. Why stay? Why move? Now ask yourself: "Am I at these crossroads?"

There is a big difference between staying in a home because you genuinely want to live in it, and you feel free to change and grow and adjust as you make your way, than to feel like you are bound to the place due to guilt, unlived dreams, and regret. In the first case, it is still worthwhile to consciously recognize the transition from before to after. There are wonderful rituals you can do that can mark this threshold.

However, if your home has become a weight either financially or emotionally, pulling you under like quicksand, you might want to consider taking small steps to expand your vision of the future. This could start with looking at real estate or rentals and seeing what speaks to you. Or you might go for walks around the neighborhood and note places that look manageable and are your style. Maybe pick up a real estate magazine during your next trip to the grocery store. Go online to check out apartment decorating or downsizing that could invite ideas and images. The options are many. Bottom line is guilt can weigh down and interfere with forward movement. Getting support around metabolizing this guilt while taking small steps toward imagining a place of your own is a helpful place to start.

The future I imagined for myself has been completely upended. What am I going to do now?

The degree of flexibility we can exercise in life as it relates to making a new plan weighs in heavily after loss. Many people like to cultivate an image of how things are going to go, and what life is going to be like in the years to come. Enter stage left: long-term grief after the death of a loved one. How much has the loss of your loved one affected the vision you had of your life? For so many of us who lose someone, that person took up a lot of space in the vision of the future. So now, on top of grieving the actual death of a loved one, we are charged with grieving the death of a dream. How many people had plans for their future that were interwoven with being a parent and having a robust family life and then lose a beloved child? Or had a plan to retire with a partner and travel just to endure an unexpected diagnosis and death? The impacts of loss reverberate throughout many structures of our lives, and we are called to adjust and evolve with this new difficult reality. Where are you on this part of the journey? Have you allowed yourself to consider a new plan or vision for your life?

I can feel some of my relationships with other people slipping away. How hard should I fight to hold on to them?

We touch on this issue elsewhere in the book, but it's important to mention here: not every relationship makes it through the gauntlet of grief. Not every friend can bear witness to intense pain and stay solidly in the relationship. Not every family member will understand or be able to show up for you in the way you wish they could. And certainly, the kinds of socializing that people do after loss can vary widely and be forever different than it was before. White-knuckling your way back to "normal" causes more harm than good because it denies the truth, which is that grief changes us. Letting yourself evolve through your grief may mean that some relationships don't make it the way you thought they might. And while cutoff isn't required, accepting reality is, and it helps us to navigate the waters of new life and choice.

EXERCISES AND RITUALS THAT CAN HELP

WHAT AM I DOING?

This is an exercise designed to help you sort out what you might still be attached to that was connected to an old idea or plan that is no longer viable or desirable. Once we get clear on what we are still holding on to, we can articulate better what we might do instead, and identify any of the blocks that might get in the way of that.

What was I going to do: I was going to live in this house until I couldn't take care of it anymore, and I figured that would be in old age. I wanted this to be the home my children came to with their own children.

Why that plan has to change: I cannot afford to stay in this house on my income, and I can't take care of it by myself.

What is hard about letting this plan go: I don't want to leave. I miss my husband, and I feel so guilty about not having this place for my children to come home to. They feel close to their dad here.

What might I do instead: I have to find a place that is smaller and more manageable. Maybe with money saved from doing that, I can start creating new memories with my grown children.

MANAGING YOUR MONEY

One way to begin the process of chipping away at this hurdle on your long journey is to take the step of finding an objective person to talk to. Whether it is a financial adviser, a person at your bank or credit union, a counselor well versed in bereavement issues, or a lawyer, it is important to talk to someone frankly about the financial reality and your hopes for the future. You may have this person in your family; however this person should not have a vested interest in what you choose to do or in your property itself. Neutrality is key and is most likely to lead to a circumstance where you can enjoy the freedom to explore your options with minimal guilt. You certainly don't want to be concerned with protecting someone else's feelings while you sort out what is best for your financial future and security.

Credit unions are incredibly helpful when it comes to paying off large sums of debt. In your area, see where there might be resources that help bereaved spouses make sound financial decisions and get their lives back on track. Remember, like grief, this is a long process, and you don't have to figure most things out overnight. But you will likely find that getting your arms and mind around the big financial picture will free up much needed energy you can use on your journey.

GETTING CLEAR AND MAKING A PLAN

——— **Make a list that includes the following:** ———

> Who do you feel most comfortable talking to about money?

> Family? (list names and why you trust their opinion)

> Friends? (list names and why you trust their opinion)

> Financial adviser? If you already have a relationship with one, you are in good shape. If you need to find one, look around in your life and see if you have friends or acquaintances who seem to have some of these things figured out, then see if they might recommend a certified financial adviser to talk to.

——— **Make a list of your financial goals.** ———

These can be as simple as making sure there is enough income to pay for basic expenses to as complex as making investments, saving for retirement, and paying for college. Get clear on what your two-year, five-year, ten-year, and twenty-year plans are.

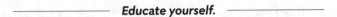

Educate yourself.

Many find themselves in an unfortunate situation where they must learn from scratch how to manage their financial lives. This often happens when one person in the couple oversees the finances, and they die suddenly. If you don't have a lot of experience talking about money or making financial decisions, this can seem like learning a new language. In many areas, there are classes and workshops that can help you learn how to engage with your financial life. Also, local libraries often have great books on how to get clear on financial realities. Invest in yourself.

WHAT HOME MEANS TO YOU

Upon hearing the word "home," some might immediately have a feeling, some might see a favorite spot, and some might think of a person. Getting clear on what home means to you can be a way to lift yourself out of the emotional pool of attachment to the core aspects of home you hold dear.

You'll need a piece of paper and something to write with for this exercise. On the paper, make one line going down the middle from top to bottom, and one line going through the middle from side to side. Label the four rectangles: People, Feelings, Sensations, and Memories.

Find a comfortable place to sit where you can be quiet and undisturbed for a little while.

Now, close your eyes, inhale, and say "home." Then, on the out breath, repeat "home." You can do this in your head or say the word out loud. Whatever works for you. Notice what comes up. Try staying with this meditation for about five minutes.

When you're done, look at your paper and let yourself write anything that comes to mind, putting each thought in the category into which it generally fits. Don't stress if one thought fits into more than one category or if one category is empty while another is full. There is no one way to experience *home*.

Next, quietly take in what you have written. Are your responses loaded with memories of older times? Specific events, like holidays or a sleepless night tending to a sick loved one? Are they sensations, like certain smells or air temperatures? Or feelings like coziness, safety, freedom? Did specific people come up in your mind and make it on your list?

Looking at your list, can you imagine how these things can migrate with you into your new dwelling and phase in life? It won't be a complete recreation of an older life, of course, but can you see how so many of the things you wrote down are there because of what you already carry with you? Your new dwelling may not have the same number of rooms, and you may not be able to bring all of the things of your life with you, but you can certainly bring with you your preferences, your memories, and your feelings, which are all portable. Look to see what floats to the top for you and you may be able to come up with specific ideas you can incorporate as soon as you arrive in your new place. These insights should help ground you in the experience of home.

CLAIMING YOUR SPACE

A lot can be said for rearranging furniture, painting rooms, and modifying decor. Claiming space in this new chapter of your life means allowing yourself to live fully in the home you have.

When you have time, take a seat in your living space. Devote this time to checking in with your dwelling. Let yourself be with the gravity of all that you have experienced in your life, and reflect on the fact that where we live, whether permanent or temporary, big or small, modern or antique, says something and somehow reflects something of us to the world and back toward ourselves. In the flow of everyday living, it's easy to lose touch with our surroundings and to treat the walls that house us as just walls, the furniture we rest on as just functional. What if we were to take some time to think about how we want to feel moving forward? Could we change things up a bit to alter the flow of energy in our day-to-day movements? Have you always wished something were a particular color or placed in a different area of a room but just never found the time or energy to do it? Allow yourself the chance to nest as you heal and make your way on your path. What do you need? Some ideas to consider are:

> Rearranging furniture
> Painting walls
> Choosing carefully what you hang on your walls. Only hang up what you like!
> Investing in some throw pillows or soft, snuggly blankets
> Bring in easy-to-care-for plants

> ➢ Claim a room, corner, or chair of one's own, if space allows—even if it's simply a chair with a little side table to create a space that is just for you, where you sit to read, write in your journal, meditate, and rest. This place should have a comfortable feel, and, if possible, face a direction that looks upon images that are at least neutral, if not pleasing (not the cat litter!).

MARKING THE TRANSITION FROM BEFORE TO AFTER

Throughout a lifetime, we pass through a series of obvious and invisible thresholds, or markers that have three key features: the before, the in-between, and the after.

Unfortunately, in modern life it is easy and common for people to flow from one time in life to another without marking the transition with any meaningful ritual or symbol. Frequently, the subtler transitions that occur go unnoticed or unrecognized for their significance. Maybe after a loved one has died and all of the accompanying burial and then legal rites have been accomplished, it is natural to think that the ceremonies and symbols to do with your loss are done, that now you have only to figure out how to live.

If you practice a faith tradition you feel connected to, you can contact your parish, mosque, temple, etc., to find out about threshold rituals that are unique to your given faith system. If you do not ascribe to a particular practice, or even if you do and would like to add something of your own to the process, here is what we have practiced ourselves and done with others wanting to more significantly symbolize moving from one phase of life to another. This ritual can also be done in a new dwelling:

Take out a piece of paper or your journal. Write on the left side a list of short sentences regarding what has been true about life since the loss of your loved one. You may write as many of them as you wish.

Then, on the right side of your page, write an alternate statement, one that reflects the opposite or the fully embraced expression of the experience.

Here are some examples:

What Has Been True about Life Since My Loved One Died	Alternate View of What Has Happened
Since my loved one has died, I've been unfocused.	I have given my mind the opportunity to deal with the chaotic pain of loss. I am ready to focus again on what I want to, even if just for brief moments as I get started.
My heart has been broken.	I allowed my heart the chance to cry to express my pain. I am ready to learn to live with the wisdom acquired from this pain and help others.
I haven't stopped crying.	I have joined my ancestors in the expression of grief. I am ready to not judge my tears and to know that they are watering the ground of the life I want to live.
I've never felt more alone.	I had to walk part of my journey alone. Now I'm ready to allow connection to stir again in my life and look at other people with openness.
My home has felt empty.	My home has not been the same since my loved one died. I am ready to fill it with new life and new memories, even small ones.

CROSSING THE THRESHOLD OF YOUR NEW SPACE

When you are done with the previous exercise, it is time to choose the threshold you will cross. The front door of your dwelling is a perfect place to do this, but you can do it anywhere. Here are the steps to follow:

> - If you are in a room, lay some string, rope, a scarf, or a rolled-up blanket on the floor that you will step over.
> - Stand on one side of your threshold. If you are at a door, start on what would be considered the outside (e.g., in an apartment dwelling, you'll start in the hallway).
> - Close your eyes.
> - Acknowledge to yourself how much you have been through.
> - Allow yourself the right of deep knowing and respect for the journey you have been on.
> - Thank your dwelling for being the container for your relationship, for your love, and for your grief.
> - Ask your dwelling to hold and to continue to support new life that is coming.
> - Open your eyes and take a step over your threshold and look around. Imagine allowing life to blossom in the walls of your dwelling while continuing to support your growing wisdom.
> - For an added element, you can also consider hanging something beautiful on your door that speaks to your heart. This can be a symbol that is part of your heritage,

an image that brings comfort, anything that reminds you that you are in your space that holds your life and your story. Make it your own and claim it.

Choosing to leave your home is a significant event. The power of it is often lost in the mayhem and stress of moving.

You are not only leaving something behind. You're also moving toward something new.

On a piece of paper or in your journal, answer these questions:

> What kind of place are you looking at or planning to move to? If you have already moved, what is your dwelling like?
> What are you imagining when you think about living there?
> What are you hoping for?
> Are you excited about anything to do with this new place?
> Are there things about this new place that, while different, will open you up to other opportunities?

Many of us are stuck because we're attached to the way we thought things were going to be. Allowing for other ideas to take root, stretching into the way things are, can allow us to experience moving as another part of our journey.

Now, like the ritual described above, you can move through a threshold crossing and invite your new place to fully become part of your story. You can do this even if where you are living is temporary.

On a separate piece of paper, write on the left side as many intentions as you can imagine for your life in this new place. Then, on the right side, next to each intention, write either how this move has brought this intention to fruition, or how you can support these intentions to come to be. For example:

Intentions for My Life in My New Home	How I Have Already or How I Plan to Bring My Intentions to Fruition
By moving into a smaller home, my intention is to save more money so I can travel with my children.	Already since moving, I've saved hundreds of dollars a month and am building up a travel savings account. Soon, I will plan our first trip.
The apartment I am looking at is in a part of town where there are a lot of things to do. I can easily step out my door and look at art or eat good food. My intention will be to do more and see more things that bring me joy.	When I move, I will make weekly dates with myself to do something simple, whether it's walk through art galleries or sit in a park and people watch.

As you reflect on this chapter, can you articulate for yourself how your life has been impacted by stress, exhaustion, big decisions to do with home, or perhaps the pull toward inaction due to fatigue? And can you identify for yourself steps you'd like to take to claim your space and let it become a place where you can rest and heal, and in which you can evolve and grow? Remember to consider that often the ways we bind ourselves to our lives is through our own fears

and patterns of guilt. If you consider what your loved one would want for you, is it easier to imagine taking steps to reclaim those parts of your life that have been stagnant? Try writing down an intention for yourself as you address these themes.

11

When Will the Other Shoe Drop?

Bracing Yourself against Future Loss

Be right here, aware of sitting here, aware of the self-definition that you're creating in your own mind. Aware of your ears listening… Aware of traffic outside. Aware of the feelings in your body. Aware of your mind grabbing at this and that. Just sit with me in this awareness.

Ram Dass, PhD, teacher and author of *Grist for the Mill*

Loss of a loved one is an experience that can be felt as an attack on a life and on the wholebody system. The stress evolving from loss can range from mild to acute and can last a few months to decades. As humans we are designed to withstand and adapt to a significant amount of stress, and, most of the time, we do. But certain stressors leave a lasting mark on the nervous system, and part of healing requires tending to those parts that are essentially "keep me safe" mechanisms. We do a lot in response to stress, which can help, and much that can hurt, especially in the long run.

A simple example of the latter is having an alcoholic drink to calm the nerves. In the moment, the drink is calming. In fact, it might even relax a person enough so they can enjoy their environment and have some fun. The problem is alcohol is toxic and requires a whole lot of the body's resources to metabolize and process. It's also addictive. One drink might lead to two, to four, and so on. The impact on the body creates a situation where someone might not have access to a calm pool of energy to respond to current and ongoing life stressors, which creates more stress.

Perhaps one of your responses is to imagine more deaths or unavoidable pain coming again in the future. Jon Kabat-Zinn, American professor emeritus of medicine and the creator of the Stress Reduction Clinic and the Center for Mindfulness in Medicine, Health Care, and Society at the University of Massachusetts Medical School, writes, "Ultimately, our habitual and automatic reactions to the stressors we encounter, particularly when we get in the habit of reacting maladaptively, determine in large measure how much stress we experience."

RESPONDING VERSUS REACTING TO STRESS

People who have experienced loss of a loved one may be going through day-to-day life wondering, "What if someone else I love dies? What if something terrible happens? What if I or someone I love gets sick?" These worries can be experienced as ongoing worries that never let up. They can also keep a person in a constant state of hyperarousal, a prime feature of post-traumatic stress disorder. It's most commonly known as the fight/flight response, and like any good defense mechanism, it works beautifully under the right circumstances, but when it runs amok and shows up when not needed, it can keep us pumped with stress hormones and their related side effects.

Topaz had many miscarriages and then made an excruciating decision to birth her baby, who had severe medical complications, early, knowing he would not survive once delivered due to his age. She calls her baby "the one who didn't make it." Topaz shared that because of these tremendous losses "on a daily basis, when my children walk out the door, from the time they were in kindergarten, I have to kiss them goodbye. I have a fleeting thought, 'This could be the last time I see my child.'"

How do you relate to stress and worry? Have you given this any thought recently? Or do you feel like the famous Energizer Bunny, going through life, continuing to stuff down as much as you can, just to get through? This might be a good time for you to check in with yourself about your worries, your stressors, and your fears and ask yourself, "What do I have control over, and what don't I?" And of those things you don't have control over, how do you feel about that? In family systems work, we often focus on reducing reactivity (those immediate and often unconscious responses to anxiety and fear that are usually not helpful) in people. The idea is to create a little bit more space between an individual and a given stressor so that the person has more time to consider, to think, and to approach a situation from a place of thoughtfulness. Kabat-Zinn calls this *responding* to stress, rather than *reacting* to stress.

WHEN CHILDREN ARE AFRAID THAT PEOPLE THEY LOVE WILL DIE

For many children, the idea of people their age dying for any reason is a blow to the otherwise strong bubble of invincibility that surrounds the growing self. Kids know a lot can happen, but death? Not death. Death is for other people, old people. To know that a person their age can die opens up the reality that they, too, can die. And not only that, everyone will die. Depending on how much experience a child has had with loss, this can be a reality shift that hits at their deepest sense of safety and security.

If your child is struggling with similar fears years after losing a loved one, chances are they are trying to make sense out of something that never quite got settled in the aftermath of their loss. Many parents have the impulse to explain away death and assure their children death will never happen to them, or at least not until they are very, very old. Parents also often promise that nothing bad will happen to themselves. But is this really a promise parents can make with full confidence? As much as we want it to be, it's not really the truth. And children, having experienced a loss, know that now. So, your job has become a bit more grounded. You are now the closest person to your child who can help them metabolize heartbreak and love. You can help them understand that the two things often dance together. You can help them see their own strength and their own capacity for courage, heartbreak, and healing.

Parents are invited to bear witness, repeatedly, to the pain and the fear with which their child struggles. It's important to refrain from making false promises. Instead, acknowledge the truth, which is: sometimes people die before it seems like they ought to and in ways that seem incredibly unfair.

What's important here is to hear their questions and encourage them to talk about what they're feeling and thinking, assuring them you will do all you can to help them, and yourself, to stay safe and healthy while living a full life. You can acknowledge that while you do all you can to take good care of yourself and others that yes, sometimes things happen. Then you can talk to your children about the resources they have *within themselves* to face whatever happens. You can talk about what courage, heartbreak, and love feel like, and give them the opportunity to express their fears and have them held, not reasoned away. Parents can help their children articulate for themselves their own strengths and own paths to courage.

CULTIVATING RESILIENCE IN THE FACE OF THE UNKNOWN

Let's get clear on what resilience is and is not. *Resilience* is defined in *Cambridge Dictionary* as: 1. the ability to be happy, successful, etc. again after something difficult or bad has happened; 2. the ability of a substance to return to its usual shape after being bent, stretched, or pressed. The two definitions of resilience house both the wonderful and problematic aspects of what has been internalized in our culture as it relates to healing from grief. To be plain, we are going for the first part of the definition in that becoming strong, healthy, and successful (whatever that means for a person) following loss are hoped for outcomes. But, returning to your original shape after loss? Not so much. It makes sense that herein lies where some of the confusion is born when it comes to our culturally internalized image of what healing looks like. You likely know this by now—we don't go back to our original form after loss. We are changed, stretched, shaped differently, and molded into something else, a different version of ourselves that incorporates this new experience, and there's nothing wrong with that.

How do we tend then, to the part of resiliency that makes sense? How do we become stronger, healthier, and successful in our lives, even though we have been heartbroken from loss? We exercise that muscle, and we practice, just like we exercise or practice anything that we are trying to develop. Researchers at Columbia University have found that utilizing growth mindset strategies helps with this, and they list the following areas as specifically helpful in growing and cultivating resilience:

- Practicing mindfulness
- Fostering hope
- Working toward forgiveness
- Practicing gratitude
- Taking care of yourself
- Maintaining a commitment to living by your deepest values
- Taking opportunities to reflect on yourself and your life
- Connecting with other people in meaningful ways

That is quite a list, to be sure, but it is worth sitting with. Like any good exercise program, especially if you're starting after a while of not working out, start slowly. Pick one aspect and work it. As you gain momentum and strength, add another, and then another.

And know this: By getting stronger and more resilient, you are not turning away from your loved one. You are creating more space in your life where you can live with their memory and your love for them in organic and true ways. Love does not disappear in the face of strength. It only grows.

QUESTIONS YOU MAY ASK YOURSELF

How do I break this cycle of fear that has developed since my loved one died?

The fight/flight response is an automatic nervous system response to fear, a reasonable outcome after the loss of a loved one. If this question resonates with you, it is important to know there are ways to heal, and not all of them are through talking—you can't necessarily think your way out of a nervous system response to a fear that has already been realized in your life. Once the trigger or instigating event has happened, the ship has sailed, at least for that moment. What your body does not know is that most likely you are okay. Your body is primed to respond to disaster; now it needs other information to come in to counter the body's response. You don't need to be ready for crisis at all times, so when you are not activated or in that fight/flight state, you are in a better place to get in touch with your senses.

In the meantime, be gentle with yourself and with others. Ask for compassion and patience and let them know you need help with this. Taking steps to not feel alone, having a plan, and taking moments to steady oneself in the face of extreme worry or fear is important.

Also, remember this—it is wise to trust your future self. Sometimes when we struggle with great fear, it is because we can't imagine ourselves dealing with something that we are afraid of happening. It can be useful to say to yourself, "I will face whatever comes my way," or "I will handle what I must." Reminding yourself of your inner strength is a broad stroke that imagines you in a position of strength. Give yourself this message over and over. If something does strongly affect you and you find yourself in a state of fear, in a quiet moment, step away, comfort yourself, and show yourself great compassion.

Since my loved one died so many people depend on me. How can I reduce my anxiety about my own health and safety?

Any person who has loved ones who rely upon them for safety, security, love, and support is bound to wonder at some point, "What would happen to them if something happened to me?" Facing this worry head-on, rather than denying the possibility or stuffing the fear, is one way to help with the anxiety that arises. This kind of chronic stress can complicate long-term grief, and, at some point, it becomes important to face the truth of your situation. Ensuring a good plan is in place for your loved ones is one of those hurdles that, once surmounted, can bring much-needed relief to these worries. Some ideas are:

- Make a will.

- Identify a guardian for your children and ensure they have agreed to this.

- Identify a trusted person to hold a copy of your will plus any other relevant information.

- Discuss with a financial adviser how to set up a trust for any dependents.

- Identify someone to care for your pet and ensure they agree to this responsibility.

Add anything to this list that can help reduce your worries. You may be surprised how much relief you feel once you've made sure that your loved ones won't have to muddle through complicated decision-making while grieving.

All these years later, I can't always predict when I'll be overcome with emotion from grief. I don't know when the next "ambush" might happen. What can I do?

This is all about riding the waves of emotion and memory and learning to recognize those things that can bring on a painful or overwhelming response. You might notice patterns over time concerning the sort of things that affect you in general. Sometimes, a certain smell, song, feeling in the air, or sound can bring on an emotional response so fast and with such power that you feel overtaken. On one end of this continuum and for those living with PTSD, these moments are considered triggers, and can bring a person right back into their trauma, with the fight/flight/freeze response fully engaged. For many others on this continuum, a certain stimulus from the environment can bring on emotional pain that is surprising, draining and can leave people wondering if they're okay. When you sense the reaction you are having is way stronger than what you might typically expect given the situation, you can take it as a signal and turn it into an opportunity to say to yourself, "I have pain here, and I need to tend to it."

Bradie shared this story of how surprised she was by an upsurge of intense emotion that came out of the blue:

It was about two years after my mom died. I was watching a Disney movie with my family, one that I'd seen years ago when I was in my teens. It was a fine night. I felt calm and peaceful. A song started, as they do in Disney movies, and I became completely overwhelmed. I started to cry and tried to stop it through breathing and sort of laughing at myself, but I just couldn't stop. I was overcome and was basically weeping. My kids were totally confused, as was I! I'd seen the movie many times and wasn't especially into it one way or the other, and I didn't love the song... There was just something about it that unlocked feelings that poured out of me. I haven't cried like that since—the kind of crying where you are just wet and soggy and tired for days after. I thought about it a lot afterward and wondered what it was about that moment that got to me. I realized it brought me back to a time in my life when my mom was okay and in some respects, life was so much more simple. It was like time shrunk and I was back in a grief place, tending to so many losses and heartbreaks. It was quite something.

Sometimes, we just can't help what gets us, but always the invitation is to ask yourself and wonder, "What was that about?"

Many people worry about their capacity to keep themselves grounded and okay when they are out in the world, worried that something will bring on a strong emotional reaction or trigger a trauma response. It's easy to see how this could evolve into other mental health conditions, especially anxiety and depression. This is where nervous system work comes in, and there are wonderful therapeutic techniques that can help with this on a body level.

Walter Brownsword, a psychologist and someone who knows grief himself, shares this bit of wisdom:

> With people I work with, a thing that comes up a lot with grief is that they are stuffing their feelings throughout most of the week and then something comes up. I encourage proactive grieving. Schedule a time and make space for it. If people do that, their body won't take over and make it happen in the middle of whatever space they are in when they can't help it. The bodily pressure to work it out isn't as strong.

Can you make dates with yourself to allow for any feelings, grief, thoughts, or worries to have a space to be aired and reflected upon?

EXERCISES AND RITUALS THAT CAN HELP

GATHERING YOUR NERVES AND GIVING THEM LOVE

If you are experiencing chronic stress or symptoms of PTSD, your nervous system needs some love and tending to. When we lose someone we love, it can be a terrible blow to how we experience the world day to day, for years to come. Often when we feel stressed or suffer from symptoms of PTSD, we do things that might feel like they are helping in the moment; however, they are simply masking an issue or dulling an acute feeling. Use of alcohol or drugs, zoning out to entertainment, and overeating are all examples of this. The best way to help your nervous system balance out and give yourself a chance to heal is to take active steps in decision-making so your fight/flight response can rest.

is a list of things you might consider doing. Choose at least one that seems like the best fit for you. Over time, you might find yourself choosing more from this list, or pursuing other ways to calm the sympathetic nervous system (fight/flight) and activate the parasympathetic nervous system (calm/relaxation). Resources are listed in the Appendix on page 358 for some of these ideas.

> Drink the recommended amount of water every day: We all know this! Why don't we do it?

> Avoid caffeinated beverages: Maybe this seems obvious, but if your nervous system is in a constant state of stress, why add to it? There are many wonderful teas and bubbly beverages that can satisfy the desire for a treat and that satisfaction might be enough to give you the bump you long for from caffeine.

> Avoid alcohol or the recreational use of drugs: Give your body a chance to find its natural regulation cycles, which

are automatically hijacked by these substances. Alcohol also interferes with a good and productive sleep.

> Get enough sleep: This cannot be overstated. Our brains do incredibly important work when we sleep. Practice good sleep hygiene by minimizing or reducing screen use right before bed. Don't drink or eat stimulating foods in the hours before bed. Avoid eating larger meals several hours before you want to sleep. Keep your sleeping space as distraction free as you can. If you enjoy reading before bed, try a good old-fashioned book, and avoid ones that are stressful or anxiety provoking. If you have difficulty falling asleep, reading a real page-turner that you can't put down might not be the best idea.

> Meditate, even for just a few minutes a day: Research shows that a regular meditation practice reduces the size of the amygdala, the part of the brain associated with the fight/flight response, and increases the size of the brain stem, the area of the brain that makes feel-good chemicals. And don't worry, you won't disable your ability to respond to an emergency or crisis. You will simply be able to respond with more clarity of thought and less reactivity.

> Get a massage or practice self-massage: The cost of getting regular massages can be prohibitive, but that doesn't mean you can't enjoy the benefits of it through self-massage. There are great online resources for this.

Maybe you can treat yourself to a soothing lotion to make it extra comforting.

> Take regular breaks from technology: *Please.* It's so important. Plenty of research exists on this, but the gist is—we need to experience life in the here and now, with our own eyes and senses and reality, and not compare our lives to others'. We also need to take regular breaks from light and stimulation coming into the mind. You are the gatekeeper of this, and only you can modulate this for yourself.

> Walk outside and let yourself notice your surroundings (if you live in a place where you feel safe doing so): If you don't, but you still want to experience nature, find a comfortable place in your home next to a window, and stream or play nature sounds like the ocean or rain. Consider practices like yoga, tai chi (tai chi is done in the water), acupuncture/acupressure, reiki, and others.

TRUST IN YOUR FUTURE SELF

When we are waiting for the other shoe to drop, we can live in a state of constant worry. "What if this happens? What if that happens? What if...?" Tune into the idea that you will be able to handle whatever comes up in the future, because something will, and you will have to no matter how elegantly or inelegantly. In the here and now, all you are dealing with is the present moment, and yes, while we have to toggle between now and later for the simple reason of planning, that's different than spending a lot of time and energy trying to prepare your mind for some cata-strophic event that may or may not happen. The key is to trust. Trust yourself.

In Pam's workshops she uses a visualization technique called "Envisioning the Future." Some of the affirmations include:

> I believe in myself; I believe in my life experience.
> I am a fully intelligent, creative being.
> My fears are transformed into my teachers empowering me to move forward with courage.

PUT DOWN YOUR SWORD WHEN YOU DON'T NEED IT

When we have experienced things that shock our nervous system, scare us, or keep us in a sustained state of stress and pressure, our systems go into the fight/flight/freeze response. For many people, this stance sticks. It's easy to imagine chronically avoid-ing overstimulating situations to keep from feeling flooded and overwhelmed. It can look something like this: "Every task I do, I do it as though it's an emergency. I just need to get through it so I can relax. But I'm finding that there is no relaxing. I just keep chasing that feeling. I feel like I am a bull charging through my life, and if I trace it back, I can see it started when my brother died, and our family fell apart. I've been in turbo mode for years, and I don't know how to stop."

Bradie refers to this as treating everything as though it were a battle. Getting to places on time, completing chores, prepar-ing for events, getting work done; these are all day-to-day tasks that many people use symbolic swords to conquer when really, all that is needed is attention. There is no need for urgency, right? Your body doesn't know that, because at one point, you needed that sword to get through all that you were going through. Your sword slayed fear. Your sword slayed exhaustion and overwhelmingness. Your sword slayed depression, anger, and despair. Maybe your sword is still slaying many of these things on the battlefield of your long journey, but it's slaying too much else. That power we cull up within ourselves, it helps. We need it, but if it never takes a rest, we stay in a chronic state of stress, and it is not good for us.

Take some time to reflect on how you respond to day-to-day tasks and stressors. Are there any stressors to which you could soften your response? List them and then come up with alternate ways you can respond to go about accomplishing what you need to. Here are some examples to get you started:

When do you use your sword? When I'm planning an extended family gathering.

Do you need a sword for this? Why do you use it? Well... sort of? Gathering with the whole family is so stressful to me! It just reminds me of who I am missing, and it feels like I have to contort myself to seem okay. My sword helps me do that. The problem is, I get angry, and I feel like I never enjoy myself, and I think people can pick up on that.

What else can you use to help you? I do want to enjoy these times, and I don't want to feel angry all the time. I can ask people to do more to help with things, like do a potluck instead of me cooking all the food. I can also take moments to just be quiet while people gather. And touch base with my heart. I can also make sure to spend time with the little kids in the family who are so sweet, and let other people help with cleanup.

Tending to yourself, your nervous system, and your heart are key here. Take the time to reflect on how you'd like to do this moving forward by answering the following questions. Think of yourself as a loved one, to yourself. What would you recommend a best friend or a loved one do? Follow that advice for yourself. You are precious. Allow yourself to think of yourself that way.

After reading this chapter, what steps have you decided to take to reduce your stress-filled concerns about future events?

Will It Ever Get Easier?

Navigating Holidays, Special Occasions, and Anniversaries

> *I worried that my father was going to die at any moment. I worried that I would die… I simply felt a yawing dizziness at the idea that life was completely out of my control.*
>
> Claire Bidwell Smith, LCPC,
>
> author of *Anxiety: The Missing Stage of Grief*

When a loved one dies, you might be faced with grief over your loss again and again. As the years have passed you may have "moved on" in many ways but might find the holidays and other celebrations particularly difficult. You're not alone. Most celebrations only happen once a year, so it follows that even after many years, you haven't had a lot of practice navigating them.

Stephanie, a member of the Fatherless Daughters Facebook group described her experience of Father's Day this way:

> *I was thinking earlier which day was the most devastating in our cycle of grieving our dads. The day they passed, their*

birthday, or Father's Day? For me they're all painful, but Father's Day for me is almost (not quite but definitely close) as painful for me as the day my dad died. I think it's because there is so much build up to Father's Day. The cards, the commercials, the pictures, the social media posts are all in our faces and there's nothing we can do.

Anniversaries, holidays, and milestones can reawaken memories and feelings that otherwise lie dormant. You may find the anniversary date is connected to a certain time of the year. For example, if your loved one died in the fall, the leaves changing might bring on sadness for many years. Be prepared for some emotional upheaval—it's completely normal. If you're sharing a holiday or lifecycle event with relatives, talk to them ahead of time about their expectations and agree on strategies to honor the person you loved.

Here are some ways you might approach these conversations:

"I know it's been a while since my daughter died. But I still enjoy hearing your stories about her so please don't hesitate to share."

"I'm so glad to be joining you, but if for some reason it gets emotionally difficult for me, I may need to leave a bit early. I know you'll understand."

"If you see me tearing up, just know I'm having a temporary feeling, and it's normal for me during these times."

"Happy Thanksgiving, everyone. I miss my husband, Bill, and today I'm remembering how thankful I am for the years we had together."

"I wish Susie were here, but I trust she is with us in spirit as she wouldn't want to miss this celebration!"

Suggestions for what to do on a death anniversary:

1. Visit their grave to place flowers or a small stone on the head-stone or visit the place where you scattered their ashes.
2. If you still have their ashes, you might consider scattering them somewhere meaningful.
3. Light a remembrance candle for them.
4. Write them a letter or a poem in your journal.
5. Do something you liked to do together—bring a friend if you need support.
6. Take a short vacation or get away from the house for a day or two.

Entertain the idea that remembrance and cycling through grief is part of the long journey and an integral part of the human experience.

THE CYCLIC NATURE OF GRIEF

One of the best reminders of my mother is growing sunflowers every year from seeds from the original "special" sunflower from Heaven I received that first birthday without her. All summer and fall I get to enjoy these with my family and think of her.

Rachel

Humans are symbolically rooted animals. We've been symboliz-ing and recognizing the power and significance of death for tens of thousands of years. There are certain smells, sounds, and cir-cumstances that bring us into the tide of remembrance and grief, and this occurs in a cyclic way. Maybe the calendar holidays and anniversaries are the tide markers for you. Or perhaps instead, or in addition, the tide that moves through and around you is con-nected to a flow of growth and opportunity for healing. We've now come to understand that grief is not linear. We don't move through a set schedule of emotional tasks, healing completely and moving on. Moreover, with passing time and growing wisdom, we revisit old pains and have the opportunity to work with our stories with increased insight and depth. These revisitings are sometimes not easy or without pain. Many of us have mental health and phys-ical ailments that are connected to these cyclical rhythms, and it's good to know about them and what we might expect, and, addi-tionally, what they might represent.

Creating space and planning for the cyclical nature of grief helps. Rather than waiting for specific dates to mark your loss, maybe you can claim space for yourself, during a time you know is rich with feeling, when you can tend to your rite of remembrance. Autumn is a season that creates this feeling for many people. What times call to you?

QUESTIONS YOU MAY ASK YOURSELF

My loved one was the glue that held the family together. Now that they're gone, we're fragmented and it's so lonely. How can we cope with this?

There are those people in families who are truly the glue that holds it all together. They might be the ones willing and able to host the holiday gatherings. They may be the holder of the family stories, lore, and history. They may or may not be the oldest member of the family. They are simply the people who show up and stay connected. Losing this person in a family system can have widespread and totally unexpected effects, especially when no one else steps in to take up the reins of family leadership. This can turn long-term grief into a family affair, which can bring everyone closer or make divisions worse.

It can take a long time for a new equilibrium to emerge in how a family operates after such a loss. For children and adults, this can be very painful and anxiety provoking, hence the journey of long-term grief. You might find that when special occasions or holidays arise, a pall of sadness falls over you, or you might wish you had somewhere else to be. You might feel discomfort and irritation with how different things are but not quite know why you're having such strong reactions.

Long-term grief isn't always clear-cut. You might not think concrete thoughts like, "Ever since my grandparents died, I find that holidays aren't as much fun and therefore I am sad." It might be more like, "I used to love the holidays but now they just make me depressed. I guess this is what growing up is all about," or, "I can't deal with going to my aunt's house for the holiday. I just want to be by myself."

This is grieving over what was and is no longer. These are chapters for which the page is turned and the only way to go back is in memory. It's a hard pill to swallow for many people, especially if family dynamics are complicated and painful.

If you struggle with this, it may be time to make a commitment to those traditions you hold dear, and to bring them back into your life in a new way—through you. Remember, you hold in your heart what you love and value, and you can access these things at any time. Can you imagine ways to bring new life to those things you miss and long for? Maybe you are the new family leader in this way and haven't assumed the position yet.

With both my parents gone and no other family I am close to, I always feel like a tagalong. I'm invited to things because people are nice enough to do that, not because I belong there. The holidays are the hardest time. I'm so sick of that feeling. What can I do?

The holidays and special occasions, more than other times during the year, can be so tenderly painful for those who have lost loved ones and for whom the fabric of connection hasn't been rebuilt. Many have no immediate or obvious options when it comes to alternatives for gathering, while others do, but they feel off or simply not okay with what they don't have anymore. Sitting in the midst of a wonderful family gathering with people who are not your family might seem nice, but there's a pain there that's deep and untouchable.

These are times to load up on tending to yourself lovingly and creatively. White-knuckling your way through the important or symbolic times might not be the best way to go. Maybe doing some ritual things that mark the passing of time and honor what you've been through would be healing, instead of hurtful.

There are also times when it helps to take action to be more intentional when it comes to how you move through holidays. Rather than waiting to see what you are invited to and maybe dreading the event itself, decide for yourself how you want to pass this time. Maybe there are organizations that need volunteers. Serving food to people is a deep act of love, and it fills people up, body and soul. Sitting with elders who have no family and listening to their stories or simply sharing space bridges worlds of loneliness and creates connection and comfort. Or, maybe you can imagine hosting a gathering or organizing an event, like a winter walk or service opportunity. As you take steps to engage with your loneliness and move toward connection on your own terms, you might find that time shared with others is more grounded and satisfying. You also might see that time spent with yourself is time well spent. You, in fact, are someone worth getting to know. And you are front and center in that relationship.

Looking at your journey from above and deciding which way you want to go next in relation to tending to your loneliness is proactive, creative, and loving. What can you imagine trying?

I can't sit through one more holiday with people who are uncomfortable talking about or saying my loved one's name. How do I handle this without creating drama?

When whole families gather in a spirit of celebration and there is a missing beloved, something is off. A chair at the table is empty. It wasn't supposed to be like this. Many in these situations feel like there is an elephant in the room and feel those with them are tip-toeing around the painful reality so evident in absence. Even years later, families can feel a heaviness, and it may very well be that the heaviness is the longing for the beloved's name to be said with ease, for them to be remembered, talked about, and cherished. That's the rub, right? Can a loved one ever be talked about openly without it somehow detracting from whatever is going on? We say absolutely, yes. Perhaps you're the one meant to do it.

The entire family might brainstorm about ways to honor this need. Giving to charities in the deceased's name is one idea, lighting a candle at the table on behalf of them, including them in prayers before meals; all of these are ideas that show how one might honor their loved one. Maybe the whole family needs to know that this is not only okay, but welcomed, and in the spirit of that kind of love, everyone might enjoy greater connection.

EXERCISES AND RITUALS THAT CAN HELP

HONORING RHYTHM

The heart of this ritual is to take time. Wherever you are, whatever your life circumstances and however busy you feel. Taking time to infuse the ritual of remembrance in a rhythmic way will allow you to move with the tides of grief rather than stand against them, which ultimately doesn't work; our bodies and souls need opportunity to process and release what we are working over, and if we don't create the space, it comes out another way, often more painfully and subconsciously.

Make a date with yourself to sit quietly. Create an atmosphere of peace around you. Some people like to wear a shawl or blanket, light a candle, turn off their phone. In your journal, or simply in your mind, reflect on how you feel now in whatever season you are in. Let your mind drift to months in the last year. How did you feel from month to month? Do you remember? Were there times that were open and spacious, or constrained and pressured?

When you consider the coming months, can you foresee times where you might wish you had space to just be? These don't have to be unique to specific dates. Just time approaching that you might want to make room to tend to your spirit.

Mark that on your calendar.

Whether you go on a walk, sit quietly in meditation, cook a favorite food, write in your journal, or pray, let it be a time just for you and your grief. You may find you long to check in with this part of yourself more frequently than you've been allowing or considering.

NATURE: THE REMINDER

If we need help remembering the cyclic reality of life and death, we need look no further than outside our front door. Mother Nature shows us day in and day out, month by month, that her cycles rule all, and if we lean into that idea, we can feel how much a part of nature we really are. Somehow we've gotten the idea that we need to maintain the same level of energy and maintain the same degree of output, no matter what time of year. Many of us fall into allowing the clock and the demands of our capitalist culture to dictate what we do and how we rest. Mother Nature doesn't give two hoots about that and instead, if we are willing to pick up what she is throwing down, insists upon rhythm. As you look out your window or travel to a park, what do you see? What temperature is the air? What are the plants and animals up to? Are there any signals that what nature is creating might be nice for you, too?

HOW TO BRING YOUR LOVED ONE TO THE GATHERING

There are infinite ways we can make space for our loved ones who are gone during special occasions. Some families do this very consciously by toasting those they have lost before beginning a meal or lighting a candle in honor of someone on a mantel or table. The first order of business is to become comfortable with the idea and know that it's a wonderful way of maintaining connection with our loved ones.

Once you've decided you want to do this, let your imagination take over. Here are some ideas:

- Make a memory table (see page 76) near a festive area of your home.
- Light a candle for your loved one and acknowledge your love for them as you enjoy the company of others.
- Make an offering as a family to an organization that your loved one would have supported, in their name.
- If you have holiday heirlooms from your loved one, talk about them and use them.
- Wear an article of clothing or jewelry you like that belonged to your loved one.
- Take a moment of quiet by yourself in the midst of activity and simply feel your feelings and send out love to those you miss. Give yourself a hug.

Yes, of course the holidays, special occasions, and anniversaries are particularly challenging. Ask yourself how you can manage a bit better next year and what your loved one would want for you in the future.

13

Some Relationships Change

This Can Be Another Loss

You find out who you are and what you want, and then
you realize that people you've known forever don't
see things the way you do. So you keep the wonderful
memories, but find yourself moving on.

Nicholas Sparks, author of *The Choice*

Nature is our best teacher when it comes to this simple fact: make a change in one place and the effects of this change can ripple out and go on for a long time and in ways seen and unseen. Maybe this is one of the reasons why people can't help themselves when they are by a body of water with rocks around; whether we skip them or throw them as far as we can, don't we watch the ripples until they disappear?

The loss of a loved one creates these disruptions or changes in relationships that are for many, unexpected. Whether we have new and complicated dynamics to sort out with family or are facing the reality that not every friend we have is going to show up for us in the way we need, these can become gnarly burrs stuck to our clothes as we navigate the long journey of grief. There may be additional grief to tend to as a result of these changes, or resentments and anger that also need tending. It's important not to forget that some of the changes people experience in relationships are generative. Some relationships deepen, mature, and heal through the alchemy of heartbreak. Have you experienced changes in your relationships since the loss of your loved ones? If so, maybe now is a good time to reflect on these changes with an attitude of curiosity and interest, rather than judgment. It's possible you'll discover some wisdom here.

NOT EVERYONE CAN WALK THE WHOLE JOURNEY WITH YOU

I was really surprised by how different friends did or didn't show up for me when my father died. Some people who I didn't consider close friends reached out a lot and even now, years later, check in to see how I am. They don't specifically say, "Hey, how are you feeling about your dad?" But just in the way they talk to me, the opening is there where I know I can talk. Other friends of mine who I thought were really close to me bailed out early, and I still carry pain about that. I don't say anything because why bother, but it makes me trust them less. They made it clear that my anguish was too much for them, so I don't share that part of myself with them anymore.

Amy

There's nothing like heartbreaking events to challenge our views on how strong we think our relationships are. People we thought we could rely on for anything and would show up for us no matter what, don't for whatever reason. And other people show up in ways we never expected. As the grief journey meanders through fields, up mountains, through dark caves, and across deserts, we may find there are different companions that show up to accompany us for a while. The important thing here is not to hold on so tightly to the reins of how we thought things were *supposed to be* that we neglect to be present with how things *are*. If we are so focused on how people have let us down, it's possible we miss the person smiling from across the road who knows grief in a similar way we do.

An added benefit to releasing the ideas of how we think others ought to be showing up for us is that we can practice asking for what we need, sharing how we really are, and simply being with someone where they are. There are many reasons why people ebb and flow in their support of those they love. It's certainly the case that sometimes folks just don't get the long-term pain of grief until they've gone through it themselves. It's also possible that they carry their own emotional baggage that makes it tough for them to be near your pain for the long haul. The point is, relationships change, and when we accept this as a natural part of life, we can relax and be open to what is there.

FAMILY CONNECTIONS CHANGE, TOO

The idea of the natural flow of relationship change is also true for families. Loss of a family member changes the structure of the family as a whole. Dr. Murray Bowen, a psychiatrist and theorist behind family systems theory, refers to the "shock wave" that runs through families after the death of a loved one. That's another reason why this idea of "going back to normal" needs to be retired from any goal to do with healing—normal doesn't exist anymore, and what's left is a new iteration in the living family. The degree to which people can be open to this reality, adjust to it, and evolve within the new family structure varies greatly. Of course, with any family, there's usually a lot of complexity that goes into how it operates, but those families that are flexible, adaptable, and foster an acceptance of honesty and responsibility walk the long journey of grief with less baggage and less reactivity.

What does this look like? For one, it's exceedingly important for family members to respect and understand not everyone is going to have the same intensity of feelings all the time. There's a difference between being together as a family and being emotionally intertwined such that one person's feelings become another's and vice versa. Families who support an honest exchange of emotions and ideas without having to share them allow for individuals to live and exist wholly in the family unit, its own organism. There tends to be an over-focus on the individual griever while ignoring the fact that a whole family is recalibrating and recovering from the shock wave of loss. Small, nuclear families where there is little extended family support or community support have a hard time because all the emotional intensity is housed within the small family. It's so much to bear! And there are often consequences of this in the many years following the loss. Medical, psychological, and behavioral problems emerge in members of a family and are often mistakenly taken at face value, rather than seen as part of a whole story that connects back to the initial loss.

If you look at grief as energy, we can imagine that it needs a place to go, to dissipate, and to transform into something else. How did you and your family adapt or adjust after the loss of your loved one? Did you have ample support from extended family? What about those family members who weren't as close to your lost loved one? Were there other community supports, friends, or acquaintance groups that could help hold and metabolize your grief? If your family has struggled to find equilibrium following the death of your loved one, it is wise to ask yourself *why*. How did each person react to their own grief and to the other's? And are there ways individual family members (starting with yourself) can take steps to fully own their grief and be interested in how other people are without taking it on?

It's natural to wonder if relationships with surviving loved ones will ever return to their past state. The short answer is "No." You have the distinction of experiencing a shared history—you've been through the loss of a loved one together and the experience can either strengthen the bond between you or cause a disruptive change in roles.

It's okay to speak honestly with your loved one and let them know how you're feeling. You may, in the process of talking, find out more about where they are in their own grief journey and learn about ways you can support one another. Honesty, coupled with kindness and understanding, is the key here.

QUESTIONS YOU MAY ASK YOURSELF

I feel changed since the death of my loved one. How do I reconcile with this change within me and its effects on how I connect with others?

To put it bluntly, when grief touches our life it changes us. It changes what's important to us. It softens us in some places, hardens us in others. Where we meet other people in the process of relating might look very different than it did before.

Jill put it this way, when reflecting on this very issue,

> *In some ways, this loss has made me more compassionate and in other ways less so. I have an infinite amount of compassion and patience for others' hardships and loss, but I'm less patient for what feels like less "justified" sadness. This was my first (and most significant) life trial, and I now have a broader appreciation for just how hard some individual's lives are. This recognition of just how hard life can be has made it harder for me to "sit with" the less significant tribulations of our lives.*

This is such a good example of thoughtful consideration of the subtle and not as subtle ways grief can shape us in the years following loss. There is always the option of shutting down, but we can also decide how we want to continue to relate and move toward those things and people who are important to us.

My social life has changed significantly. What do I do now?

Going at life alone can be lonely. The problem is socializing doesn't always fix the feeling. You may still find it uncomfortable to be with people who don't really understand what you've experienced or who you can't be yourself around, even if you've known them for years. If you haven't done it in a while, taking steps to invite others into your world takes courage, but it can be as simple as inviting a friend to go bowling, on a walk, or to a movie. It can be as big as going on an organized tour vacation with other single folks. If you find yourself longing to be with people in a light and social way, taking a chance to move toward what you want is a first step.

In some cases, simply sorting out how to move forward in relationships that were defined in part by your deceased loved one can be extra complicated and bound up in loyalties, shoulds, guilt, and devotion.

These issues don't resolve themselves overnight or in any particular order. It takes time, consideration, and honest reflection on the truth of where you are and where you've been. Be patient with yourself and with those you love, always understanding that the loss of your loved one changed everything, and it's okay not to fight that.

EXERCISES AND RITUALS THAT CAN HELP

WHAT ROADS DO I WANT COMPANY ON?

When we've been hurt or let down, sometimes an auto-response is to not want or need anything from anyone. Then suddenly, we find ourselves more alone than ever. In the process of moving forward from loss, we have to consider reaching out to reengage. When thinking about how you might like to invite people back into your life, take a look at what you are doing, or what others whom you love are doing. These don't all have to be specific to grief, but more generally, to life. Although, there may be some parts of your grief journey where it would be wonderful to have companionship. Here are some examples to consider:

> I'd love to travel to a place my loved one wanted to visit. Would I like company? Who would it be?

> I'd like to honor the ten-year anniversary of my loved one's death, and the road I've been on since then. I know someone who hosts dreamwork retreats that sound wonderful, and I know just whom to ask to do it with me.

> I'd like to visit the home I grew up in and wonder if my brother would like to join me for a walk there and talk about our lives.

> I'd like to take an art class to tap into my creativity. I'll ask a few friends of mine if they'd like to do it with me. If they can't, that's okay. I'll be open to whom I meet.

> I've had my eye on a silent meditation retreat at a local monastery. I would like to make a date with myself to do this, to honor my own spirit and relationship with myself.

Let yourself imagine those things you'd like to do and with whom. Ideas you come up with are automatically part of your journey and even if they don't specifically connect to your loved one, they are part of your path. Who will join you?

SAYING "YES" AND "NO" AUTHENTICALLY AND WITHOUT GUILT

Pam once gave a well-attended workshop entitled, "What You Don't NO Can Hurt You," where participants were encouraged to unearth those activities and people to whom they have been saying "yes" without considering their own wants and needs. Try this. Make a list of things you've said "yes" to in the past that no longer serve you. Perhaps you've included the bowling league on your list, a daily two-mile hike, volunteering to drive the soccer team, or being the only one providing the coffee-hour desserts at your church. Without thinking too much, quickly write the words "yes" or "no" next to each activity (or person) on the list. When you're done, notice how many "nos" there are and begin to make decisions to put your energies elsewhere—into people and activities that give you a good feeling and that support your grief journey.

MOVING THE FAMILY MOBILE

As a result of one family member's death, relational positions have no doubt changed. Here is a way to visualize those changes. Sit quietly, close your eyes, and imagine a mobile dangling from the ceiling, the individual parts of the mobile representing the members of your family. Now touch one of them and notice how the relationship with the others changes—some move closer, others move further apart. This visualization demonstrates a sometimes painful change in the family system and is a natural result of the loss of your loved one. Reflecting on this visualization, are there conversations you'd like to have with family members about shifting roles and their feelings about them?

Change is inevitable in life. After significant loss it feels like nothing will ever be the same in every part of life, including your relationships. It's up to you. Based on what you've read in this chapter, do you intend to keep moving forward?

14

"I'm a Different Person Now"

Discovering Who You Are Without Your Loved One

True belonging alters and re-creates your identity.
When that belonging is fractured or lost, something of
our deepest self departs. To open yourself is to risk losing
yourself.

John O'Donohue, poet and author of *Eternal Echoes:*
Celtic Reflections on Our Yearning to Belong

"Who am I without you?" is a question that plagues so many suffering from loss. Whether it's loss of a spouse, a child, a sibling, a parent, a grandparent, a friend, or a beloved pet, some of us are so tied to who we are in relation to a loved one that when they are no longer with us, it's as though we're walking around with a partially empty self.

Sometimes these losses affect how we experience our identity in our family, our social circles, and in our communities. These all may need to be flexibly reshaped to allow for your new reality. The extent to which the loss of your loved one affects meaningful and deeply held aspects of your identity dictates how much you might struggle in the years following your loss. It's easy to forget that what we do, how we operate in the world, relate to others, and the roles we play are deeply ingrained in our histories. Partnership, parenting, work life, hobbies, and spiritual and religious life are all areas where we express our self-identity. Is it time to ask yourself, "Who am I without my loved one?"

Mary struggles with this issue. She lost her husband about two years ago and loved how he made her feel about herself. She told us,

> *I know it's been a long time since Jeff died, but I really miss just being with him. He got me. He saw the real me and he didn't try to change what he saw, like so many people in my life do. Now I feel like I'm pretending when I'm with people. I hate dating because I'm not real! I'd rather be alone than pretend.*

We experience and project our identities in individual ways that are part of relationships, and part of larger groups: "I enjoy long drives," "I'm Jeff's partner," or "I'm an activist." Some people adopt the qualities or interests of a lost loved one to hold on to part of what made them unique.

GETTING IN TOUCH WITH YOU AGAIN

> *Life would have been different if he were here because of his sense of humor in tough times, his general wisdom, his decisiveness.*
>
> Holly

Were your choices and identities deeply tied to each other's? Were you inseparable siblings and each other's best friends? Were you connected to your child and your role as a parent in family and in community? With your partner, did you plan your day around what each was doing? When you imagine walking through the door, what part of you symbolically enters first? You the partner? The parent? The mechanic? The minister? Which part of you leads the way into society? These are important questions to ask yourself as you reckon with the question "Who am I without you?" In other words, "Who is walking the journey now?" Ilene, who lost her husband six years ago, wrestles with this. "I should be over this by now. I don't know how to be me without Gary. I think I got my personality enhanced by him. He made me look better, more at ease. I still don't know how to be comfortable in social situations. I feel like I died, too, and they just forgot to bury me."

Getting in touch with the "I" in your relationship is a big step to take, but it needs to happen in little increments. You don't have to create a totally new you. You don't have to become someone else. If you and your loved one enjoyed gardening together, you can still garden. If you found deep connection and meaning in volunteering or serving your community, you may find that taking initial steps back into this part of you will reignite your own identity.

Begin where you are. Bradie talks with her clients about trying this: As you look around or go about your day, notice when you feel a pull, an awareness, or an urge toward something pleasing. Let yourself move toward that thing, whether it's pursuing it or simply naming it. If it's a song on the radio you like, enjoy it.

Maybe turn up the volume. If it's observing a beautiful sunset, let yourself pause there for a moment to soak it in. If it's the taste of a yummy food, savor it and let yourself taste every little bit, even if it's just for a moment. All those little moments you have with yourself are the real, true important parts of you!

FEELING STRONGER AND SETTING BOUNDARIES

> *Since my husband died, I've discovered who can be*
> *with me for the long run and who is too uncomfortable.*
> *I let go of friendships I thought were strong and was*
> *surprised by some that were.*
>
> Michelle

You often don't know what you're capable of until you're forced to face your greatest fears. Sometimes only in retrospect we can marvel at what we've accomplished. Take a moment to notice and reflect on where you've been since you lost your loved one. You've traveled difficult roads and it's time you commended yourself for that, even if simply getting out of bed sometimes felt like running a marathon.

In the years following a painful loss, people often report feeling like they finally learned how to say "no" to things. They've developed boundaries because they simply could not do everything they had been doing prior. Some told us that through their grief they realized how precious life was and decided to stop participating in things they didn't value. Instead, they chose to pursue those things that resonated more with their soul's purpose. Some feel pride at how they stayed strong for their children and kept life going when all they really wanted to do was succumb to the weight of sadness and fear.

QUESTIONS YOU MAY ASK YOURSELF

My loved one was my muse, and I haven't created anything new since their death. How can I recapture that side of myself?

A muse is a person who inspires creativity in another person. They are often thought of as a romantic figure, but this is not always the case. In this context, it can be anyone who brings out the light in us, the shine, the scintillating parts of our nature that would otherwise lay dormant, or perhaps underexpressed. This can be a grandparent whose eyes always twinkle when they hear you sing. A child who brings out the softness and patience of unconditional love. A sibling who knows you better than anyone and celebrates your every success. A friend who picks up the phone no matter what time you call, ready to hear what is on your mind.

Love is creativity. Love is hope and energy. When we lose someone we love deeply and who inspires in us an energy flow that liberates those qualities that make us shine, we ache in ways both to do with loss of our loved one as well as loss of access to that part of ourselves. This can look like deep depression for some, flatness, lack of luster, purposelessness. It can be scary and deeply disorienting, and it can go on for a long time.

The thing about a muse is that they somehow carried the key to something already inside of you. It existed before they saw it or smiled with glee at your gifts—those gifts are still there. The reasons for sharing them deserve a revisit, and your beloved muse is one way to do it because the clogged-up energy, love, and creativity needs a place to go.

Loneliness is part of the conversation, too, because when connection with others is part of how we connect to the rushing energy of our own creativity, we can feel as if we are essentially cut off from our spirit when our muse dies. This can be fundamentally destabilizing and can leave many a griever feeling anywhere from flattened out to existentially depressed for years.

Might it be worth considering that you can still access your love in a creative way? Can you offer your creativity and love energy to your loved one as you go about the work of making, creating, and giving? It might look something like this:

- Take a few moments before starting the creative endeavor or loving action.
- Get settled in your body. Steady your breathing.
- Notice your surroundings and tune into the little things. The sounds, the smells, the textures...
- Offer what you are about to do to your loved one. Invite them to enjoy what you are doing.
- Acknowledge to yourself that it may feel clunky for a while, that you're feeling rusty and you need their help.
- Let yourself cry if you feel the urge to and keep at it.

You may feel very tired after you try this the first few times, and you might wonder if it's even worth it. We suggest it most assuredly is, and that you have a chance to bring back into your life active use of your gifts that are now touched by the deepest experience of loss. What alchemy will transform your gifts into something new? Do you want to find out?

My priorities have changed, permanently, since the loss of my loved one. How do I release the pressure I feel to still be the old me?

This has been mentioned before, but it's worth restating here. Priorities often change when we are on the long grief journey. Over the years you may have found that things that seemed important before simply aren't anymore. That's okay. Sometimes priorities shift due to changes in responsibilities. Are you a single parent now? Are you caretaking for a widowed parent? Are you ministering to children who are suffering the loss of a sibling, while you try to stabilize from your own grief after the loss of a child? Are you suddenly without a partner and sorting out all kinds of life decisions? These life issues don't just resolve themselves in the year's time following the loss (remember that pesky internalized idea about how quickly we are supposed to be over grief?). No, these are the things that permanently change a life's circumstances and require significant adjustments to what are top priorities. This can have cascading effects on how time is spent and with whom, how money is spent and on what, and whom you reach out to when in need of comfort, support, and advice. When you look at it like that, doesn't it make sense that your priorities have shifted?

It seems like nobody understands what I'm going through and that's making it hard to connect with people. How can I stop feeling like a stranger with people who know me?

Without sounding "judgy," there are lots of folks who do not *get* grief, and unless they are truly interested in understanding where you're coming from, they're not going to until they go through it themselves. So, it's not uncommon to feel like people just do not understand you, nor you them for that matter. It can be a lonely feeling when there aren't enough other people in your life who *do* understand where you're coming from. If this is the case for you, it's important to reach out and find people who do.

And speaking of "judgy," it's the pits to steep in that mental space for a long time. Grievers who feel misunderstood and angry often judge those whom they feel have let them down. This could be with people who grieved the same loss but appear to be carrying on just fine. It could be with people whom you considered friends and who dropped the ball over time. Ultimately, we experience the most freedom and spaciousness when we accept ourselves where we are, accept others where they are, and respect our right to be just where we are on our paths.

But what is the secret antidote to judgy-ness? Curiosity. Take this example: "I do not understand how my sister can be moving along like we didn't lose our mother. She's doing all kinds of things, traveling, posting pictures on Instagram—you'd never know what we all went through. She must not have been as affected as me and really must be kind of heartless." Now flip this around a little and play with the thinking. "I do not understand how she can be moving along the way she is. I still feel stuck and like I can't sort out which way to go with my grief. I wonder how she is feeling and what she is doing to cope. It seems like we have different ways of handling this, and I'd love to understand how she is getting through."

You see how one angle is about cutoff judgment, and it hovers around the idea that people ought to grieve in the same way. The other angle opens up a line of inquiry and interest that could lead to more intimacy and understanding between people. When we take comparisons out of the equation and replace them with inquiry, we often learn a lot more about ourselves and other people.

EXERCISES AND RITUALS THAT CAN HELP

ACKNOWLEDGE HOW YOU'VE CHANGED

The death of a loved one changes us, sometimes in small ways, sometimes in grand ways. In the process of living, we forget to take stock and make note. How have you changed? Take out your journal and take a moment to quietly reflect on this question. Write down anything that comes to mind, no matter how small. Hopefully this exercise creates an awareness of your strengths that can help you move forward.

THIS ISN'T THE END OF THE STORY— WHAT COMES NEXT?

One way to be curious about what comes next in your life is to suppose for a moment that you are the writer, the director, and the actor in your own movie. As the writer, you get to create the next scene(s) in your life. As the director, you move the characters and yourself into situations that best illustrate the story. And as the actor, you decide if this is the movie you want to be in. All choices you have the innate ability to take on. You can fantasize and write about this or just close your eyes and put yourself in a "movie" of your own creation. What comes next? Interesting, huh?

MAKING CONTACT WITH YOURSELF

Connecting with yourself is important as you make your way on the long journey through grief. The heartache caused by loss can obscure those parts of us that were once fully alive. As you take more steps into your life by seeking enjoyment, contentment, and meaning, you will experience more energy, which can be reallocated to activities that resonate deeply with your true self. Carl Jung wrote, "What did you do as a child that made the hours pass like minutes? Herein lies the key to what you should be doing in your worldly pursuits."

Have a piece of paper or a journal and a pen/pencil available. Sit comfortably and close your eyes. Let your mind drift to a time in your life when you had a moment of deep absorption in an interest, hobby, or activity. Stay there for a while. Try to notice what you were doing, how old you were, the conditions of life surrounding your experience. Were you with people, or were you alone?

Now answer these questions:

> What were you doing?

Is what you were doing something you do now? If yes, why? If no, why not?

Can you imagine creating more time in your life to allow for moments of engaging with a personal interest, hobby, or pastime? If yes, what is it and how? If no, why not?

> Is there something else you can imagine that would, even if just for a few moments, bring you some enjoyment? This can be as simple as looking out your window at the sky or taking a walk.

Try this. Make a date with yourself to do just that and enter it into your calendar. For example, you can write in something like, "On Saturday morning, I will sit at my kitchen table and paint with my watercolors," or "On Friday night, I will go to a used bookstore and browse the poetry section." It's important to be *specific*, which will help you clarify and keep your commitment. Specificity creates the space you need in which to act.

As you reclaim your life and your space in it, with all of what makes you *you*, opportunities will arise that naturally add to and support your innate curiosity and interest. Don't fall into the trap of, "I can't do that anymore because I'd need to get all the stuff to do it," or "I don't have time." Take the first step and allow yourself to enjoy, even if at first, it's just for a few moments.

Applying all of this to your plan moving forward, what can you consider? Write in your journal, open up, be creative, and set an intention for yourself. You never know where your story will bring you.

15

Helping Children Cope with Long-Term Grief While Tending to Yourself

It can be tough to help kids deal with grief when you're grieving as well. It's important to take care of yourself...

Amy Morin, LCSW, psychotherapist

A life built around a core sense of absence is its own type of grief and for many is difficult to describe in words. The journey begins early if your child lost a significant loved one at an age where they don't hold any memories of them. If you're helping your child grow up with the absence of a precious loved one, you already know you have a crucial role to play. It's important to keep their deceased loved one in consciousness, by name and by image, to tell stories about them, saying their name in fluid, nonwhispered ways. Consider also this truth: children will grieve and will process their grief in some way, no matter what we do. The more open we are, and the more space we can hold for them, the more fluid their experience will be.

SPOTTING LONG-TERM GRIEF IN CHILDREN

When a child loses a parent...that child grows up feeling
different and alone. A story is written in a secret place
in that child's mind—a story of loss and pain and the
triumph over that pain.

Maxine Harris, PhD, author of *The Loss That Is Forever:*
The Lifelong Impact of the Death of a Mother or Father

As much as we'd like to insulate ourselves from untimely loss, it's proven to be impossible. Some people lose a loved one when they're infants, and others after a long life lived together. There is no official roadmap detailing how loss will impact a life, but some themes emerge worth considering.

Here we write as though you are a parent or caregiver to a child who has lost a significant loved one, but if you are reading this section with yourself in mind, hold a space for remembrance of your age and your thinking and needs from that time. So often as children go through their own grieving process, they are supported by people who are also grieving and who have varying levels of knowledge about developmental ages and stages and the needs associated with them. Those who are in the acute stage of grieving don't generally have a lot of extra energy to spare.

Let's begin with what unifies us all in the experience of long-term grief, regardless of the age you are at the time of loss. In the beginning, common feelings and reactions include anger, ambivalence, longing, and the persistent striving to recover the person lost. Age is what tends to dictate how these emotional reactions appear and are understood or expressed. As a rule, adults have more life experience than children and have more reference points for identifying feelings and for asking for what they need. Children are often confused about what their feelings are about and may even struggle with naming them. Anger can feel more like an urge. Persistent longing might be expressed through obsessive ritual and magical thinking. When young children lose a parent, sibling, or other precious loved one, the effects can last for years, especially if they are not supported by the important adults in their lives in a way that allows all of the feelings and fears to be expressed and processed. Michael described how his granddaughter continues to process the death of her father who passed away five years ago.

My granddaughter has hundreds of cuddly toys. So many around her bed that she can't get in it! She fixates on keeping them all in the same order. She is ten now and she doesn't look to be abandoning her teddy bears any time soon. We just accept it.

It's so important for caregivers, teachers, and other adults to know that even years after a child loses a dear loved one, especially a parent or sibling, issues can arise which look like anxiety, depression, attention deficit disorder, autism, obsessive-compulsive disorder, and academic delays. In a child's life, loss changes the shape, texture, flow, and rhythm of most everything. It doesn't mean they can't go on to live wonderful enriching lives, but it does mean the relevant and important adults in their lives need to keep an ear open to underlying issues as they express themselves.

Older children and adults understand time and finality, whereas infants, toddlers, and young children do not. *Forever* can be both an impossible concept to understand as well as terrifying when applied to the deceased loved one. It's easy to see how immediate grief reactions can evolve and morph into long-term and unresolved grief as the child learns to have a relationship with someone who isn't there. Even years later, people of all ages report "seeing" their loved ones in passing cars or in groups of people. Pam swears she saw her father sitting in a diner eighteen months after his death. "I saw him sitting in the window from the parking lot wearing his favorite baseball hat, and I almost approached him!" This kind of seeking behavior is found in people of all ages.

No matter the age a child is when they lose an important loved one, they are likely to regress to behaviors from a younger developmental stage, at least for a while. Children who were potty-trained may bed wet again for a time. Teenagers may want to sleep in their parent's room or may not feel comfortable going out. Moreover, adults may wish for someone else to manage the nuts and bolts of life, responsibility feeling too burdensome and stressful. Herein lies the potential for a complicated battle of the needs. It's easy to imagine that if an adult is feeling the pains of grief for a long time and needs a release of pressure, it might be doubly hard to care for children who suddenly are not only grieving but are also doing things that are unexpected, appear immature, or even are annoying. The way children's caregivers respond to these regressions has a lot to do with the way grief is metabolized in the long run. That's why getting support and gaining increased understanding of how children express grief is so very important.

A LIFE REDEFINED

> *Ian was twelve when he lost his father. When he was twenty, he asked, "I wonder what kind of man I would have been if I'd had my father all this time." Now he's forty-one and told us, "I still miss him every day."*
>
> Pam

Another thing to remember is that at every developmental stage or milestone, life is redefined. Graduations, new jobs, greater independence, a committed relationship, parenthood—all these things that come to pass in a life stand out as one more life event a parent didn't witness, and one more moment to grieve. Over a lifetime, metabolizing this loss and incorporating it into one's identity is the goal.

Those who lost a loved one at a young age might not feel free to talk about them. Some feel as though bringing up their name or names will make others uncomfortable. Some suffer from feelings of sadness and jealousy when they witness others having close and bonded relationships. There is a sense of difference, of otherness that marks a person's life and can make special moments at best bittersweet, at worst, emotionally intolerable. It seems there is a value placed on the recency of loss. The further back one's loss goes, the less room it gets to take up in conversation. Meanwhile, the person who lost someone at an early age may feel like this fact of their life is the first part of them that enters a room, the rest shaped by this loss.

Whether we're healing our inner child, tending to our adult wounds, or helping another person on their long journey, it helps us to be oriented to where a person was in life when they sustained their profound loss. It can also help us serve ourselves from a tender and compassionate point of view.

QUESTIONS YOU MAY ASK YOURSELF

How do I support my adolescent child who is continuing to struggle?

Anger is very common, as is depression, anxiety, and reactivity. It can be difficult to stay present with someone who's displaying any or all of these emotions, so it's a good idea to get your own support, especially if you are grieving, too.

You don't have to have all the answers. You don't have to explain the why of things, or to try and make sense of death. Sitting with your adolescent and holding their vast array of feelings and fears, getting in touch with your own memories of being around their age, and helping them navigate the bumpy part of their road is your role. It's okay to be honest about how you experience grief, about what you do to stay afloat, and of the long view you're taking. Offering them an image of an adult making their way on the journey is very valuable—teenagers need their mentors and guides.

Leah, mother of a teenager who lost his father, shared how she is approaching this painful issue:

> I just try to be around and available a lot. Sitting at the table, not consumed by something but just doing something simple. I always hope my son will just start talking, and it doesn't really work like that, but he'll sometimes just be with me, put his head on my shoulder. I know if I push, I'll be shut out, so I am learning how to bide my time and hopefully not blow it if he ever wants to talk about anything.

We lost a member of our family, and that loss is affecting other family members in big ways that my child is picking up on. How do I make sure my child doesn't get overwhelmed by these external feelings from others?

This is an issue we've addressed elsewhere, but it bears restating here. The death of a loved one sends shock waves through a family, particularly if it was a person who was a significant part of the life of the family—a parent, a child, a sibling, a grandparent. These losses have tendrils and reach into the corners of different family members' psyches.

Here is an example: A child loses a grandparent who they don't know well or haven't spent much time with. They understand this is hard and have feelings that are hard to describe, but generally, the loss is not felt in a profound way. However, the child's mother is devastated by the loss of her parent. Over the next few years, mother goes from acutely distraught to chronically stressed by having to manage all of what goes with losing a parent, while dealing with ongoing grief. This child went from having a mother who was one way, to a mother who became almost a different person for years. So, the child on paper might not be grieving for the grandparent, but is grieving for the change in his mother, which again, might be hard to put into words or talk about, depending on the age of the child. The child's behavior might look like a form of anxiety. We might see regressed behaviors. We might see stress and distraction in school, or other issues pop up. You can see how it would be easy to say, "Oh, Johnny has anxiety, and we need to treat that." Or "Lucy has ADHD, so let's put things in place for that, and check out medications," when really what is happening is that the child is carrying around a huge sense of worry, maybe fear, and certainly energy resources are going toward maintaining a feeling of emotional safety.

There may also be situations where the death of a loved one brings up ongoing *new* stressors. If a child's loved one died from a genetic condition that runs in families, now children and other family members may need to be regularly monitored. Depending on how this rolls out in the forthcoming years, there could easily be significant stress for the child about things that are on the order of existential and maybe even terrifying. They might wonder, "Am I going to die? Is my sibling going to die? My parent?" We need to be aware of and sensitive to the fact that children pick up the stressors of family like sponges. And while sometimes there's not much that can be done about the facts of a situation, a whole lot sure does fall on the primary caregiver when it comes to keeping themselves intact enough to be able to support their children and keep things open and talkable.

How do I address my own continuing grief while also tending to my children's grief?

So much falls on the shoulders of parents who are tending to their own long-term grief after loss. There's really no way around it. It's important to know: No one does this perfectly. There is no perfect here. It's more of a long continuum that we can look to that goes from:

Complete Shut Down ←——→ Open Communication

The closer we can get to the right side of this continuum, the better. And generally, adults do better when they take care of themselves and have their own ways to process, unpack, and work through their emotions. Usually, this will mean adults are working to contain their own feelings enough to make space for their children's, that they are stretching into more ways to manage anxiety and reduce their reactivity, and generally don't drop the caregiving ball. Therapy, asking for support from friends and family, engaging in grief groups where processing and venting can take place in a supported and useful way, and educating oneself on what different developmental stages are all about are all effective steps people can take to own themselves and honor their responsibilities.

Also, remember that tending lovingly to yourself is part of the deal. We make the mistake of thinking that tending to ourselves has to be fancy or time-consuming self-care. Massages are nice. Retreats are nice. All of that is great, but guess what? They're often expensive and not always practical, and if we wait for the perfect time to do something big in order for us to take care of ourselves, we miss all of the small opportunities we have to love on ourselves and reduce stress and pressure. You don't have to go to an hour-and-a-half yoga session—you can do a five-minute sun salutation at home. You don't have to book a spa day and spend hundreds of dollars on a treatment whose effects will disappear as soon as you walk into your house. You can take an extra ten minutes to get ready in the morning, lovingly, or savor that cup of warm cocoa, or notice the fact that every morning when you look out the window, the sky is different. Are you busting through life like everything is an emergency? If so, can you take some moments to slow down, look around, and just be?

I'm worried about the well-being of my children who I think are still grieving. When should I get help?

Have you noticed any significant changes in their behavior that might indicate a need for professional intervention? In children this might look like ongoing and intense separation anxiety, school struggles and an inability to focus, depression, a deep need to control things in the environment, nervous habits like tics or ritual and repetitive behavior, or strong emotional ups and downs. In older children, you might see increased rebelliousness or withdrawing from family, experimentation with or increased use of drugs and alcohol, drops in grades, or withdrawal from formerly enjoyable activities. These are worrisome issues for parents and often it's hard to manage the anxiety that comes from them.

If you're worried, a good first step would be talk with your pediatrician and your own therapist. Depending on the age of your child, sometimes it is better for parents to get support for their own anxiety and worries before initiating a therapy for their child. It's also a good idea for that to continue even if children are in therapy. Doing as much as you can to ensure that your struggling child and children aren't on their own in working through grief is very important.

For younger children, having a place to work things out in ways that are developmentally appropriate is very helpful. Play therapy, which is described in the Appendix on page 363, is shown to be very effective in helping children process grief. Older children and teens can benefit from an array of therapies, including groups where they can talk with other children who have experienced loss. They are, after all, in a special group now, and know things about grief that others don't.

When and if you see evidence your child or children are struggling in ways that are interfering with them enjoying life and participating in even basic life activities, it's time to talk to someone.

My child lost a close friend. What can I do to help them through this?

If you are helping your child process the loss of their friend, these suggestions are worth considering:

- Listen and don't try to solve problems or make promises that you cannot possibly follow through on with complete certainty.

- Take care of your own emotions. Notice if you've been impacted by the loss of your child's friend and take the necessary steps to get the help you need so that you can truly be with your child in their struggle. Sometimes parents can inadvertently pass along their own pain and anxiety if they do not process it on their own.

- Something happening to parents is often a child's worst fear. Help them by organically referring to their "safe" people, those people who would be there for them no matter what. Some parents like to put the names and phone numbers of those people on the refrigerator or some other common space where they can be seen often. This expands the safety net under children, which provides background comfort. Life is big. It helps to know you have people looking out for you.

- Explore with your child whether they would like to do anything to acknowledge their friend's birthday or the anniversary of their death. They can go to an important place and lay flowers, donate money or time to an organization that is relevant to their friend's life, or they can bring a gift to their friend's parents.

EXERCISES AND RITUALS THAT CAN HELP

MAKING THE MOST OF A MOVE FROM A FAMILY HOME

After the loss of a spouse or caregiver, it may be necessary for you to move your family to a new home. Moving is hard for children, no matter their age. If you are leaving your family home following the death of a loved one, even if it is years later, it can be even harder. Your children are on a long grief journey, too, and moving out of the family home is part of it. They will have their own reactions, associations, fears, anxieties, and needs related to moving through this part of their trek, and they will need a strong guide to get them through.

The following exercises can be done with your child as you prepare to leave your home as well as when you are in your new one. These can be modified to allow for developmental and age variations.

Time to Take Some Pictures

Like going through old family albums, sometimes we enjoy revisiting our past and shared memories with others to whom we are close. Many find great comfort in doing this, so why not make your muse your family home?

Before you start packing up your house, take photos of it. Make sure to capture images of your favorite spots both inside and out. Take pictures from inside looking out windows to remember the views you had from different areas. This can be a lovely set of images to revisit and will be especially nice for children as they grow up and may have foggy memories of where they once lived.

Visit Important Places and People to Say Goodbye

There might be places and people you will want to visit to say goodbye to especially if you are leaving the town in which you live. In the month or two leading up to the move, sit with the child and make a list of the people and places that have been important to you all. You may already be planning a gathering of saying goodbye to close friends and family, but what about those folks you see all the time but whom you wouldn't necessarily invite to a going-away party? Like the owners of the country store, or the folks at the post office? These are the faces and personalities that color a life. As far as places, maybe the local toy store? Or the park on the corner of the neighborhood? Plan with your child to visit these people and places and what to do when you are there. This can be as simple as saying "bye and thanks," or giving a flower, or feeding the squirrels. Take pictures of special places and people so that you can revisit them any time. Get creative and don't be surprised if your child has a lot of feelings while doing this. Sometimes moves can be so overwhelming and so stressful that we forget to give children the chance to have their own process, and they are swept along on the current of adult stress, just to get jettisoned into a new space and new life with no ceremony.

Make a Calendar with Your Kids

Children have a different relationship with time than adults do. Cognitively, time moves from a very immediate experience to having a sense of past, present, and future over the course of many years. Grounding a move in time can help children of all ages get clear on what is happening when and what is going to happen.

What you'll need:

> A calendar big enough to write several things in a space for each day
> Thin markers of varying colors
> Little stickers (especially for young kids)
> A place to hang the calendar in a visible place, like the kitchen

Once you have had the conversation with your child(ren) about moving, start to orient them to time and action. Together, write the date of the move on your calendar. If you can, put a picture of your new place on the calendar. Include specific things that will be happening and things you can have them help with on moving day such as packing up dishes, visiting with neighbors to say goodbye, and packing up their bedroom. On days your child helps pack or is engaged in anything to do with moving (going to the store to buy boxes is not exciting, but their participation is sometimes necessary and important), put a sticker on the calendar celebrating their efforts. Children often like to check which day they are on and you can let them cross out each as you make your way to the moving day. This makes what can be a surreal and existential experience into one more tangible and recognizable.

Moving Vision Board or Album

You might be thinking, "Seriously, I'm about to move and you want me to make a photo album?" Yes, but don't worry. This doesn't have to be the winner of a creativity award. It can be an album, a bulletin board, a big piece of paper on the refrigerator with well-organized pictures on it. Here's the idea: You will be showing your child(ren) the reality of moving. You can go as far back as you want. If you lived in a place before you had your child, you can put a picture of that, then a picture of any place you lived after that and then a picture of the place you are going. You can even put pictures of places where you lived as a child. The idea here is to show them, in pictures, that people move, which will assure them it will be okay, that places change and people can move through them. As much as you can, let them participate in making this, and perhaps add pages to do with what they love about their present home and what they want in their future home.

X Marks the Spot

For a child of any age (and for us adults) leaving the home where we lived with our deceased loved one can be excruciating. It can feel as though we are leaving them behind, and it's hard to reconcile that feeling with the reality that we carry their memory and our love for them wherever we go. Children of all ages benefit from concrete ways of marking where they've been.

Ask them and yourself: "How do you want to leave your mark before you head out for this new chapter in life?" Here are some ideas, but let your imaginations soar! You can adapt this exercise to your unique living circumstances.

> Plant a sturdy perennial in a part of your yard that will likely be left alone for a while
> Sprinkle wildflower seeds
> Write a note or even just a word and bury it in the yard
> Leave a message in a bottle for the new owners/renters (kids are often very curious about who moves in after they leave and enjoy having a bridge to them, even if it is never through an actual relationship)
> In a cupboard, the back of a closet, or other hidden place allow your child to put their initials in small lettering

Have fun with this. Allow for plenty of feelings. Do this when you are not in a rush or frantic about that last room that needs to get packed up. Take your time. You are going through this, too.

ANCESTOR VENERATION

Veneration means great respect and reverence. In the case of ancestor veneration, we are talking about a specific practice or ritual designed to pay that respect to our departed family. People all over the world do this to some extent, for a variety of reasons, ranging from asking ancestors for help in current problems, helping to ensure the deceased's comfort in the afterlife, and maintaining connections and family order.

There are so many ways to do this that are beyond the scope of what we can describe here, but if you find yourself drawn to the idea of working in ritual that is also connected to those who came before you, there are many resources for this. Mallorie Vaudoise wrote a wonderful book entitled *Honoring Your Ancestors: A Guide to Ancestor Veneration*. In it she shares the following: "Ancestor veneration can refer to any ritual or spiritual practice that reconnects you with the people who came before. Doing genealogical research, cooking your grandmother's favorite recipe, learning the folk music and dance from your cultural background, and speaking to the dead in your dreams are all examples of ancestor veneration. They complement a wide variety of spiritual paths."

This can bring great comfort to children who are struggling with loss, as it tends to the idea that our people are part of a large and long story.

IDENTIFY RELEVANT SYMBOLS

We are a symbolic species. For as long as we've been making pictures on cave walls and making imprints in sand, we've been showing in images those things that are important to us and that carry meaning. Children and adults are often soothed when we do this for those we have lost. Some connect certain animals to a deceased loved one, or a set of numbers. or time on a clock. Some have spiritual images that capture the heart of a loved one in a home, on a mantel, or even in a wallet. We can support children in this end to do the same thing, to help them facilitate a

conscious engagement with how their loved one can be repre-
sented in their lives. Some examples of this are:

> Giving children items that belonged to their loved one
that are meaningful to them
> Noticing the wildlife in your area and considering the
symbolic meaning of certain animals
> If you have ancestral ties to certain places, considering
customs and rituals from those areas that are relevant to
your loved one and working those into your family
> Preparing foods your loved one enjoyed on special occa-
sions and talking about this openly

Whatever you do, allow for it to be creative, flexible, and
even eccentric. What's nice about this is that it creates the idea
that our loved ones are with us, and we can think about them and
send them love whenever we want.

NOTICE THE RHYTHMS

This is one of those get-in-through-the-backdoor ideas that
can help ground us and our children to earth, life, and the reality of the cycle of life. The more tuned in we are to the flow of
nature and all that goes with it, the more we can stretch into the
idea that we are, in fact, part of the cycle of life. Nature is at the
same time beautiful and life giving, and powerfully destructive.
Depending on where you live, there are different relationships
and rituals to do with the seasons. Here in the northeast, the

seasons are distinct and are culturally marked by the planting/ growing/harvesting months. It's so easy to go through life in our hypercapitalist, "always moving at the same rate" culture, but if you take one giant step back and notice the backdrop, you see that there's this whole other thing going on. By tuning in to the distinct smells and excitement of each season, we feel more and more part of this dynamic whole. We reap the benefits of this in many ways, not the least of which is creating space in our hearts and minds that we have rhythms, too. Sometimes we are high energy and out, and sometimes we are quiet and within and need to tend to our aches and pains. Adults can help children find this spaciousness in themselves by slowing down enough to see we are part of nature, too.

It's hard work supporting children through their long grief process. How are you taking care of yourself as you do so? If there were any suggestions in this chapter that resonated with you, take a moment to make note of them and make a plan to implement them. It's never too late to help a child who is grieving.

16

When There Was Pain in Your Relationship

Although grief stems from the end or loss of a relationship in some form, it can also be the beginning of a much larger journey—a journey into the very meaning of your life.

Sameet M. Kumar, PhD, author of *Grieving Mindfully*

Sometimes the most painful relationships are the hardest to grieve. There's a reason for that, and you're not alone if this rings true for you. Grief is hard enough to contend with when the relationship you had with your loved one was relatively conflict-free. When pain was a main thread in your emotional tie to a person, you've not only lost someone you love, but you've also lost someone you might have hoped to have some kind of healing with. Even when the relationship was painful enough that there was a necessary ending, it doesn't mean there was no relationship. In fact, you were still in a relationship, just the cutoff kind. Ann Marie shared this:

My husband cheated on me with another woman and was in bed with her when he died. Of course, I'm terribly hurt and angry about the betrayal, but I'm still grieving his death and my family thinks I'm crazy.

Family systems theory suggests that, in fact, relationships where there was emotional cutoff can carry more energy than those where individuals were still connected, even if dysfunctionally. This is all to say that none of us gets out of this grief business unscathed, and some have a lot of extra work to do when their relationship was filled with unfinished business because healing from that is part of it, too.

HEALING THE WOUNDED HEART WHILE GRIEVING

> *My grief was and is about the anger I couldn't voice to my mother when she was alive, but my mother being the person she was, also gave me many funny, wonderful memories, even if many of them were a result of her lack of self-awareness or denial about the limits of physical reality.*
>
> Maya

A quick walk down the self-help and psychology aisles at the bookstore reveals books about all kinds of complicated relationships involving parents, siblings, grandparents, and issues to do with addiction in families; mental health disorders and personality disorder; circumstances of living such as poverty, divorce, blended families, and more. Why might this be so? Because the business of life is *difficult*. Families are but a group of people who live together, bonded by promise, DNA, or both. Love, affection, commitment, hope, dependence, trust, nurturance, and companionship—all are part of family relationships to greater or lesser degrees, providing varied textures and expressions of family life in the world.

When you're born there is no guarantee you will arrive in a family that has it all together. Some of us had a loved one who struggled with a ferocious temper, some had an addiction, some had emotional needs so deep they looked to their family members or others to fill them.

When we lose a loved one with whom there has been a complicated, painful, or traumatic relationship, we are often left with a confusing set of emotions with which to contend. Moving on through the long journey has a lot of off-ramps that sometimes lead to dead ends and other times lead to interesting backroads not shown on the main map. The dead ends are the roads with names like, "Get Over It! They Were Abusive," or "They're Gone, You Can Finally Live Your Own Life." You might be able to hang out on those roads for a little while, but for so many, there is a natural pull to get back on the one leading to real healing. Hopefully we can backtrack to find another road named, "Learning to Sit with Reality and Grieve What Was and What I Wish I Had."

Brenna's father died from a yearslong addiction to alcohol and drugs. She was heartbroken from the long and drawn-out way he died. The various ways she fortified herself against the pain when he was alive became walls that needed dismantling before she could begin to truly heal herself. As she removed each brick and wooden board surrounding her soft, tender pain, she was able to see how much she was trying to protect herself from repeated heartbreak. Over the course of her healing, in her mind her father became a whole man again, the one who was so happy she was born, played with her when she was little, and who loved his family. Bottom line: he was many things, including someone who succumbed to addiction and died from it. She described it this way:

I had a pretty strained relationship with my dad before he passed away. I hadn't spoken to him for three or four years because I was so upset with him and the things he had done to my family. I vividly remember times I'd see him at my brother's baseball games or a church mass my grandparents dragged us all to, and he'd try to talk to me or tell me he loved me, but I couldn't even look him in the eyes. When he passed away, I felt so guilty. Now that it was impossible to talk to him, I wanted nothing more than to tell him how sorry I was and that I loved him. It took me a while to process and work through removing this heavy burden. Ultimately, I think it made me realize the significance of mending important relationships because you never know what could happen to someone.

Processing the loss of a loved one for whom we carry anger, resentment, fear, or traumatic memory is an ongoing act of

self- compassion. For many, there is no possibility of reconcilia-
tion, no time to heal together or be vindicated, so constant sorrow
becomes the norm. This can feel like a burden to those left behind
if they believe this sort of healing can only happen with the loved
one themselves. Pam described her process like this:

> My father died when I was in my forties. We had a compli-
> cated relationship, most of it due to his struggle with alcohol-
> ism and his abusive treatment of my mother. When he died
> of cancer, I felt a mix of relief that his pain had ended, but
> sadness that we might never completely resolve things between
> us. Closure of our difficult relationship took many years of
> therapy.

Some relationships are so abusive and neglectful, it takes a lifetime of work to climb out from under the rubble created by their
menacing and toxic words, their physical attacks, or their devastating neglect. Different from ongoing intense grief, some describe
feeling nothing at all. No relief, no sadness. Just flatness. Maureen
shared that her father died several years ago and that it was hard
to talk about because of what it seemed like people *wanted* her to
feel. She wrote,

> I got the news and got on with my day. He was a horrible
> person, and I hadn't seen him in over ten years. He'd never met
> my children and was in no way a part of my life. It wasn't a
> relief. I felt it was just information and that freaks people out.

These stories all capture the following reality: no matter the relationship we have with our loved ones, sometimes grieving their death can be complicated and thorny. You might think you're doing fine on the grief journey but then something comes up and there you are in a patch of burrs; it takes a while to pluck out all of the spiky bits. Our loved ones teach us not just about love and connection, but also about loss, pain, anger, and grief, and not just when they die. The lessons are ongoing and fold into, over and over again, the life we continue to live.

INHERITED GRIEF AND TRAUMA

My maternal grandmother died when my mother was eight. When I was in my twenties, my mother told me the story of discovering her mother's body in the bathtub. After that, my mother lived in a Catholic orphanage until she was grown. My grandmother's legacy was passed to me. How could my mother say goodbye to the mother she did not know very well? How do you say goodbye to "absence"? My grandmother's death, handed down to me, redacted by my mother, was the invisible defining character of my mother's motherhood.

Maya

In some families, inherited grief and trauma run through generations like a river. The ways in which this affects relationships and health are varied and intricate and often dictate how parents relate to their children. If grief and its associated trauma are not consciously and compassionately dealt with in the previous generation, the effects can travel down through the family tree, creating dysfunction. Perhaps the parent has significant anxiety from the result of a psychic legacy that results in holding the child too closely. The child senses something is wrong through unconscious clues or a story they might have heard, but the parent hasn't processed the reason for their anxiety, and they can't make the connection. For example, a mother told us that her father had died tragically on an amusement park ride. Each time she took her children to a park with rides, she subconsciously operated out of that trauma and prevented her children from fully enjoying themselves, pulling them back from even the gentlest amusements in fear.

INTERGENERATIONAL HEALING AND EVOLUTION

My mom lost her mother to suicide when she was six months old, the result of postpartum depression. This loss impacted my mom her whole life. Prior to doing hospice work, I worked in a family and children's program for eighteen years, supporting mothers with their pregnancy and young parents with their new baby's first year of life. This was my life's work. I felt I was able to use the love and generosity given to me by my parents to help heal my mom, myself, and the pain of a previous generation... I was able to recognize, let go of,

and integrate the gifts received from the tragic loss of my
ancestor, my maternal grandmother. I learned and was
able to name the universal experience of mental illness in
family systems.

Jeanne

We don't always know when we are healing generational wounds, but we are so lucky when we start to tune into that powerful flow of evolution. It's not easy, but it's possible to bump out the story a bit and take an eagle's view of what has been going on in your family. An easy example might be the theme of addiction. How many of us have in our family stories of addiction or abusive use of substances? These stories can always be looked at from the wholly personal point of view that is concerned mostly with how one person's behavior affected you individually. But very often, if we step back, and back again, and take a good look at the bigger family story, we often see that addiction was borne from addiction, which was borne from some form of trauma, which was borne from some other trauma or grief. Then we can zoom in and focus on our own lives and behaviors. We can ask ourselves, "Am I continuing to participate in the flow of this pattern of addiction, trauma, or grief? Or might I make some adjustment and get more conscious about what I am doing in my life, here and now, to heal. To grow. To move on?" These are big moments in a family, and they often change the way future generations experience the world.

One way to think of it is, let's not let all of the pain and heartbreak be for nothing. Even if a particular issue wasn't your personal journey, you can harness the wisdom that is connected to the pain your loved ones experienced and make use of it as you make your own decisions and live your life.

QUESTIONS YOU MAY ASK YOURSELF

I have a lot of unhealed wounds with my loved one. How do I move on when there was so much pain in our relationship?

When people have the opportunity to work through their issues with their loved ones before death, they've received a great gift. It's harder when you never got the chance for closure. If you want to address unfinished business on your own, know this first: you are doing important work. The work is as real as if your loved one were sitting with you at the table hashing things out. This important work is with your own psyche, with the themes and story lines you are attached to as a result of whatever has taken place. When you're ready, some form of therapy, spiritual guidance, family research, journaling, and/or letter writing are all things you can do to help you on this part of the journey.

Why am I still grieving such a complicated relationship?

To put it simply, you're still grieving because either there is more grieving to do, or because there is pain from your relationship you are still processing. Grieving those people we loved but with whom we shared tangled, painful, abusive, toxic, or neglectful relationships is so difficult because there's so much to sort out. The same person when remembered on one day can elicit a feeling of love and longing while on another can plummet the griever into a pit of terrible memory. With that terrible memory, there might be associated sensations, recollections of traumatic moments, flashes of rage, and tidal waves of regret and sorrow. And death being what it is, there is no possibility of working it through with the deceased. Sarah described it beautifully when she said,

> Grieving a painful relationship is a personal experience between you and the deceased. It's an extremely lonely place to be because others close to you cannot truly understand the depth of your emotions or how to help. There are so many unresolved questions and issues that will never be answered or resolved. As the years move on and the pain lessens, you get to a place where you can sit with grief longer. You start to take back your life and become the person you want to be.

This truly is work you are doing with yourself, in relation to your loved one, and it isn't easy.

EXERCISES AND RITUALS THAT CAN HELP

WISDOM I AM CULTIVATING FROM THIS RELATIONSHIP

Closure after the loss of a loved one with whom you had a com-plicated relationship takes time. It is also not finite. Closure sounds as though a particular issue gets neatly tidied up, and after dusting off your hands you get on with it. However, closure is more about understanding and metabolizing the reality of the *whole* picture, so the patterns borne from the relationship no longer control life from an unconscious place. As we travel on the path, we pick up new bits of wisdom that have the potential to get woven into the bigger tapestry of our lives, adding color, texture, and truth. Settling into that truth, with each new addition of wisdom, is closure.

Getting clear on what you learned from your relationship can help with this process. Try this. At the top of a piece of paper, write the following:

Issue with my loved one

What I learned from this issue

Wisdom I am cultivating

Then write out the reality of your relationship with your loved one. Get clear on what you did accomplish through this relationship, no matter how painful. Here is an example.

Issue with my loved one: My mother was neglectful.

What I learned from this issue: I learned how to take care of myself and meet my own needs.

Wisdom I am cultivating: It is very hard for me to rely on other people. I am learning that I can stretch into trusting other people while always knowing I can take care of myself.

Yearning for your deceased loved one, for what you had or what you hoped to have, is also part of the ongoing experience of grief. Yearning is an ache that never totally subsides. Rather than trying to squash it, consider embracing it. One way that love lives on is in maintaining a relationship with our loved ones after they die. Transforming this yearning into a new form of relationship can be a way to move along down the road on your journey, offering new views and greater comfort.

MANIFEST WHAT YOU YEARN FOR

It's important to know there are those wounds that are still wide open when a loved one dies with whom we shared pain, heartache, and trauma that can become the source of suffering in the future. It can be so frustrating, especially when you feel like you've worked through many things and have come to understand so much about your relationship. But some wounds leave a scar and while we can move on and find our way, we need to be compassionate with ourselves when our scars hurt.

The most painful thing about death is that it makes it official: we aren't going to work out in this lifetime the issues that existed between us, at least not together. Grieving that fact is a necessary part of your journey, and you may have to do it more than you think. It's also important to know that what you longed for with your loved one is likely something you can manifest in your life and in your heart. We can always work with matters of the heart. How can we do that? By naming them. Name what you longed for with your loved one, what you wish you had, what you craved, and see if there are simple or creative ways to meet those needs in your life now. It would look something like this:

What I longed for: I longed to not feel afraid in my own home and to not feel like I was always walking on eggshells.

How can I bring this into my life now? I can devote time, resources, and energy into learning how to manage my own anger and frustration so I don't make my children feel the same way. I can be the dad I wished I had. I can also pursue relationships with friends that are generative and compassionate.

RELEASING WHAT'S NOT YOURS TO CARRY

Sometimes part of what makes grief so painful is that we're carrying the whole of the relationship we are trying to heal from as though all of the responsibility for how it went is on us. Or we don't carry any of it, putting it all on our deceased loved one. But for certain situations that typically involve clear abuse of power, it's usually a little bit of both, and getting clear on that helps to make our long grief process more digestible.

Bradie often quotes her cousin who once said, "I'm going to put that down because it's not mine to carry." It makes so much sense! We need to carry the responsibility of what is ours and release what is not. Well, how the heck do you do that? Try this:

The relationship and why it was troubled: My mother was so cold. She made everything sterile and controlled. There was no flexibility in our house.

What was theirs to carry: Their mental health and their fear of losing control.

What is mine to carry: I take responsibility for how I acted toward her eventually. I never learned how to talk to her in a respectful way. I was either superficial or explosive. I avoided going home for the holidays and never figured out how to relate to her.

What have I been carrying that I need to let go of:
I was not responsible for the whole of our relationship. We were both unmoving, and she had work to do, too, that she never did. I may never know why, but I know that I wasn't responsible for her personality being what it was.

Doing this exercise can be very illuminating. You might find you've been carrying around with you extra baggage that is not yours to carry. In putting the baggage down, you may find over time that you have more of a chance to look at your own life and your own heart and take full ownership of how you are in the world. Ultimately, it's liberating. It's courageous. And it's worth it.

As you take stock of where you've been on your long grief journey, particularly if you are processing the death of someone with whom you shared a complicated or painful relationship, can you draw from this chapter any ideas on how you'd like to move forward? Make note of them and practice acceptance. It's a deep stretch for many to make, but worth it. When we claim the truth in all of its messiness, we take control back and give ourselves the chance to more thoughtfully live our lives.

17

Guilt and Regret

The Challenges and Rewards

No one ever told me that grief felt so like fear.

C. S. Lewis, *A Grief Observed*

We have stories stored in the deeper and darker parts of our psyches, moments that, when we reflect on them, can bring us to our knees with the deep pain of wishing we had done something differently, or that our paths with the people we love could have led elsewhere. Some of us carry the weight of these stories like boulders on our shoulders, weighing us down and making our road so much harder to walk.

How we relate to these aspects of ourselves is important to consider, often glossed over in a culture that insists upon "no regrets!" and the avoidance of pain. These cultural commitments are doing a great disservice because we are often left without a roadmap on how to reckon with guilt and how to relate to regret—both important parts of the human condition that need some airtime. As a result of this, we struggle mightily with grief as well as with choices when it comes to taking steps forward on our journey.

THE DIFFERENCE BETWEEN GUILT AND REGRET

"If only" is the game of guilt that plagues many
survivors… As we yearn to make sense of the senseless,
often the only route of control we have is to blame
ourselves… work to let it go. Don't give in to the guilt.

Pamela D. Blair, PhD, *I Wasn't Ready to Say Goodbye*

There are specific differences between guilt and regret that bear mention as we sort through these weighty topics, but there are also areas where they overlap. Good old *Merriam-Webster* lets us know that guilt is: "the fact of having committed a breach of conduct especially violating law and involving penalty; the state of one who has committed an offense especially consciously; feelings of deserving blame especially for imagined offenses or from a sense of inadequacy." Regret, on the other hand, means: "to mourn the loss or death of; to miss very much; sorrow aroused by circumstances beyond one's control or power to repair; an expression of distressing emotion."

It's no wonder these emotional experiences lay in the more privately held chasms of our lives. Like any real feeling, it has its generative aspect and its destructive ones. What we are aiming for here is to pull these emotional mandates into the open so they can be used on your journey. It's also important to recognize when you've been relating to their destructive elements. Shame, self-attack, holding guilt that's not yours to carry, or not allowing yourself to move forward are the destructive relationships we can have with these emotions. It's probably why culture wants to diminish these feelings. Discernment is key here.

So, guilt generally speaks to something we've done that involves some sort of breach. It doesn't always have to be around something we were conscious of, but it often involves some moral or ethical mandate that ought to have dictated our behavior but that we ignored or didn't know about in time. These offenses sometimes require apology, sometimes honoring consequences. Almost always, for true freedom, they require acknowledgment and honesty, even if simply with oneself.

Regret is a bit weightier and touches on guilt, remorse, and even longing. It covers our reactions to specific events and choices we had some degree of control over, as well as those we did not. We can regret the truth about a relationship that was pained, even if we carry no responsibility for how the person we were relating to behaved. We tend to regret roads taken or those we passed by Fault is not a necessary component for regret, whereas it typically is with guilt.

What might this look like on the grief journey? How can we distinguish between these two painful emotional hurdles? Let's look at some examples.

REGRET IS A TEACHER

I have this one memory that visits me often. I remember pushing my mother's hand away from my son in a fit of

impatience. I was mad at her on a scale that felt almost
untalkable, and in that briefest of moments, that little action,
it felt like I hit her soul. We never talked about it, but I carry it
with me now, all these years later after her death. I apologize
to her spirit all the time for being that rude and hurtful, and I
wish I could go back and be different. More patient and softer.

Margie

This is regret. Captured here is the story of reckoning with the truth about how things are and afforded here is the opportunity to allow regret to be the teacher it is. Margie can grab hold of this and not only wish she were different years ago but tend to that part of herself now. Can patience and softness be cultivated in her current relationships? Is there work to do to heal from the wounds that existed between her and her mother? Can she reflect on how her anger and resentment flowed through her hands and her expressions and evolve, grow, and grieve? We can do this with any regret, no matter the size. As long as we are alive, we can look to each day as a new opportunity to make use of what we learn.

We get into trouble when we only stay fixated on the regret itself. What is the use of regretting being impatient if you don't cultivate patience in the here and now? What is the use of regretting not telling someone how you felt about them when they were alive if you don't do that now? Use this teachable moment to help shape the life you are currently living; in fact, you may find that the pain of regret transforms into softness, kindness to yourself and others, and much greater empathy for all people.

ATTENDING TO GUILT

Let's take an example here of someone who drove under the influence of alcohol and was responsible for another person's death. This is a clear-cut situation, and as our legal system mandates, there are consequences for this action a person must honor. To the human heart though, guilt does not end when punishments do. How can a person move from the hell of their own making into a life marked by the wisdom earned through their mistakes? And what about accidents? According to the creators of the organization Accidental Impacts, about 30,000 people every year are involved in causing harm to others, sometimes resulting in death.

If guilt is a factor in your grief journey, you may be wondering if you have the right to grieve, or if you are allowed to bear the full weight of this shared human experience. Of course you are. Grief spares no one. But your journey involves taking roads that have to do with redemption and deep acceptance of what has happened. It's really a job for all people, but sometimes what we are facing can be so big and so overwhelming that we avoid it. If you don't already have someone clearly identified as a guide on this particular road, it would be good to find someone. A qualified therapist or trusted religious or spiritual adviser are options to consider, as they tend to be people accustomed to sitting with, and not minimizing, the complexity of being human.

PUT DOWN GUILT THAT'S NOT YOURS

Maybe the guilt you feel is nonsensical in that you truly had no culpability in your loved one's death or did not ever consciously hurt them or intend to inflict pain. In that case, the work for you might revolve around a core pattern of taking responsibility for things that are not yours to take on. Or maybe magical thinking has you looking for ways to reason that if you had done something differently, your loved one would still be alive. This is tender and important work where the if-onlys live. Remaining in this tortured land keeps us from living the life we have now.

Sometimes families are committed to making one person the holder of the community guilt. There are people who heavily identify with the idea that they themselves were the problem, and if they had been different, there would've been a different outcome. Beware the family that organizes around blame. Ask yourself: "Am I holding blame that's not mine to carry?" If so, why? What would happen if you decided not to carry a certain story any longer, like the story of: "If I had been a better son, my father wouldn't have become an alcoholic," or, "If I hadn't been so concerned with my own family, I would have noticed that my friend was suicidal, and I could have prevented her from making that decision."

Very often we try to carry the weight of the responsibility for things we simply don't know how to grieve or are afraid to grieve.

QUESTIONS YOU MAY ASK YOURSELF

I suffer from intrusive thoughts that feel punishing and judgmental. How do I get out from under this weight?

In two words: *with compassion.* This is the only way.

When the truth of guilt turns back on itself in a way that

is only punishing, shaming, and judgmental, there can be no growth, as guilt only serves to keep you frozen in place. We often keep ourselves from growing and evolving because we feel we don't deserve it. Sometimes we are fully aware of this. Sometimes it is unconscious and is only recognizable by its effects. This might look like a life constrained at every turn. There might be addiction, isolation, or shutting down of creativity. Allowing ourselves to be vulnerable enough to accept and work with the material of our own lives can help.

We can't get away from the fact that what we choose to do at one point in our lives is not necessarily what we would choose if either we had to live it over again or if we were faced with a similar dilemma now. That's just part of it, right? Factors in life at any given time set up an array of conditions that support one decision over another, one set of choices over another. Getting clear on what was operating for us at any given time gives us the chance to look back on our lives, excavate the wisdom that came from the decisions and mistakes we made, and then move forward with greater clarity around who we are and what we want.

There are so many roads open before me. How do I know if I'm making the right choice?

As you make your way toward meaning and wholeness, you may find yourself stuck at different crossroads or in various terrains. Crossroads might be marked with signs that point you in opposing directions like this:

This Way to a New House ←——→ Stay Where You Are

Turn Your Child's Room into a Craft Room ⟷ Keep Their Room as They Left It

Personal Interests This Way ⟷ Familiar Routine This Way

How do you choose? How do you know which way to go? Many struggle with the choices that lay at crossroads because an often not talked about aspect of grief is choice. When we move toward one thing, we naturally turn away from another. In turning away from something or someone, an opportunity or a desire, we are faced with grief, and this is none too easy.

In day-to-day living this comes up all the time in small, seemingly insignificant ways. Think about sitting down in a restaurant you haven't been to before. You know the food is supposed to be fantastic, and you've heard the head chef specializes in combining flavors in unique and refreshing ways. You're handed a long menu with too many choices. You want to try several things that look great, but you have to pick one and you worry, "What if I don't like it? What if I wish I picked what my friend ordered? What if I regret my choice?" So, you go with what you always get, the burger. You know you like burgers. You get them all the time. Boom. You're done. Now you don't have to worry about making a mistake or choosing wrong or, more significantly, you don't have to deal with the dreaded feeling of regret.

That is a cheeky example of the crossroads of choice, only meant to reflect that we humans do it all the time. How we relate to choice and regret weighs in heavily here as we talk about much bigger and more profound moments of choice in a life where the landscape changed due to death.

Regret and grief are bonded cousins. They relate to one another deeply, and it's why these crossroads cannot be underestimated for their power and complexity. Maybe you had experiences in your life where, when you tried to make big decisions, things didn't go as well as you'd hoped. Maybe you had relationships with caregivers where you were not allowed to flex your choice-making muscles and were conditioned to defer to others who "knew better," leaving you in the wake of their opinions and choices. Maybe you've had luck with avoiding decision-making altogether and have lived a life where you respond more to what happens rather than taking the wheel and directing your own path. Or maybe you've been the decision-maker your whole life and you are tired. One way or another, you have a relationship with choice and therefore, to some extent, with regret.

Part of you might be saying, "But sometimes it's just nice to get the burger!" Yes! Sometimes you just need to rest with what you know. If that happens to be where you are on the grief journey, that's okay. Maybe tomorrow you'll get the dish with an herb you've never tried, or the fruity dessert you've never heard of. We contract and expand, contract and expand, like an accordion. This is as natural as breathing. Allow yourself to expand when you feel the call to do so, even if the call is from a distant, unknown part of the map in your hand.

Guilt, blame, and silence are themes in my family. How do I free myself from their impact?

Sometimes things happen so fast—if we could go back in time to prevent a catastrophe we would. There are millions of stories like this. When your actions or nonactions are connected to the death of a loved one, this is a specific type of grief that can carry through generations.

Here is a story from Bradie that exemplifies this:

My paternal grandparents had a son before my father was born. His name was James (Jimmy). Growing up, I knew of Jimmy, but didn't really know him. It was kind of a ghost of a story that I heard about, but I don't know how. When Jimmy was two years old, apparently my grandmother had gotten him dressed up for Christmas pictures. She put him out in the yard, made sure the gate was closed and ran inside to get a couple of things before leaving the house. When she came back outside, she saw the gate was open. My grandmother ran to the pond and found Jimmy, drowned in the water. According to the lore, my grandmother found out that night that she was pregnant with my father. Her family blamed her for this tragic accident, and it impaired her ability to parent my father. She did, but the clogged-up trauma that was unprocessed, toxicity from blame and guilt, and her own lived pain from her family of origin resulted in troubled relationships and an ability to go only so far when it came to expressing love, vulnerability, and softness. I think about my grandmother a lot, and I wonder what she would have been like if Jimmy didn't die, or if rather than being blamed, she had been loved, supported, and nurtured through her grief. As an adult and a mother, I truly cannot imagine how she managed. I guess it matters what we consider "managing."

Is this a recognizable experience in your life or family? How have guilt, blame, and silence shaped the experience of grief in your life? Is there a way you can imagine changing this pattern? One key step to take, even if it's not with your immediate family, is to make your pain discoverable with someone you trust.

I lost my loved one unexpectedly and can't help but feel that if I had done something different, they might still be here today. How do I move past this sense of guilt?
Anyone who has faced the accidental death of a loved one would agree, there are things that happen in life so suddenly, so unexpectedly, and so tragic that the heart is seared permanently by the demarcation between before and after. In situations like this, not only are you faced with the hard work of grieving through unexpected loss, but there is an added layer of perhaps witnessing the accident, being with your loved one when they died, having to inform their families, or, for some, the feeling that if you'd made different decisions, your loved one would still be alive.

Connor was swimming in the Atlantic Ocean with friends while on a short weekend getaway. It was after tourist season, the beaches were quiet, and no lifeguards were on duty. The group knew the waters fairly well but were unaware of a strong rip current that had come through, and they were pulled further out to sea. One of his friends did not make it back to shore. Talking years later about the moment in time when he lost sight of his friend, it was clear the images and feelings were still fresh—he was at times still frozen in grief, fear, anger, and guilt. Whenever something good or generative happened or even hinted at happening, Connor became anxious, thinking: "How can I do this when he can't? What would his parents think?" He had assumed the roles of judge, jury, and executioner in his own life, simply because he survived what his friend did not. He was caught in a terrible grief/guilt undertow of his own mind.

So many people have stories just like this one. If you've experienced something similar and are having a difficult time reclaiming your own life, consider that the road you are on is marked with signs that read: "This Way to Acceptance," or "Horrible Accidents Happen—It's Not Your Fault." Try looking for side roads named, "Honor Your Loved One by Valuing Life," and "Wisdom This Way." Which one would you decide to traverse first? Make sure to look around and pick up any gems of wisdom along the way. You have had an experience that has shaped the rest of your life. Is it possible to let that be generative? What would this look like for you?

You have likely heard this before, but truly living means fully engaging with love, loss, heartbreak, and boundless joy. The depth and breadth of the human experience is vast, and it can be difficult keeping the heart open. Take small steps. Open a little door first and walk through. This might mean taking a day trip to a beautiful place and letting yourself enjoy it. Try offering your joy to your friend and send them love. You can experience both at the same time and stretch into that place where all of it is real. Then you may find yourself walking on the road named, "I Am Here for All of It."

EXERCISES AND RITUALS THAT CAN HELP

REGRET AND WISDOM GAINED

In the years after a loved one has died, there are many choices to make, and if a person is struggling with regret having to do with their relationship with the deceased, they can feel frozen in place. This exercise is meant to clear up the relationship between what you regret and the wisdom you gained from your traumatic journey.

Grab a blank piece of paper or open your journal to a clean page. Make two equal columns—one column that says "Regrets," the other, "Wisdom Gained." See if you can think of ten things you regret in your life and list them in the Regret column. Then next to each one, list what lesson or wisdom you gained.

Regret: I regret being impatient with my mom. I was angry with her and didn't talk about it, but I acted out in other ways and I know this hurt her.

Wisdom Gained: I've learned to be more honest and to not passively punish someone for things I'm mad about but won't communicate. This has made my relationships better, even if it's hard to be honest about my feelings sometimes.

Can you see that with any moment in which we have regret, we also have the opportunity to access our innate wisdom? These are the hard-won jewels of living a life filled with all the ups and downs and choices and crossroads we face as humans.

LETTING THE TRUTH OUT AND IN

We are hurt by the unacknowledged pains we carry that are forced down into the depths of our hidden selves. It's a mistake to think that hiding guilt or regret will make it go away. In fact, it's the opposite. The more you allow for your truer feelings to come out and be expressed, the less potential energy they carry. Make no mistake: We know this is not easy. We are basically suggesting you do one of the hardest things any of us can do—lay bare our biggest and most tender pains. If this feels untenable to you now, that's okay. Just think about it. When you are ready to let the truth out and into your heart and psyche here are some steps you can take:

> Consider how you want to share your truth. Do you want to begin by writing or dictating thoughts and stories on a recorder? By enlisting the help of a therapist? Or spiritual/religious guide? It's important, if you're going to talk to another person about guilt or regret, that it be someone who is not reactive or unable to be objective. You don't want someone adding to what you are holding. You just need someone to hold your stories and bear witness to your journey.

> When you notice that it's hard for you to say something or acknowledge a truth, make note of that. There's energy there. What are you afraid will happen?

> Avoid making excuses or rationalizations or minimizing things. This just lessens the impact of what you are trying to do, which is to free yourself from the binds of unprocessed guilt and regret.

> Let yourself learn and turn your learning into wisdom in your day-to-day life. None of us makes it through life without making decisions that teach us a whole lot of things.

I DON'T NEED THIS

Sometimes the noise in your head can get overwhelmingly loud when it's all about how you've struggled, stumbled, or made mistakes. The noise can be intrusive thoughts, punishing self-attack, and even shame. Here's how we work with this. We recommend taking out your journal and asking yourself these questions:

> What purpose do these thoughts serve?

> How are these thoughts beneficial to my being right now?

> Do I need to keep revisiting guilt and regret?

> Is there anger to process or make use of?

Scan your body, releasing the pain where you are holding it. Tap into the wisdom of the story.

Remember, life is not about achieving perfection. It can be about growing and evolving. How have you grown? After reading this chapter maybe you've gathered some new insights into guilt and regret. Ask yourself two important questions: What can you do about it now, and what would your loved one want for you?

18

When Catastrophic Things Happen

Let me be a beacon for others by telling the hardy myths
of survival. Help me bring purpose and significance to
the fresh narrative I am living.

Pixie Lighthorse, author of *Prayers of Honoring Grief*

Some of us are attached to the idea that if we plan well enough, prepare well enough, maybe even pray enough, we will be spared having to face catastrophe. Others carry the feeling that no matter how well we plan, something might happen to overwhelm us, and we feel anxious about it. Some of us know firsthand what it is to face horror and despair head-on. There are major themes that arise in the years following a catastrophic event, and there are specific challenges that make realizing a new way of life more difficult.

In this chapter, we talk about the personal and collective loss that is often traumatic and shocking, and which demands an unusual amount of readjustment or ongoing stress in the following years. Natural disasters, war, mass shootings, pandemics, acts of terror, violent crime—all losses containing realities that set apart the experience of grief. In the world of the griever, this can make healing even more challenging. What some might find helpful on their grief journey, others might find not only unhelpful, but insulting and harmful.

In this chapter, we touch on themes that current research and personal stories tell us about losing loved ones in ways that are hard to reconcile and that we might find impossible to move on from. We talk about what making peace with reality looks like and address the ever-burdensome pressure to find that elusive sense of closure. We also share some of what current practice suggests as it relates to what is helpful in reclaiming your life.

AMBIGUOUS LOSS

My husband was a therapist. He had cyclical depression, and, in hindsight, he suffered from something more than depression. When he would get depressed, he wasn't in reality. He would decide something and then that would be true even though that wasn't what the reality was. Our marriage was challenging because he suffered from mental illness. My dealing with his loss is very multilayered. I had had other experiences of him being suicidal, but he couldn't even put a BandAid on a scraped knee, that's how squeamish he was… So the fact that he drove down to the park and shot himself in the head is beyond comprehension. There are still days I go, "He's dead?"

Alaiya

Psychologist and researcher Pauline Boss has written extensively about ambiguous loss, which is characterized by loss without closure. This loss can be psychological or physical. In this book, we'll focus on the latter.

Physical ambiguous loss occurs when people disappear "without proof of death." The Boxing Day Tsunami of 2004 took the lives of over 200,000 people. Many families lost loved ones who were swept away in the rising waters, never to be found. Earthquakes, hurricanes, tornadoes, and floods are all natural events in many parts of the world that suddenly steal people from their families and communities. The terrorist attack on 9/11 in New York City, Washington, DC, and Pennsylvania, stands out as another episode where many bodies were not recovered, and families were forced to grieve on a national stage with no conclusion.

In many cases, loved ones are not only dealing with this ambiguous loss of loved ones, but they're also faced with losing their homes, their communities, and the social structure in which they, live all at once. Hurricane Katrina in 2005 devastated communities in Mississippi, Louisiana, and Florida, and took lives in a reported seven states. Two years following the hurricane, 135 people were still missing. When traumas add up, one on top of the other before there is adequate time for a person to stabilize and build up strength again, there is great suffering.

It's important to know that there are certain realities that go hand in hand with these kinds of losses, both in terms of their effects and what is helpful in reclaiming life while incorporating ambiguous loss into the fold. First of all, it is very normal for people to freeze. With this kind of loss, and this kind of stress, and without a clear path forward supported by cultural and community ritual, engagement, and niceties, people suffering this kind of loss remain in a sort of limbo state.

Being in limbo for too long is detrimental to human functioning. Why? What naturally comes to mind is the very human and very natural hope for closure. Closure doesn't mean "getting over it," or "moving on," or not grieving anymore. It is the punctuation at the end of the sentence. It is the experience of knowing what is true so that it's possible to make a decision on how and in which direction to take the next steps.

The COVID-19 pandemic is an example. Young adults fresh out of high school, college, or graduate school were primed and ready to begin their lives. Some had specific plans that were canceled or postponed. Others weren't quite sure what they'd do but knew where they were going and with whom, and what kinds of jobs or training they'd be looking for. But now, with the entire world in this state of perpetual waiting, they feel stuck, many back at the family home, many in their rented dwellings with no jobs, no prospects—a perpetual waiting. At the same time, millions of people are grieving and afraid. At the time of this writing, there have been over 6.1 million deaths worldwide from COVID-19. Depression and anxiety, sleeplessness, and addictive behaviors are common and becoming severe for many people. It could be argued that most people the world over are living in a state of ambiguous grief in its psychological form right now, while millions also suffer from the loss of loved ones and a lost future without them.

CONCURRENT STRESSORS AND TRAUMAS

A known contributor to ongoing and pervasive grief is the experience of concurrent stressors in the years following loss. This can happen for anyone going through any sort of grieving at any time but is almost always a reality after catastrophic or traumatic loss. After natural disasters, including epidemics and pandemics, issues like food insecurity and unemployment are major sources of stress.

When people lose loved ones to natural disasters or to the side effects of them, they are also faced with overcoming the loss of community, and of routine and ritual around the bedrock upon which grieving might happen.

Multiple family members dying is also an extreme experience of concurrent stress where, in one fell swoop, entire families are reshaped around gaping chasms where there used to be life and hope.

Those fighting in wars and those caught as civilians between warring groups are extremely vulnerable to prolonged grief, depression, PTSD, and anxiety.

From another perspective, there are those civilians and persecuted groups that are the victims of these wars. The scars from war injury carry through generations as grief stalls in deference to survival.

This is all to say, there are so many layers of what one might experience at a time of catastrophic loss. These are the experiences requiring a deep excavation of the self to find all of the compassion, patience, kindness, empathy, and perspective that is possible to find. These things can be applied to oneself and to one's community. It is important to release any idea of grief being linear. In fact, count on it being nonlinear, tangential, and creative in getting its needs met. Sometimes grief will look like mourning the loss of a loved one. Sometimes grief will look like community engagement and support and hard work. Sometimes it will look like activism and courage. Other times it will be private and tender. There's no one way, and *there is no timeline*.

BREAKS IN RITUAL AND CEREMONY

Every day people die alone or in places without family, but during certain acute times of loss, this happens on a much larger scale. As a major rite of passage, death has through time immemorial been ritualized and sanctified through prayer, presence, and ceremony. The thought of loved ones transitioning from life to death without the support of family by their side can be a tremendously painful one. Funeral rites are another deep part of the human social fiber. They are woven into myth, story, religious text, music, and art. We rely on these in many respects not just to usher the dead into the afterlife, but to usher the survivors into new life without their loved one. Funeral rites are important and often bound by significant rules, traditions, and customs. What happens when people can't have that? During the COVID-19 pandemic, especially in the first year, no one could gather. People had to mourn in ways absolutely disparate from how they would normally. Many did their best to keep hold of their customary practices, but who would have ever imagined holding funeral ceremonies via Zoom?

Who would have ever imagined we wouldn't be able to hold and physically comfort or receive comfort from fellow loved ones and grievers?

These pains happen all over the world for different reasons. Consider people who are not able to practice their faith with freedom due to conflict or lose loved ones in civil war and must flee. Here again, we have trauma laid on top of trauma. These wounds heal at a different pace and need specific tending.

PERSONAL AND COLLECTIVE RESPONSES

It's been almost twenty years since I lost my husband in the 9/11 attacks. Not a day goes by where I don't think of him and replay that horrific time. When I see footage of other terrorist attacks around the world, my whole body reacts.

J.

In many cases, the personal mourning process for those left behind following a collective experience is public and politicized. Unlike most family or community-centric losses where the bereavement process happens on the personal stage, in acts of terror, episodes of mass gun violence, highly publicized murders, wars, or loss during the COVID-19 pandemic, there is a bigger and more exposed terrain mourners must navigate. This, for many, feels invasive and as though there are eyes on them in their most vulnerable and heartbroken moments.

Ongoing social and political commentary in the media surrounding a particular death or group of deaths continues to make the personal public. This creates a situation where, for many, there is a disconnect between the big conversation about what happened and the impact on one's own family and future.

Then there are the years following the event. What researchers and individuals have found is that there is no one way to heal from this kind of grief. Some enjoy participating in yearly memorials for their lost loved ones, while others feel they conjure up such powerful feelings of grief and loss that they are more detrimental than helpful. Some find therapeutic groups to be comforting while others find them to be triggering and overwhelming.

In these collective traumatic experiences, to the degree we can, tending to both individual grief and community grief is important and relevant to healing.

QUESTIONS YOU MAY ASK YOURSELF

My family has been significantly impacted by loss. How do we begin to heal as a whole?

Families are impacted to a great degree as a result of this terrible pain. The whole system is reorganized as a result of their loss, especially in the immediate aftermath—this is a reactive reorganization. The reaction is white-hot shock and grief, so it would make sense that over time, adjustments need to be made where reactivity can evolve into generative growth.

Here is one example to explain this thinking. A family is

reeling after the murder of a young adult family member. The parents are beside themselves with shock, grief, despair, and anger. They are struggling to find their way through legal issues and formal matters. Their relationship is struggling to hold the new and heavy burden of surviving this incredible stress. They have other children who are still living at home and who, up until this tragedy, relied on their parents to be the strong and supportive ones. Now they are broken. The surviving children consciously and unconsciously take on new roles to accommodate the stress and anxiety in the home. Some are adaptive and healthy, some are not. After years of living in this compromised state, it is not too late to reflect on the journey the family has been on, acknowledge what has taken place, and how different family members tried to keep their heads above water. It is never too late to make meaning of your family's story and talk about how you want to move forward, maybe with permissions to let go of roles taken on that are no longer needed. You see? We can always keep talking and understanding more deeply those things that impact our lives and how we can move on together.

Feelings of helplessness have me frozen. How do I begin to move forward?

A significant precipitant to post-traumatic stress disorder is a felt sense of intense powerlessness and overwhelming helplessness as a result of a catastrophic event. As we have said before, with losses such as these, almost every aspect of life has changed, and even if one has been able to carve out a bit of "normalcy," there may still be a nagging sense of things not being right. Research lets us know that finding our agency, in whatever way we can, helps unequivocally. Helplessness breeds fear. Agency breeds bravery. Are there small steps you can imagine taking that could initiate an experience of increasing power in one's own life? This may be as simple as deciding to donate money to a cause connected to your loved one's death, to as complicated as joining said cause and adding your voice to the chorus of activism and truth to power. Every small step leads to more steps. You may find a newfound voice and healing along the way.

I keep replaying my loved one's death over and over in my mind. How can I stop these thoughts from destroying me?

Another aspect of complicated and long-term grieving is the experience of intrusive thoughts and images and turning over and over again in the mind experiences that were either had or imagined. Sometimes this is our mind's way of trying to make sense out of what happened. Sometimes it's an effort to practice dealing with pain in a different way. Other times it's because in a specific moment of time, our mind was seared with a shocking pain that, in a sense, has a record player in our mind replaying a moment. Sometimes these thoughts are imaginary as we try to sort through what our loved one experienced when we were not with them. We are trying to complete the story in our own mind, but it turns into personal torture instead.

However painful, the brain does this with trauma, and it is

very normal. There are ways to help our minds heal from these repetitive thoughts, and a lot of these ways are not helped through cognitive-thinking routes. Our bodies and nervous systems need help getting back online and out of the groove of the traumatic moment and aftermath. Eye movement desensitization and reprocessing (EMDR), somatic reprocessing, tapping, and acupuncture are all techniques that are helpful in this area. It's not to diminish the benefits of talking through experience, but when the nervous system and fear centers of our brains have been hijacked by trauma, we need to help those parts of ourselves regain equilibrium so that the rest of our emotional work can carry on in a way that is not flooding.

EXERCISES AND RITUALS THAT CAN HELP

FIND YOUR POWER

What researchers have found is that, even years after loss due to natural disasters, when people engage with what they can do to help, to make meaning and improve situations, conditions tend to change and life is experienced differently. With intention and a subtle change in focus, adjustments can be made to our thinking and our behaviors that create new openings for healing. Little bit by little bit, we can move the arrow in a different direction.

Identifying and reconnecting with our strengths helps us with this, and it takes practice. Saying positive things about yourself is required. For some, this is very difficult. This could be due to an awareness issue (some people just don't know what their strengths are) or a reluctance to claim space and take pride in yourself. In everyday life, there are many ways your strengths show up that seem like typical modes of being in the world. You're making your way through a difficult journey that takes *strength*. In any hero's tale, there is a moment when the hero must dig deep to find their power, their will to keep going, and recommit to their efforts to stay on the journey. In recognizing and accessing your strengths, you find the power you need to recommit to your journey, and to yourself.

Consider these prompts and work to keep your responses focused on the positive. For example, if an answer that comes to mind is "I'm stubborn," that can be reframed as, "Once I get my mind set on something, I don't give up."

- I'm a capable person because

  _____

- In my life, people have told me that I'm X *(compliments only)*

  _____

- In my life I'm most proud of X *(it's okay to brag)*

  _____

- The personality trait*(s)* that allowed me to do thing*(s)* I am most proud of is/are

  _____

- One of the biggest obstacles I overcame was

  _____

- I overcame it by

  _____

- I wish people knew that I'm

  _____

- When I daydream about doing something, it's

  _____

- The person or people who see my strengths and support them are

  _____

- One of the ways I can cultivate a strength I love is

  _____

- Places and situations in my life that call for my strengths are

  _____

TRANSFORMING RUMINATION INTO WISDOM

If you are struggling with ruminative thinking (excessively thinking about something, usually in a negative way) and/or avoidant styles of managing emotions, look at this as a signal that something wants to be processed and metabolized. We go over and over again a repetitive loop of thoughts, memories, and experiences when we are trying to gain mastery over something or stretch into a different way of managing a similar situation, should it come to pass. Do you ever do this when you keep going over an argument you may have had with someone, or when you keep imagining yourself saying this thing or responding that way? It's our attempt to do the thing differently, whatever it is. So what are you practicing at?

Try this: In your journal make three columns. From left to right, and put the following in each column: Repetitive Thought/ Argument, How I Imagine Myself Responding, What Am I Practicing?

It can look like this:

Repetitive Thought/Argument: I keep reliving the day that my daughter left for school and never came home. I keep going over and over in my mind how mad I was that we were all late and that I didn't kiss her goodbye. I can't stop thinking about it. It is my personal hell.

How I imagine myself responding: I try to imagine holding her and kissing her and not caring so much about being late. I imagine smelling her hair and looking into her eyes with love. I wish that were the last way she saw me.

What am I practicing? I am trying to practice remembering that we had many moments like that, and she was so deeply loved. I am practicing forgiving myself. I'm practicing remembering to be present with the people I love now.

The purpose of this exercise is to gather some insight into your repetitive or ruminative thinking. Throw your arms around it and try to sort out what you are trying to make sense of. It can help to clarify the main themes so you can incorporate them into your life now. Is there action you want to take but are scared? Are there things you need to say to someone but don't know how?

COMMUNITY MEMORIAL

A community memorial is a beautiful way to celebrate the life of your loved one. You might want to choose to put this physical memorial in a place they loved spending time. The memorial could be a park bench in their name, or a community garden. You might also choose a crowdfunding fundraiser for a school scholarship or other cause.

CLAIM YOUR RIGHT TO RITUAL

Ceremony and ritual are not relegated to a specific time frame. If you feel like you did not have the funeral or services you would have wanted for your loved one, you can have another one! In fact, some people do something to honor their deceased loved ones every year! It is never too late. There just may be a time when it is easier and safer to do.

GET INVOLVED AND GET CREATIVE

Research shows that people who foster active coping mechanisms and cultivate self-efficacy in their lives do better. What does *do better* mean? They tend to find ways to live in the here and now with a sense of meaning and hope. Well, how do you do that? There are myriad ways, big and small, that can help with this. Think about where your energy is and notice if you respond to any of the ideas in this list:

> ➢ Volunteer with organizations that help rebuild homes and businesses that have been devastated by natural disaster.

> Learn a new skill, like knitting, or learn a new language, or practice painting.

> If you are proficient at a skill, teach it to others.

> Join organizations that are related to the theme surrounding your loved one's death and add your voice and your wisdom. You have that, and your voice is important.

> Plant a garden outside or in pots inside.

> Participate in community events. If socializing is too overwhelming, volunteer behind the scenes.

> Talk about how you are and ask others how they are doing. Be real. It's better than trying to put a mask on every day. You don't have to feel good to be honest.

> If you have the lifestyle for it, get a pet. The act of taking care of another creature and petting an animal is deeply comforting.

> Say your loved one's name. If you are talking about your life or recalling memories, allow yourself to tell the stories that involve them and allow people to know about your life and your experience. This can be in small doses like, "My son loved this chocolate," or "Every year on the first snow, my dad would go out in his long johns and do a funny dance." Or, they can be longer stories shared over coffee with a trusted friend or confidant.

This chapter is about finding your power and accessing it in the face of catastrophes outside your control. If ever

there were a time to wrestle with these questions, it's now. Research lets us know that when we face head-on and engage with what is in front of us and figure out how to be with it all, we are stronger. Are there ideas here that resonate with you, or did you come up with your own as you read? Write them down and get detailed on how you'd like to see them through.

19

When You Are Walking with Someone Else on Their Long Journey

*For people in full grief who have no community or
an extended family of like mind, but might have one
real friend to watch over them while they go splashing
through grief's messy and ecstatic route to beauty, the
best thing to do is get both of you down to the sea.*

Martín Prechtel, author of *The Smell of Rain on Dust*

Occasionally, we're called upon to show up for people in ways that we have no training for and for which we have no how-to manual. We are invited to sit in the presence of a person who is struck down by grief. We are asked to bear witness, to not look away or minimize, to hold space for the most exquisite of pains. This is not easy for anyone, but it is part of life and relationships.

Years after someone has lost a loved one, you might still find yourself in a place where you need to offer support, and you might be tired. Likely, the feelings and intensity of expression are not as acute as they were directly after the loss, but maybe issues come up unexpectedly when you were otherwise enjoying a pleasant moment with your loved one. Maybe you are supporting someone you care for deeply, but who has changed so much since their loss, you feel like you're with a different person. Maybe you feel hopeless when it comes to helping them clean out their loved one's belongings. Perhaps you're trying to help your spouse overcome the devastating depression that has settled over them after the loss of your shared child, or your friend to move on after the loss of a mutual friend. When you're with this person, sometimes you just want to talk about something else.

If you find yourself here, there are some themes to consider that could be useful to you.

ACCEPT THAT YOUR LOVED ONE MIGHT NEVER BE THE SAME

> Loss of a loved person is one of the most intensely painful experiences any human being can suffer. And not only is it painful to experience, but it is also painful to witness, if only because we are so impotent to help. To the bereaved nothing but the return of the lost person can bring true comfort... Whether an author is discussing the effects of loss on an adult or a child, there is a tendency to underestimate how intensely distressing and disabling loss usually is and for how long the distress, and often the disablement, commonly lasts.
>
> John Bowlby, CBE, psychiatrist and psychoanalyst

A repeating theme in this book, and in others that cover the painful topic of grief, is that nothing feels like it did before a loved one died. There will always be the empty chair at the table, the spot on the couch that no one wants to sit in, and the bed that is now always made. The person you are supporting through their long journey is carrying around this difference in their heart and for some, it takes a toll. Widowed parents may seem tearful all the time. Children who have lost a sibling may still be struggling to find their place in this new family structure. Your friend may not be able to tolerate being with you and your child after losing her own. Sometimes sitting with reality, both theirs and yours, is the hardest part. Deep and ongoing grief leaves a mark. It's best not to pretend it isn't there.

This is when some soul searching will be helpful. Can you tolerate the changes you see in your loved one? Can you be with this different version of them? Sitting with someone who is still mired in grief can be very painful, particularly when you have been able to move on from your own loss. This can happen in families, especially when one or a few people are still very much struggling, while others seem to be doing all right. To alleviate painful feelings, sometimes the most patient of us want to yell, "Would you just get over it and get back to normal!"

Often what brings people to therapy is when others in their world can no longer deal with the way they're acting. Well, this can happen with grief, too. How many times has the refrain been uttered, "I love her, but she's so hard to be with because she's so sad all the time."

It's a good idea to have a heart-to-heart with yourself periodically. Ask yourself if being with your loved one's pain is hard on you. Ask yourself why. Do you feel responsible for making them feel better? The answer is: you are not responsible for making them feel better. Do you feel if you just had the magic words, you'd be able to say something to take away their pain? Because you can't.

Does being with their grief remind you of your own and stir up old pain? If it does, you might want to think on how you're showing up for your loved one and consider getting extra support. Whatever the issue, check in with yourself and get clear on how you feel about the person you are supporting. If resentment, impatience, anger, or guilt are coming up, allow yourself to take some time off to tend to yourself. You are not the answer to your loved one's pain.

LIGHTENING THEIR LOAD

> *Even ten-plus years after my losses, the thing that grounds me the most and brings me the most comfort and peace is when a person shares how much **they** miss my special person. Not sure if that makes any sense, but people who reach out at random times saying they miss my dad because of x, y, or z just do so much for me. It feels less isolating.*
>
> Ali

Now that we have determined you can't be everything to everyone, let's talk about what you can do to help someone on their journey. What follows is a collection of ideas gathered from years of conversations with people about what has helped them as they traversed the road of grief.

- Remember the anniversary of the loved one's death. You can acknowledge this with a phone call, a card, a simple text saying, "Just thinking of you today and sending love," or an invitation to go to the cemetery with your loved one.
- If it makes sense, acknowledge birthdays and anniversaries. Bradie always calls her grandmother on her grandfather's birthday and on their wedding anniversary, just to say hi and to acknowledge that this might be an emotional day.
- Say the deceased's name. Don't avoid bringing them up in conversation or telling stories about them. Out of sight is not out of mind, and many people relish the chance to hear about their loved ones.
- Avoid comparing your grieving loved one to anyone else as a means of urging them toward a different way of being. Shame can easily come from being compared to someone who has appeared to grieve "better," or for less time.
- Take note if they start saying things that sound worrisome. Always consult with a mental health professional if you feel concerned about personal safety.
- Give what you can, but not more. Inauthentic giving can

create seeds of resentment, which sours a relationship and can unwittingly conjure up feelings of shame and embarrassment in the bereaved. Just be honest when you're not up for doing something.

- Periodically, ask specifically how they are doing. Give them the opportunity to talk about what they're feeling and what their current struggles are.

- Offer to help with big jobs (if possible) like cleaning out storage units, bedrooms, closets, or homes. Don't be surprised if you get a "no" in response. But don't hesitate to offer.

- Model working through grief. If you are also grieving, allow yourself to talk about your process and what you are stuck on. Sometimes having the chance to help someone else can lift us out of our own pain.

Do you have any ideas to add to this list? Write them in your journal.

THE DIFFERENCE BETWEEN HELPING AND ENABLING

Helping and being supportive is one thing. Making excuses, covering up, and allowing for unhealthy patterns is another. In the addiction community, we refer to this as enabling, and this is often part of codependent relationships.

Think of it this way. Helping is doing something for anyone who is unable to do it for themselves. Enabling is doing something for an individual who could and should be doing it for themselves. Sometimes this gets murky, and when we think we are helping, we are really encouraging a loved one to continue living in an unhealthy, self-destructive way.

Pam remembers one particularly difficult case where Susan refused to move back into the apartment she shared with her husband, Sid. Nine years had passed since his heart attack and death, and Susan had moved into her daughter's very small apartment in the same building. She didn't mind sleeping on the pullout couch in the middle of the living room. Her daughter had a disabled adult child also living with her. Meanwhile, Susan still paid rent for the apartment she lived in with Sid and everything on Sid's desk was in the exact position where he left it. The book he was reading was open to the same page, and all of his clothes and shoes were still in the closet.

What could Susan's daughter do to help her mother move on? How could she stop being an enabler?

So often when we make little concessions for people who are suffering, they start off just like that—little. It must have made perfect sense to Susan and Susan's daughter that she stay in her apartment for a few nights after Sid died. Family very often want to be together when facing unbearable grief. But then it went on and on. Perhaps Susan had very compelling reasons for wanting to stay, and maybe Susan's daughter didn't mind too much at first because she was grieving, too. But, years later, nothing had changed. The system became calcified because Susan's daughter was unable to take a stand. Not one, but three lives were put on hold. It was time to change things, but how?

Susan will likely need support. Therapeutic at least, but maybe even adult social services. Getting connected with systems that have the infrastructure to support adults on multiple levels is not a bad thing. In fact, it's adaptive and smart, especially when there are no other family members who can help support Susan as she reclaims her life.

You see where we're going with this? You don't have to do it alone. Reaching out to agencies, hospice organizations, therapists, and religious organizations can very much help get people the support they need. Sometimes, opening up the system a bit by inviting in help is just what can get the roads cleared again.

QUESTIONS YOU MAY ASK YOURSELF

Why am I not enough to help?

When people are struggling deeply with ongoing grief, no one is good enough, because no one is the beloved's deceased. This is what makes supporting the grieving person so challenging at times. It is essential that you have your own support person with whom you can talk to about how you feel, why you are also hurting. You need to be able to express frustration and anger in a totally guilt-free zone.

It's also helpful to get very clear on what you can and cannot do. This is a personal conversation with yourself and provides the bedrock from which to offer what you can but not overextend. It can sound something like this: "Every part of me wants to make sure my dad is not alone every weekend. I want to extend an open invitation to whatever we're doing, but I know that is not sustainable or good for him or me. So, I will invite him over this Sunday to watch the football game and have dinner and extend offers like that when it makes sense." You address the longing you might have to be everything to someone you love, but you reel it in before you make promises you can't keep. Think about it. It's not fair to resent people you overextend to when you are the one offering the overextension to begin with.

You can also make this an opportunity to talk seriously with your loved one. Communications like this can go a long way: "I know I'm not your son, and I can never replace him. I would never dream of trying to, but I love you and I am with you." In saying things like this, you acknowledge the reality that the person they love and lost is irreplaceable, but you are there for support if and when they need it.

I'm going through a tough time in my own life right now and am finding it hard to be there for my grieving loved one. How can I continue to show up for them while tending to myself?

Let's not forget that you might be grieving, too. You might be grieving the same loss as your loved one, or someone who is unique to your life and family. You get to take a step back and tend to yourself. Yes. You can have that, too.

The rest of life does not stop just because we or someone we love is grieving. Maybe you are going through a divorce, lost a job, or are struggling with issues with your children or finances or health. Maybe, just maybe, you're tapped out. In these cases, you get to claim space for yourself to tend to your own needs. You can do this with love and compassion. You can say things like, "I love you and I know you are struggling, but right now I don't feel strong and don't have much extra to give. I'm sorry I can't continue to meet every week for lunch. I just need to pull in my energy to deal with my health (or family, grief, divorce, etc.)." Or something like this, "It's been so important to me to be there for you as you've walked the road of grief, but after losing my sister, I am crushed and need to take care of myself."

Maybe your loved one can show up for you now. Maybe they can't. But no matter what, you get to take the space you need to deal with your own pain and your own life.

I find myself getting frustrated with my loved one who seems stuck after the death of someone close to them. How do I keep myself from being impatient with them?

Here is something important to remember: you don't have to understand where your loved one is coming from to be supportive and kind. You don't. You might be a "pick yourself up by the bootstraps" kind of person, and you might not be able to appreciate what gets in the way for people who cannot do that. That's okay! The key is not to judge. Judgment breeds in Comparison Swamp, Gossip Creek, and Exhaustion Desert. Avoid these places on the long journey of supporting someone you love. Don't compare your sister, who is grieving the death of her dog years later to the neighbors who just got a new pup after their previous one died. Don't gossip with your aunt about your grandmother's habit of talking to her deceased son. And don't blame your loved one for the exhaustion you feel. Grab the reigns of your own behavior so that you give what you can when appropriate and allow for others to live their lives as they see fit. You don't have to see things the same way. You just have to be there and be real.

And always remember, it is not on you to take away someone's tears or create situations where you think tears might not come. In fact, it's best in most circumstances to manage other people less and manage yourself more. How are you doing? Are you taking good care of yourself? Are you allowing for your own love and grief to flow? Tending lovingly to self very often translates to deep loving of others because you are allowing them to manage themselves. If you can do that, you are gazing upon Mount Respect.

EXERCISES AND RITUALS THAT CAN HELP

CREATE SPACE FOR YOUR OWN FEELINGS

Sometimes, when you are in a position to support a loved one for years as they struggle, it can feel as though you'll never get to the other side of a sad tunnel. And many people struggle with feelings of guilt and resentment as more and more time goes by.

Take a moment to ask yourself:

Are you experiencing burnout? This could look like strong feelings of impatience, annoyance, and sometimes outright anger and resentment.

Do you feel resentful because you're also grieving the loss and you haven't gotten to express your pain?

Have you forgotten ways to tend to yourself? If so, write down at least three things you can do to focus attention on yourself and your needs.

HANG UP THE SUPERHERO CAPE

Something to remind yourself of is that you cannot take the pain of loss away from someone else. Instead of trying to wrest grief from someone's heart, try this: Every time you go to talk with or share time with your loved one, tell yourself first: "I can't take their feelings from them. I can only be with them."

You might be wondering what you *can* do. You can bear witness and let someone be where they are. You can ask them what they might find helpful if something specific is going on. You can remember important dates and reach out when your heart calls you to do so. Believe it or not, in our culture that remains so focused on people getting over grief fast, these actions are really rather big. They might not be as dramatic as Superman making the world spin backward so he could go back in time, but they are deeply felt and heroic moves when it comes to the heart. Let yourself off the hook of *solving* anything so you can just *be* with everything.

BOUNDARIES ARE NOT MEAN

Simply put, a boundary is the space where one person stops and another starts. Emotionally, it's taking seriously what's okay for you and what's not when it comes to how you relate to others and how they relate to you. It's being able to say "no" when you want to and not feeling like you have to sacrifice what is important or essential to you in order to keep someone else happy. Boundaries, when held and respected, engender feelings of respect, responsibility, and equity.

The fact is, you simply can't be there all the time for someone, no matter what. Or, even if you can, you might not want to. This has nothing to do with love or commitment. It's more about the idea that you have a life, just like everyone else does, and you get to live it, even when those you love are hurting. When this simple fact is ignored, resentment and bitterness grow. These are far more destructive elements in a relationship.

Are you feeling like boundaries have been an issue in your relationship with someone in your life who is grieving? Use the prompts below to get clear on what's happening and how you might make some adjustments to hold space for yourself.

The issue that is making me feel resentful: Whenever my loved one is having a hard day, they reach out and need support and I'm tapped out.

What I do now: I drop whatever I'm doing because I know they need support and don't know what else they'd do if I couldn't talk.

What I can do instead: I can answer the phone and tell them I am not able to talk right now and tell them when I can.

What I'm afraid will happen: They will think they are not important to me or that I'm always too busy. They will feel alone.

How I can address that fear: I can tell them how much I love them and can do two things: I can let them know I want to be a support for them, but I'm finding that I can't always drop whatever I'm doing to talk. I can also brainstorm with them other ways they might tend to themselves when they are struggling.

You've just read some ideas about supporting someone through their grief journey while tending to yourself at the same time. Did any of the ideas resonate with you? Take some time to write about this in your journal and make a plan to treat yourself with as much love and respect as you do for those you are supporting.

20

Walking toward a New Day

Cry out! Don't be stolid and silent
with your pain. Lament! And let the milk
of loving flow into you.
The hard rain and wind
are ways the cloud has
to take care of us.
Be patient.
Respond to every call
that excites your spirit.
Ignore those that make you fearful
and sad, that degrade you
back towards disease and death.

Rumi, excerpt from "Cry Out in Your Weakness"

In the book *The Bridge of San Luis Rey* by Thornton Wilder, we read about a bridge that collapsed in Peru back in the eighteenth century, killing five people. The tragedy was witnessed by a monk as he was about to step out onto the bridge and he's left wondering—as we tend to do when bad things happen—"Was there some purpose to this?" or "Was it just random?" The truth is always more complicated, and the narrator concludes:

> *But soon we shall die and all memory of these five will have left the earth, and we ourselves shall be loved for a while and forgotten. But the love will have been enough; all those impulses of love return to the love that made them. Even memory is not necessary for love. There is a land of the living and a land of the dead, and the bridge is love, the only survival, the only meaning.*

The love goes on, the grief goes on, and so does life. We hope to make meaning and move forward after saying goodbye, and we find it's a long journey—longer than we expected, as first we crawl before we learn to walk. We dream of reaching out into the world and of lifting ourselves up into a greater understanding. In looking back on the long journey, you begin to see how each phase of your life began at a decisive threshold where you went from one way of being to another. Your world, your sense of self after all the mourning and loss, holds the promise of you expanding and stretching into new possibilities. It's up to you to see all your pain and sorrow as an opportunity, as grief has the enormous potential to be transformative psychologically and spiritually.

Grief evolves and changes with time, and our response to it continues to shape us. Love goes on the journey with us—one day at a time. The gift in the journey is that we continue to evolve because of our experiences with grief and grieving the death of a loved one is only the beginning.

There is no doubt. Grief has changed you forever and is offering you the choice of carving out a larger, wisdom-filled life. Many of us get to a place on the journey of grief and wonder why we ought to keep going because the process of healing and growing is often painful and scary. Every experience you have, every explosion of love and joy, and every devastation of heartache and pain is part of the whole human story. Since the beginning of time, we have been birthing-surviving-dying-grieving, over and over again, and so we are called to search for meaning and the wisdom that comes with it.

WHERE ARE YOU NOW, AND WHAT DO YOU NEED?

When you reflect on the time since your loved one died, can you parse out if there are some aspects of life that have gone more smoothly than others? When you take your car to the mechanic, it helps if you can describe to them what you're hearing, seeing, smelling, or feeling as you drive. If we couldn't do that, or worse, if *they* couldn't, they'd end up fixing things that didn't need fixing and perhaps not find the actual issue.

With long-term grief, you may have struggled to find your individual strengths like using your coping skills, finding your sense of self amid chaos, and accessing strength, courage, or beliefs. Or maybe, when looking back, you see that your family handled your grief miserably, and maybe members of your family were locked in their own grief cycle to the degree that everyone was an isolated ship, tending to their own stormy and scary emotions in isolation, rather than with others who knew and loved the deceased as much as you did. Or maybe it was society and the culture you live in that let you down. Where are you now? Which direction do you want to go on your journey? Are you about to step onto a road marked by tending to your own courage and power? Is there healing left to do as it relates to articulating for yourself *your* experience? Are you about to rediscover aspects of yourself that might have been overwhelmed by the chaos of grief? Is the next leg of your journey going to be marked by deep reflection on your family of origin and getting clear on what happened to you and your loved ones when you sustained the loss? Maybe you will come to understand your loved ones more, and they you, as you make sense of your story. Perhaps you will do this work with a therapist, a spiritual guide, or through journaling and letter writing.

QUESTIONS YOU MAY ASK YOURSELF

Will making meaning and regaining a sense of purpose ease my pain?

As you move away from nonacceptance in whatever form and toward meaning, you may find that you have more energy to channel into things that are of importance to you. Meaning can be expressed in a variety of life-giving ways, some profound, some more subtle. As Maya told us, "Life is all about what you love, what you learn, and what you choose to do with that."

Here is how Fred Guttenberg, author of *Find the Helpers*, whose fourteen-year-old daughter Jaime was killed at Parkland High School, describes his move toward meaning-making:

> *How do I respond to what happened to my daughter other than making sure I visit her at the cemetery? Quite simply, by becoming her voice and fighting the lobby and the legislators who worked together to weaken our gun laws and to put our children and loved ones at risk of gun violence... As Jaime's voice, Jaime and I will work together to pass gun safety legislation and to defeat the legislators who put the needs of this lobby over the needs of public safety.*

You may have lost parts of yourself as a result of the death of your loved one, but you most likely came into contact with formerly unknown aspects of yourself in the process of struggling toward a new day. The depth of our pain opens doors for us. We catch glimpses of our courage, our passion, our rage, and our longing for peace. We learn about love and hope, strength and compassion. When we wail, we cry out within the echoes of our ancestors. And when we emerge from the darkness, we see through new eyes.

Whether this leads to meaning for you is entirely up to you.

Diane told us that she has a new appreciation for life. She wrote the following, on what would have been her daughter's seventeenth birthday:

Losing you was the hardest thing I've ever had to deal with. It broke me into a million pieces, but I knew you didn't want me to stay in that dark and painful place. I want to live with passion and purpose and be the kindhearted person that you were.

Inspiration and meaning-making comes in many forms. There's the actor who lost his father suddenly when he was twelve. Years later he's using that experience of loss and grief whenever he's asked to portray a character who needs to convey that pain. Or the musician whose mother died of cancer and is writing beautifully inspired music dedicated to her.

What if I can't move on?

Maybe you haven't taken some needed action, and your grief journey has stalled out and created a powerful and exhausting malaise. Or is it possible you're judging yourself too harshly or misinterpreting what is meant by "moving on"? Or perhaps it's because you haven't yet shaken the meaning out of your experience of loss. Either way, the process takes time and often evolves ever so subtly. Like a flag moving in the wind, long-term grief moves and changes over time. If your self-imposed expectation of "getting over it" is weighing on you, it will undoubtedly stall the natural process of evolving. If you think you're a failure at grieving, this thought will undoubtedly have a negative impact on how you approach the years following your loss. The simplest antidote is to set an intention—either big or small in scope—remembering that each day we're alive is a gift.

Brenna's new beginning was in realizing how she was treating herself. "I've had a lot of time to process not only the grief, but the negative ways I was treating my body as a result of my own personal demons. I come from a family of addicts, and my father is not the only one to succumb to his addiction. I do not need to be the next." Meaning can be as rooted and relevant to the here and now. Breaking family patterns and using the wisdom gained from her loss to dig into her own health and choices—this is meaning in real time, and for Brenna it will change the course of her future.

I'd like to move forward with my life. What does that look like?

Crossing the threshold to a new day means you may need to see yourself as leaving behind the You number one and embracing You number two—a different, enhanced version of yourself that has emerged from the ashes of loss. Learning how to embrace You number two is key to moving on to a new day. You have changed, in many ways. What are they? What do you know now about living with grief that you didn't know before? What hard-won wisdom can you carry into your life and relationships now?

Remember this:

- Grieving and loss can be a catalyst for growth, change, and transformation and can become an impetus for maturity and growth and fuel for living.
- If you can focus on meaning-making from your loss, your efforts can enhance your mental and physical health.

- You have a greater capacity to recognize grief in other people. Compassion grows, as does empathy. Have you ever had the experience of sitting with someone who just gets it? Who sees you and understands, on a visceral level, what you are saying? The broken heart in us reaches the broken heart in others. When this happens, loneliness evaporates.

EXERCISES AND RITUALS THAT CAN HELP

CRYSTALIZE THE GIFT AND HONOR IT

Take a moment when you have time and quiet, and let your mind drift. As you relax, taking steady breaths, think about your loved one and the specific light they added to your life. Let yourself rest in whatever images come up. Was it laughter, protection, connectedness, or adventure? Was it comfort, beauty, support, or touch? Write down as many things that come to mind. As you reflect on your list, pick the top two or three that resonate with you the most and meditate on them. How might you harness the power of these qualities and make use of them in your life?

RELEASE PRESSURE, APPLY LOVE

We've hit this point repeatedly in this book, but it bears mentioning again: there's no rule about what meaning looks like for people. Also, making meaning from our losses and pains might look one way at one time and completely different at another.

When we are seekers of meaning, wisdom, and healing, we are consistently stretching, adjusting, and growing. Doing this gently is key. We can't force healing. We can only allow the room for it to occur.

There's also no recipe for the perfect new day. Pressure is what makes grief so unbearable at times, and it's time to check your valves to make sure there are no pressing in places you don't want pressed, and that there are no clogs where you're wishing there was flow.

How do we do this? Check in with yourself by answering these questions in your journal.

> **Am I feeling pressure coming from others to be different, feel differently, or grieve differently?** If so, make a list of these pressures. It might read something like, "My family wants me to enjoy the winter holidays again and act like my old self," or "Friends seem to have fallen off and I think it's because I've changed. I don't like doing the same things anymore and must not be as much fun."

> **Can I transform pressure into hope?** Here's what we mean by that: take that first statement from above, "My family wants me to enjoy the winter holidays again and act like my old self." With care, we can transform that into a wish or a loving hope. Imagine if that statement was transformed into this: "I love you and I know the holidays are painful for you. They will

always feel different now, and I hope that over time, you will be able to carry your love for your loved one while also enjoying the family and friends you have who love you and want you to be okay." By doing this, we can maybe tap into the underlying wish that is operating for people and release the idea that you are doing something wrong.

> **Am I judging myself?** What are those judgments? Next to each, do the same thing and write an alternate statement that reflects love instead of judgment.

LOOK TOWARD THE HORIZON

Whether you live in a place with sweeping views or tall buildings side by side or some place in between, we all have in our mind's eye *the horizon* and what lies beyond it. Some close their eyes and see the ocean, some see mountains, some see the sky. Looking toward and beyond the horizon can give us a moment to look outside of ourselves and our personal experience.

When here and now starts to feel shaky and that things just aren't working out, look to the horizon (whether in person or in your imagination, or even a picture) and breathe. Just be in that space. Let your eyes drift and take in what you see. And remember this always: there is a new day on the horizon, another chance to wake up and tend to yourself, your heart, and your life.

A New Day

happens unannounced
begins the unending
loss and gain
with cries
with pain
asking to bend
breaking us open
heartache unspoken
screaming
the unanswerable
inviting us
"come this way"
we walk in darkness
toward the light of
hope from hopelessness
a new day awaits

Pamela D. Blair

21

Specific Kinds of Loss

Grief, when it comes, is nothing we expect it to be.

Joan Didion, author of *The Year of Magical Thinking*

While writing *The Long Grief Journey*, topics came up that were specific to certain losses and experiences. We wanted to have a space for some of these topics in the hopes that every griever—no matter who you lost, how you lost them, and where you are on your journey—will find yourself in this book.

LOSS OF A PARENT

My mourning changed over the years. I replaced the sadness with a certainty that I'll always have the memory of her. It fills me with joy and pride that she is my mother. And that my granddaughter is named after her.

Brita

The loss of a parent, whether anticipated or sudden, brings about different levels and timetables of grief. If the death was anticipated, you may have had the chance to put a support system in place and an opportunity to say goodbye. Ideally, you had the opportunity to say what you needed to one another. Perhaps you were able to process the reality of loss with your parent as they were dying, an auspicious and painful rite of passage for both of you.

When a death is sudden and unexpected, shock happens first, an emotional and psychological wave of disbelief that, according to loved ones' descriptions, makes it difficult to think, see, and understand what is happening. Shock takes us out of the here and now to protect the system from being overwhelmed to the degree we can't recover. Sorrel put it like this, after the sudden loss of her mother:

> There's a club for people who lose loved ones suddenly and unexpectedly... In my personal experience, this club typically meets on a secret, ad-hoc-only basis with loose agenda items like "shameful resentment, etc.," or feeling awful for actually being jealous of a friend who got to hold their loved one's hand and say "I love you" as they took their final breath. But again, there's no need to explain yourself... Everyone in this club gets it.

Whatever your personal circumstances, it's unfair to expect you will simply get over their death within a certain timeframe. Deb lost her mom when she was just sixteen. Now, forty-six years later, we asked her how she was feeling about that early loss. "Does the sharp pain soften over time? Yes, but still, almost fifty years later, I think of her almost every day and wish we'd had more time."

There is an internalized message many have articulated in their yearslong processing of grief, which goes something like this: "It's the natural order of things. My parents were supposed to die before me and they did, so I feel I'm supposed to handle this better," or, "My parents were old and sick when they died. I feel selfish for wanting them back, but I do." For good or bad, our parents shaped the environments into which we were born, and when we were young, they set an example of how, or how not, to interact with the world. Some turned against their influences and others mirrored them. As we age, some of us may not fully come out of our parents' shadows.

Release the idea that getting over grief means you're no longer grieving. Instead, allow for the reality that profound loss changes you and calls you to move into a different version of yourself. Let yourself be curious about what these changes mean. How are you different? How has your parent's absence impacted your life? How has grief allowed you to see humanity, our world, and your place in it?

Questions You May Ask Yourself

Is it possible that the decisions I'm making as an adult are influenced by my early loss of my parent?

Yes. There is no doubt about it. Everything we do is impacted by what we've experienced in our lives. Loss of a parent as a child is one of those experiences that changes the literal landscape of a life. Not only that, how adults responded to the loss impacted things, too. Was your grief supported, accepted, and worked through? Was someone else's grief so powerful and intense that it overshadowed yours? Did the impact of your parent's death cause a ripple effect of other stressors that you and your family had to contend with? What developmental milestones did you go through without the support of your parent? These are just a few examples of questions you can ask yourself as you reflect on how loss of a parent impacted your life, particularly when young.

Another theme people who lost their parent as a child described was feeling disconnected from those who had not had that same experience. It's traumatic for many and relating to those who grew up with both parents and who did not experience similar life consequences and stressors can be difficult. It's like living on a different planet. Brenna shared,

> I feel that my experiences with grief at a young age have made it challenging to relate to partners. I have dated people with very few traumatic past experiences, and they often did not understand my situation. This would make me feel irrationally upset, and I would feel isolated as if these people could not begin to understand the difficulties I've faced.

It's easy to imagine patterns emerging of difficult relationships, reactivity, and loneliness that is impossible to assuage. The side effects of that are many, and until grief is fully processed and understood, these patterns are likely to repeat.

So often we make decisions or react to things from a place in ourselves we are not fully conscious of. We try to heal wounds and gain mastery over events that knocked us down. At every crossroads, there are many parts of us that show up and participate in decision-making. It's often the effects of our decisions or our reactions to things that let us know that something is amiss. When we find ourselves continually asking ourselves, "Why do I keep doing this?" or "Why does this keep happening to me?" we have a clue that there's something deeper to look at. Many a time, grief is the culprit.

The following exercise is offered as means of connecting with your parent and with the space they left empty when they died. People of all ages can do this, and it doesn't matter how old you were when your parent passed away.

My surviving parent is dating/remarrying again, and I'm having strong feelings. What do I do with them?

There are so many things in life for which you simply cannot prepare. For example, managing the unexpected feelings that arise when a surviving parent decides to date, cohabitate with a partner, or remarry.

It's normal to idealize your deceased parent, even to the extent where they seem practically perfect in your eyes. This natural response to grief might cause you to think no one will be able to replace them. Adult children of a widowed parent may be surprised by the complicated set of emotions that arise when faced with a perceived interloper. They may cognitively be able to tell themselves things like, "My father deserves to have love and a companion," or "I can't be everything for my mother, and of course I know she can love another person." Yet, there are pestering and unrelenting thoughts and feelings that have nothing to do with logic—thoughts and feelings threatened by life changes requiring you to stretch yet again.

An adult child of a widowed parent is in a very different place than a child who is still living at home with their surviving parent. The family dynamic, the emotional and psychological well-being of the family members, and the time that has passed since their parent's death all weigh heavily here as their surviving parent takes steps to enter a new relationship.

If you are struggling with a new relationship your parent is enjoying, try these things:

- Practice letting feelings pass like water through a sieve.
- Be curious about your feelings rather than judgmental of them.
- Talk openly about the conflict you may be feeling with your surviving parent or, better yet, a professional or someone who can process these conflicts with you.
- Allow yourself to easily talk about your deceased parent (or spouse if you are supporting your child in their adjustment).

- Consider life and your family story as having chapters, and this is simply the start of a new chapter.
- Take the long view and recognize the reality that you have your journey and your parent has theirs.
- Bottom line: know you have the right to take the time to adjust and assimilate to new information and to a new relationship.

Exercise

WRITE A LETTER

Sharing with your parent details about your ongoing life is a beautiful way to stay connected to them. Can you take time to write, or simply say to them out loud, what is happening in your world that you think they would have enjoyed knowing about? This speaks to the idea of maintaining a connection with them. It might not come naturally at first, but over time you might find yourself updating them with ease.

Here's an example:

Dear Mom,

I decided to make your stew recipe and I'm proud to say it came out great. As the smell filled the kitchen, it reminded me of you. I love you.

LOSS OF A PARTNER

The key task is to accept the reality of the death, experience the pain of grief, adjust to life without the deceased, and memorialize the loved one in order to move on.

Pamela D. Blair, *Getting Older Better*

The emotional and relational impact of losing a partner is varied and complex. Feelings of isolation, depression, loneliness, guilt, and regret can continue well beyond the culturally allotted time for grieving. A less often discussed aspect of long-term grief is the relationship the surviving person continues to feel with their deceased partner. Moving through and healing from this loss does not mean severing the relationship or getting over it. Many experience an ongoing dialogue with their partner and continue to feel a relationship and connection. This carries through into day-to-day living as well as into new relationships and remarriage. Can one actively live while maintaining a felt connection to a partner who has died? Does this have to be a secret, hidden aspect of loss, or is there a way to weave this significant partner into a living reality? The years of shared memories, physical bonding, child rearing, or other meaningful interactions create a deep connection and to varying degrees shape our identities. When that connection is broken, it has the potential to threaten the remaining partner's purpose for living.

Questions You May Ask Yourself

I always considered myself an independent person, but now I'm lonely without a partner. What happened?

There's a huge difference between these two words, *alone* and *lonely*. As an independent person, or one who was self-dependent, you were probably okay being alone from time to time when your partner was alive. You enjoyed a day to yourself, a long walk on a nice day, traveling with friends, or having your own hobbies. Some people, when alone, become highly creative. Introverts are often at their best when they take time to be alone. Under those circumstances, you chose how you spent your time, but your loved one's death was not a choice. Being alone by choice before the loss is different than the loneliness that you're feeling now. It makes sense. You haven't lost your independent nature, you're simply and profoundly lonely.

You can surround yourself with a group of twenty people and still feel lonely if you fail to connect with them. Taking steps to connect with others may be a challenge, as it requires you to be a bit vulnerable and open. Work to find a way to make this happen. You can still be an independent person and depend on others to support you as you gain the courage to open up.

Social support and relationship expansion can have healing and helpful effects when connected to and supportive of those things you hold dear. Things like political views, religious ideals, and even personality traits have the opportunity to take a backseat when long-term grief is the common experience people share.

Bradie recalls a client who, years after losing her spouse, chose to continue attending a loss and bereavement group. She's made connections with others in the group who, outside of the group, might never have crossed her path. Grief breaks down boundaries that are often set by culture.

I'm still grieving my deceased former partner even though I'm now with a new partner. How can I keep my connection with my deceased partner without hurting my current relationship?

If you had a deep, bonded connection with your former partner, try not to judge yourself because you still have moments of grief. Perhaps you felt your deceased love was your soulmate, or you still believe they were the only chance you had at that kind of love. We're here to tell you that you will never love that way again. But you can love again! Every relationship is unique in intensity, bonding, and expectation. In addition, if you had children together, depending on their ages, you will still be grieving with them to some degree as life goes on.

If you're in a trusting, supportive relationship with your current partner, you might try communicating to them that a connection to your deceased partner is helpful to you, not because you love the deceased more than them, but because of your shared history. In addition, you might use your journal to communicate privately with your lost loved one, especially if you have concerns about the children you had together.

I'm a senior citizen and I lost my partner. It feels like I'm having more trouble moving on than younger people I know who've lost their partners. Am I?

You may be right. Chances are you were in a long-term relationship where you became deeply bonded and dependent on one another over the years. You might also be experiencing uncomfortable thoughts of never meeting anyone else and spending your elder years alone.

Married or not, making big changes at later stages in life can be more challenging for a variety of reasons health and finances among them. Here's the paradox: over the age of fifty, change gets harder, and it can also seem more urgent. Perhaps your life was more settled, and patterns of behavior were firmly ingrained. You may have lived in the same house or town for years, been together with the same partner for a long time, and worked in the same field all that time. Or, just as the notion of retirement began to loom up ahead on the mental horizon, the death of your partner threw your plans off track.

People over fifty may be experiencing empty-nest syndrome, mostly free of the demands of young children at the same time as grieving the loss of a partner. John and Andrew raised two beautiful children together. Two weeks after they dropped their eldest at college, John was diagnosed with an aggressive form of cancer and died within the year. The sudden change of status from being part of a couple raising children together can easily throw a person off balance.

Exercise

QUIET REMEMBRANCE

On significant dates that may only be important to you, enjoy quiet moments of remembrance. You can do this by lighting a candle with your partner in mind, displaying a certain flower that is symbolic of something, or having a special treat on a birthday or anniversary. Taking space for things like this can be very grounding and soothing and need not require permission from anyone else in your life.

LOSS OF A CHILD

The truth is that many people die way before their time. People in the prime of their lives die from illness, violence, and accidents. Infants, children, teens, adults—these deaths can bring us to our knees. When death happens out of order, we have extra work to do. We are left having to reckon with the blows to our senses of stability and fairness in a world that can be incredibly unstable and unfair. The death of someone young is part of this disordered story. The unifying bond between those who have lost children is that the life they were nurturing did not last long. Illness, infection, birth complications, genetic factors, sudden infant death syndrome, and accidents all might be the "why" their child died. But the *why* never answered for the parents and families is, "Why *my* baby?"

People who lose their adult children ask the same question.

The relationship has changed over the years. Perhaps your role has been to offer advice or support. Maybe you were friends who did things together that gave you joy. At this point in life, you might have been physically and emotionally dependent on your adult child and looked to them to provide care. This role reversal can be especially difficult for older parents, making anger and sadness particularly acute.

Years later, you may still be struggling to find balance after suffering such a tremendous loss. How do you talk about yourself or consider yourself in the larger social scale? Do you keep your loss private, unsure of how to talk openly about your child? Is your child remembered in family celebrations? How do you answer when asked how many children you have? These moments in life can throw a blanket of despair over a struggling parent. And when there is a disconnect between how one parent feels versus another, relational strain can emerge that sets couples on opposite poles.

Questions You May Ask Yourself

People have said that having another child will help. Will it?
For many couples the question might eventually be, "Should we have another child?" Depending on how your child died, perhaps you're questioning now if you'll ever be able to have a healthy child or deliver a baby safely.

In her book *How to Go on Living When Someone You Love Dies*, Therese A. Rando, PhD, suggests the following:: "It is important that you not get pregnant too soon after the death of your child.

You must first achieve some resolution of his/her loss." She goes on to suggest you've got to review the fantasized or real relationship you had with your child, and that you shouldn't feel that having another child will resolve your grief. If you decide to have another child, there will be many things to consider, especially whether you and your partner are ready and in agreement.

Children are sometimes burdened with the unlived dreams of their parents. It is mighty hard work for mothers and fathers to allow their children to blossom into who they are, rather than who parents wished themselves to be. This dynamic can be exacerbated by parents who compare their living child to the idealized version of their deceased child. The ramifications of this can play out over a lifetime. It is unassimilated and long-term grief that supplies the energy for patterns to play out as a result of this unsuccessful attempt to heal. If you sense that you or your loved one is struggling with this, it's important to talk to someone about it. When grief gets stuck this way, it can be as if you've lost not just one child, but your child who is living and remains unknown because of the role he or she has been assigned to play.

But do not assume that any children born to parents who have already lost a child are doomed to fill a replacement role! This is not inevitable as the human heart has oceans of love contained within it. Of course parents can grow their families and welcome new life into the fold. Maintaining a bond with their deceased child in fact would make this easier. Think of it this way: If parents try to get over the loss of their child and attempt to carry on without sufficient time to grieve or have the idea that they shouldn't talk about them, a hidden story is created. Hidden stories take on a powerful and controlling energy of their own. It becomes easier to place on subsequent children the hopes, fears, and ideas parents had for their deceased child. It's easy to do because all of the energy and truth of story is clogged up in the pipes of grief and emotion.

If the parents' deceased child takes up residence in the psyche and story of the family, there is no need to transfer the hopes for the lost child onto their living children. If they talk freely about their deceased child, have pictures of them around, include them actively in the family story, and ritualize connection with them, whether through marking birthdays or visiting the cemetery as a family, then the memory of the lost child is kept as their own person separate from the living children. There is more air around the whole family to relate to this part of their shared story.

Children are often very interested in their parents' lives and what happened before they were born. If you lost a child before your living children were born, it's a good idea to tell them the story of their sibling. Children want to know their family history and the child you lost is an important part of it.

How can I stay tuned in to my partner when we are healing in different ways?

There is a common yet very difficult theme for couples with differing grieving styles, as they have longer-term effects on each other as individuals and impacts on their visions of their future.

It gets a little more complicated when you want to step out

and talk with others but find you can't. Perhaps there is a barrier blocking the flow toward community and shared healing. Maybe it's your own fear; maybe it's your partner's. After such a profound loss, it's natural for parents to want to cocoon and stay in a dark, safe place for a long time. Letting the outside world in is like opening the blinds and allowing sunshine to blast rays on pitch black. It can feel destabilizing when one person wants to stay safe in their quiet den when the other feels drawn to moving out into the world. Stephen shared,

I feel like I'm living on a different planet than my spouse. It's been over three years since our daughter died, and I want to start living my life a little bit, but my wife can't join me. The movies, a vacation, dining with close friends. I feel suffocated by her grief, and it feels like I have to work harder to stay okay because she is so depressed.

The job here is to be honest with yourself and your partner, to continue to support one another as you have been, and to know that how things are now are not how they will always be. Long-term grief has no time limit or strict form. It changes shape and color, texture and vividness. Adjusting with those changes is what is important.

It is often the case that parents grieve in different ways and for varied lengths of time. We cannot apply our own grief experience to another with any intention of comparison or judgment. But it's very important that when one person in a partnership might need to camp out for a lot longer at a certain stop on the journey, that the other figures out how to keep moving on theirs. It may well be a good time for both of you to seek out support together to get some guidance on how to manage this difference between you without it turning into a wedge in your relationship. Couples therapy, pastoral counseling, and individual therapy are all good places to start. For many, traversing the terrain of grief strengthens the relationship. Greg put it this way:

The first few years after our daughter's death were really challenging for Jill and me. We just grieved in different ways, and it was difficult to have the person I relied on most in life struggling with the same tragedy I was. We both had an unshakable confidence that we'd make it through this together and that was helpful. And we did make it. In the long run, it made me love and respect Jill more and our relationship is even stronger.

One of the biggest things couples face throughout a relationship is to not take on management of the other's feelings and experience of life. It is possible to have conversations about your individual needs and to articulate for yourselves how you might go about meeting them. When you stay present, loving, and honest, it is possible to release the idea that you have to change how your partner feels. This is not always easy, especially if you are receiving messages from your partner that, in fact, your going out with friends is making them feel really bad! Most important is that both partners do their best to take full responsibility for their own feelings and actions. Trust is the kingpin of relationship. One that has been impacted by the loss of a child is in special need of extra layers of trust, reliability, and openness.

Am I the only one who feels like people just don't get the agony of miscarriage?

People who don't know what it's like to lose a pregnancy might say, "At least you know you can get pregnant." "You can try again." "It happens all the time." "You should be happy you didn't come to term because something must've been wrong with the fetus."

Statistics from the Center for Disease Control tell us that between 10 to 15 percent of pregnancies end in miscarriage every year in the United States. The majority occur during the first trimester, with about 1 to 5 percent occurring in the second trimester. Miscarriages are defined as occurring before twenty weeks of pregnancy, while stillbirths occur after twenty weeks. In the United States alone, stillborn babies account for 24,000 deaths each year.

There might be assumptions made about how parents are doing depending on how long they were pregnant. Yes, it's a different experience miscarrying at seven weeks than delivering a full-term stillborn baby. But for many hopeful parents, it's no less a major loss. Mothers describe their thinking and emotions like this, even years after their loss:

- I feel worried I will never be able to have a baby after having three miscarriages in a row. I'm grieving the loss of my pregnancies and the hope of being a mother.

- I have awful memories of when I miscarried. I think about it sometimes and blame myself for not being healthy enough.

- People in my family say, "Just try again when your body is stronger." I know they don't mean it this way, but that implies it was my fault that I couldn't grow my baby.

- I saw who my real friends were after I delivered our stillborn son at twenty-nine weeks. Only one person didn't feed me platitudes and just let me cry.

- It's been ten years since I had a late miscarriage. I'll never forget the confusion and despair I felt. Now I find myself feeling like someone is going to take my living child from me.

The hard part about sorting out long-term grief and its effects is that it is slow moving, incremental, and not always obvious. Over time, this can create epic undercurrents that evolve into riptides that end in sweeping otherwise perfectly good relationships out to sea.

For women and couples who have had many miscarriages or unsuccessful IVF procedures, there comes a time when the image one had of what family was going to look like might be forced into something else, something different.

Consider Holly's story:

Just prior to my husband John's diagnosis of pancreatic cancer we had undergone several unsuccessful rounds of IVF, involving three miscarriages as well as a miscarriage prior to my daughter's birth. These losses resulted in us both having to accept that the family we hoped for was not to be. Due to my husband's diagnosis, we were unable to proceed with adoption or fostering, which held great meaning for us as we wanted her to have siblings. I've had to accept that my daughter's childhood will look different than my own and will be unlike what I wanted for her. I think the experience of trauma from living the worst-case scenario with both the miscarriages and John's death has led to a lower threshold for me in terms of how I cope with other uncertainties in life. There are some things that don't bother me the way they might have or that I can brush off more easily; however, there are other things like having to decide to put my dog to sleep or making decisions that impact my daughter's life that trigger a sense of doom or catastrophic thinking. I think this is all trauma related, but I am still working to understand it.

Intrusive thoughts and vivid memories of miscarrying or learning of the death of their unborn child can weigh heavily for years. Arriving at random times, these thoughts can color the experience of subsequent pregnancies. Death and life are so close, and it's hard to stay grounded when fear, traumatic memory, and anxiety carry into years when new experiences demand their own attention.

The long grief journey after miscarriage and stillbirth, like all grief journeys, is about moving through life with death. A gentle hold of both the idea that death is as natural as life and the fact that losing a pregnancy is heartbreaking and potentially traumatizing is the task here. Both are true. Stretching into the capacity to sit with these truths while navigating each day is where the long journey can lead to more freedom to live life in the here and now.

Is it okay to want to talk about my child?

The topic of death does interesting things to conversation. If you are talking to someone who has not lost a loved one, very often there can be an awkward moment, a pause, a look. It can be subtle enough that the moment can recover, but noticeable enough so the parent picks up the other person's discomfort with not knowing what to say. Over time, this can chip away at the right any parent has to say their child's name, to refer to them, tell stories about them, and include them in current life. If you find yourself without enough people with whom you can say your child's name, find a support group, whether online or in person, where you can share your experiences of the child with others. You may in fact be far enough along in your grief journey that you can be of service to others who are in the immediate aftermath of loss. You carry wisdom, even if it feels like despair. For those who are lost you could be the one to carry the map that remains hidden to those who are new on the road of grief.

Remember: what's comforting to you may not be helpful or comforting to your spouse, your children, or other family. This is not a dismissal of your feelings or of theirs. Sometimes the hard work of grieving in a family is figuring out where to get certain needs met that others you are close with cannot provide. While meeting your own needs, make sure not to expect others to have the same ones you do.

Parents who have lost their children carry the relationship with them and there may be, even years later, issues to work out. Allow for that. Make space for the whole relationship to be truthfully talked about and processed. You might face memories or truths that make you weep, but you will also see that the business of relating to other humans is a fine mess, and as much as we can, we need to wrangle with it. Talk to a therapist, support group, or person studied in grief who can walk this road with you. You will still have a relationship with your child at the end of it that can bring comfort and a sense of peace.

Exercises

NAME WHAT YOU WANT

When one loses a child, they are often changed in surprising ways. Maybe you were someone who once enjoyed the company of other parents, but now find them overwhelming. Maybe you participated in certain activities or hobbies with them that are no longer relevant or enjoyable to you. It's a vulnerable spot on the journey when you want to reengage or begin living actively when the ground feels wobbly beneath your feet. It can be helpful to get clear on exactly what you want to do. You might feel certain about some things, nervous about others, and very clear on the hard "nos". The next step is imagining yourself doing these things and how you'd do them. By yourself? With a friend? With a group?

Take out a piece of paper and on the left, write "What I Want to Do." Then, write the word "Feeling," then write, "With Whom?" And finally, "When." Look at the following examples:

What I Want to Do	Feeling	With Whom?	When
Go to Montreal	Nervous	Deb	Springtime, for my birthday
Join a knitting group	Comfortable	By myself; I'll see people there I know	Next month
Go to dinner	Fine if it's a quiet place and not a place I went with my child	My two close friends with whom I can talk openly about my child	A night that works for all of us, next month
Attend a conference out of town	Nervous	By myself	Summer

TIME TO TAKE A BREATH

You're going about your day, and you find yourself ambushed by emotion after having painful thoughts about your child. Pay attention to your body. Are your shoulders raised up by your ears? Is your breathing shallow? Deep breathing is one of the best ways to clear your mind and lower stress in the body when you start to feel angry or frustrated. When you practice breathing deeply, it sends a message to the brain to calm down and relax the body. Try this:

- Sit or lie flat in a comfortable position.

- Put your hand on the belly just below your ribs and your other hand on your chest.

- Breathe deeply, in through your nose, allowing your belly to push your hand out. Your chest shouldn't move.

- Breathe out through pursed lips. Breathe in through your nose. Feel the hand on your belly go in, and push all the air out.

- Do this breathing exercise three to ten times. Take your time with each breath.

- Then notice how you feel when you're done. Replace the painful memory of your child with one that captures your love.

LOSS OF A SIBLING

...the full impact of our brother's or sister's death begins to seep into our consciousness at precisely the same time when others might expect us to be feeling better.

TJ Wray, author of *Surviving the Death of a Sibling*

Sibling death is one of the least acknowledged types of loss, especially in adulthood. Immediately following a death, the focus of support is usually on the parents having lost their child, not on the surviving children who have lost their sibling. To add to the pain, the sibling often has less input than others into the funeral, memorial service, or other arrangements. Condolences offered to them may start with questions about how the deceased's parents are doing.

Lingering grief long after the loss of a sibling can be complicated for several reasons. Ambivalence often present in sibling relationships may give rise to guilt, which is a known contributor to complicated mourning. Suppose you had a close relationship with your sibling or a more distant one. Either extreme (and everything in between) can bring on feelings of abandonment or guilt long after your brother's or sister's death. You may continue to experience anger, sadness, and regret if the relationship was never what you wished it could have been.

Your survival itself might be another source of guilt, especially if you recall the times when you wished your sibling would go away or disappear. These are all normal reactions to sibling loss, so try not to judge yourself too harshly if these feelings continue to come up for you. Another factor that complicates sibling grief is the need to support your parents in their grief. This can draw on your energy and emotional reserves, making it harder to care for yourself. You may question if you have the right to mourn as deeply as they do—or as the surviving spouse or children do. Know that you had and still do have the right to mourn, and that you deserve the same support and care as others affected by their death.

Questions You May Ask Yourself

It's been three years since my sibling died. I'm an adult and I should be able to handle it. Why am I feeling anxiety like I never have before?

Our family makes up the structure of our lives, whether we see its members frequently or not. Even with large age spans between some siblings, there is a feeling of being part of a group—the group born of your parents. Like any group, when one member leaves or dies, this can be unsettling or anxiety provoking. Being an adult does not mean being part of a family group becomes less important. Even if your sibling didn't have an active presence in your day-to-day life, they held a symbolic place in the story of your life. Their death can make you feel older or signal that your family is becoming smaller. In addition, if your sibling died of a genetic disease and you share the same genes and are of a similar age, a sibling's death might increase concerns about your own mortality.

How close you are to your sibling—or not—does not always dictate how we move through grief in the years following their death. Steve, whose brother died from COVID-19, puts it this way:

He was my older brother by thirteen years. We grew up at different times in the world, but in our later years we began to find some commonality and our relationship was expanding into new and different places. We began to find time to talk every few weeks and were closer than we had ever been when his life was cut short. I feel his loss every day, and now I'm the only sibling left.

Janie on the other hand shared,

My sister and I texted throughout every day. We were always cracking each other up or helping each other deal with hard stuff like marital stress, worries about our kids, issues with our parents. But mostly, I just always felt like I was at home with her, and she was who I wanted to hang out with when I had free time. The hole in my life since my sister died is indescribable. I can't find solid ground. I truly thought we'd grow old together. Even years out, I just have this pit in my stomach all the time. It's like nervousness, but I think of it as loneliness now. Just an empty space that no one can fill.

In some cases, the death of a sibling may have made you an only child or the eldest child, creating a profound shift in the role you may have held for most or all your life. Your new role can make it difficult to wade through the many complicated emotions arising when a sibling dies. If your parents are still living, some adults who've lost an adult sibling experience a change in their relationship. Since siblings often feel their grief isn't fully acknowledged and their parents are focused on overcoming *their* loss, they can feel abandoned by their parents who have been disabled by their own grief.

I was, by default, put in the role of having to care for others in my family after my sibling died. I know I must tend to myself and my grief, but how?

Perhaps your focus on being there for someone else resulted in putting your own grief on the back burner. It's common for surviving siblings to support others in the family or take on the role of caregiver. Caregivers in this situation might focus so much energy on others that they become overstressed, which can result in depression. Unacknowledged feelings can eventually become burdensome and heavy, which could interfere with the flow of grief and regaining a sense of identity in this new life reality. To resolve this, you must confront your own sadness and pain. As they say, if you allow yourself to feel it, you can heal it.

There were five of us and my oldest sister was the one all of us turned to. Now that she's gone, they're all turning to me. How do I make it clear that I don't want that position in our family?

The oldest sibling often takes on the role of parent, especially if the parents were emotionally or physically unavailable. The death of a sibling upsets the birth order within a family, robbing surviving siblings of the individual strengths, characteristics, and identities that are tightly linked to each individual within the family. One road on the journey of healing can be about building certain strengths within yourself that your sibling so naturally carried. When they die, you don't just get over this as much as you are called to grow through it. Part of this growing through will likely be a process of identifying which aspects of your sibling you want to pick up, and which ones you and your siblings may simply have to adjust to not having. Maybe your deceased sibling was really good at hosting whole family gatherings around the holidays, and now family are hoping you'll become the new host. Are you up for that? Or will this be something that you will all have to talk about and maybe come up with a new way of being together?

Exercise

MAKING SPACE FOR GRIEF

If you feel like grief got stuck somewhere, and you need to spend time contemplating and being with the emotions of your grief, allow for that and make space for the experience. It might be the case that when your sibling died, you were so concerned for your family you didn't allow yourself to fully go through your own grief process. Sometimes we need to double back on the roads we've traveled to see what we missed along the way. You could do things like:

> Take a couple of days off from work and plan to be alone so you have time and don't have to worry about putting on a good face for work or social engagements.

> Go someplace that holds meaning to either you or both you and your sibling. Visiting a body of water, like an ocean, lake, or river can be especially meaningful because they symbolize eternal life as well as

movement through time. Bring enough food and drink so you can stay for a while, settle in, and allow yourself to commune with your sibling. Pay attention to what comes up for you, what animals come around, cloud formations, a passing breeze. Just be with what nature is offering you as you connect with the love you shared.

> You might enjoy going to a quiet place of worship where you can just sit and be. You might also consider making an appointment with a person of faith who serves in a given place of worship so you can talk to and process your loss and loneliness.

> Some enjoy acknowledging special days like birthdays, date of death, or some other event that was relevant to their relationship. Getting a treat of some kind on their birthday, lighting a candle, making a wish for them, going to a favorite restaurant and ordering something they might have ordered, or doing something you used to do together as children can be a wonderful way to keep your sibling in your life routinely and enjoyably.

> Consider writing a letter to your sibling or journaling about them. Maybe there are things you wish you had said or regrets you need to air out. This can be therapeutic because it gives shape to what can typically feel like an out-of-control feeling.

LOSS OF A GRANDPARENT

> *After finding out from the physician that Grandpa was*
> *in his last weeks, I drove home from the hospital alone*
> *and called my father, crying on the phone telling him his*
> *father was dying. When I took a moment to catch my*
> *breath he just said, "Well, it's inevitable."*
>
> Andrea

In our society, loss of a grandparent is sometimes viewed as a minor occurrence because death is expected of the elderly, and people don't often extend traditional condolences. You might even find that your job won't give you time off. Yet many among us have had, for a variety of reasons, the experience of deeply knowing our grandparents, and even our great-grandparents, and suffer their losses as we might suffer the loss of our parents, especially if we were raised by them. Haddy, a man who lost his grandmother when he was in his thirties told us, "In my experience, a parent could also mean a grandparent, and their loss is tremendous, too, for many of us who were raised by them." While death may be timely when one is of a certain age, it does not mean that the power and duration of the grief is less. Empathy for long-term grief is hard to come by because in our culture where many families live so far apart, a much larger number of people grow up seeing their grandparents only once or twice a year, if that. These might be pretty peripheral and obligatory relationships that just don't carry the heart and depth that others enjoy. On the other hand, you may have had a meaningful relationship in your early life before distance took over.

The lack of research done on the specific impact of the loss of a grandparent, in our view, speaks to the cultural implications of how we see the aged in the West. You can observe it playing out in how people responded to COVID-19 and its impact on our world's most vulnerable. In the early stages of the pandemic, many people behaved as though it wasn't that big of a deal because at first it was thought that only the elderly and those with pre-existing medical conditions were in any danger of severe illness or death. That view exposed the opinion that many have: the elderly are disposable. Tell that to the people who have actually lost a parent or grandparent to the disease, those who have had to bear witness to their suffering without being able to hold them and usher them through the transition of death with soft words, affection, and prayers.

Pam, whose grandmother died at the age of 102 in 1997, said,

I still miss her. She moved in with us when I was ten and became the one stabilizing presence in my chaotic childhood home. As I moved into adulthood, and she moved with my mother and father to Florida, I learned to live without her physical presence and drew on her legacy of love and strength of character. In my mind I can still hear her speaking in her Swedish accent with the smell of butter sizzling in the small frying pan as she made a mountain of Swedish pancakes for us on Saturday mornings. One of my greatest challenges was trying to make those thin pancakes for my own children, but I will never duplicate the love she put into them—and all of us.

For you who years later continue to long for and deeply miss the love and support you had in relationship with your grandparent, your grief is real, it's valid, and you are on the long journey, too. No one gets to determine for you how much and for how long you get to grieve.

If you had the kind of relationship with your grandparent that leaves you heartbroken, it's important to take the space and time you need to heal. You may not always find people who understand or can relate to your grief, but there are those who will.

If you didn't have a parent-like relationship with your grandparent, it doesn't mean their loss isn't significant. Did you love your grandparent dearly but never felt you had the opportunity to spend as much time with them as they, or you, would have liked? Some of you may have lost your grandparent before you were old enough to have a mature, close relationship with them. Perhaps you are suffering some regret about unanswered questions or things you left unsaid. And you may be left with the impossible wishes that begin with, "I could have..." or "I should have..."

Questions You May Ask Yourself

I carry unsettling memories of my grandparent and am having a hard time, even years later, dealing with their death. How do I reconcile with this?

Susie, whose grandfather lived with them when she was growing up, remembers her grandfather drinking too much and falling down drunk in the front yard for all the neighbors to see. Arnie was devastated to find out at his grandmother's funeral that she once participated in a store robbery. These are tough memories to deal with, especially if unspoken and unprocessed. It might be time to talk with a professional or talk openly about them with a close friend. Secrets can cause shame but can be diffused by open conversations with someone you trust.

The loss of my grandparent when I was a child was my first experience with death. But it's only now, years later, that I seem to be having a difficult time with it. Why is that?

Many people experience the death of at least one of their grandparents in childhood or early adulthood. For many, this is their first experience with loss. Although grief is always individual, age can influence a person's understanding and response to the loss. At the time of their death, you might have felt as though you had to prioritize the needs of other family members and had little or no energy to attend to your own needs. And here you are now, years later, puzzled as to why you're feeling their loss so profoundly.

It would be ideal if all families could grieve together, however, often they do not. Sometimes in families, there is a real disconnect between how the grandparent related to their own children versus their grandchildren. Family squabbles, old wounds, and resentments can make grieving very confusing for children.

Exercises

ACKNOWLEDGING THE GIFTS

There's no way around it: we're here because our ancestors survived. What can you draw from their stories, their courage, their fortitude, and their determination? Some of us might have wonderful stories and memories to carry with us. Others might not. As you think about your grandparent, what did you get from them that you can carry with you on your journey and into your life? A great ear for music? A strong work ethic? Empathy? Good recipes? Tradition? Think about this question and actively make use of the answers.

YOUR LOVE HAS A PLACE—LET'S FIND IT

Energy can neither be created nor destroyed, but it may transform from one type to another. This is the principle of conservation of energy and is the first law of thermodynamics. Many believe that love itself is the highest form of energy. We can imagine that love does not go anywhere, it just changes form. The love you have for your grandparent is still there and needs a way to be expressed. Can you imagine taking this precious energy and directing it in a way it can be used, experienced, and healing? Try this exercise:

How I showed my love: I used to knit with my grandmother every night before bed.

How might I show it now? I can volunteer at a local nursing home and knit with the people there. I can also donate knitting supplies to those who don't have many resources and offer them in honor of my grandmother.

LOSS OF A FRIEND

I have always regarded my stories of strange adventures
with Marcus as a cherished gift. Like a pocket full of
shiny pennies I could pull out and share. For the first
year after his death these stories brought me pain, but
now I can think of them and share them again with the
same joy I had before his death. It saddens me that there
will be no new adventures (one of the hardest parts of
losing him), but my precious memories are how I keep
him with me.

Sonya

The people we share our closest friendships with are our chosen family on earth. Some are part of our story for many decades, linking childhood to adolescence and on to adulthood in a series of stories and memories, bonding us together in ways that require no language. Others grow out of defining life transitions, moments, and events such as college, a job, or raising school-aged children together. And some friendships are simply born from an immediate sparkly alchemy that feels like a recognition between spirits.

About three years ago, Pam and her husband buried two of their closest friends within weeks of each other.

They took our shared histories with them. Just like that. Two
people, husband and wife, close friends and off they went with
the stories of our lives together. Who will ever know us as well

as they did? We shared thirty years of challenging kids and wonderful grandchildren; thirty years of religious and political arguments and agreements; thirty years of shared tears and joys. We spoke in a kind of shorthand, a private language where we would often finish each other's sentences. How do you ever replace that?

It's a universal truth: we can't replace people we've lost. But at some point, we can allow the love we felt for our friend to work on us and open us up to the people in our lives, and appreciate them for who they are, and allow them to appreciate us. We can find people in whom we can confide, friends who will hold us up when we are down, and who will be there for us as part of our unique life's fabric.

A few years ago, someone said to Pam, "You've got to make younger friends… they last longer!" Pam replied, "Well, that didn't work—over the years, three of our four friends who passed *were* younger." If only we could make a series of chess moves and decisions that would protect us from such grievous pain. But no one move or set of circumstances can assuredly spare us. Young children, teenagers, adults, and the elderly are all in the same stream of life when it comes to friendship. Simply put, when you're engaged in friendship, you're engaged in love. The way grief plays out from loss of a friend can be as tangled and painful as any other.

Question You May Ask Yourself

I've tried making new friends, but how do I open myself up to these new experiences?

No one will ever replace your friend, and that is okay. If you have people asking you to do some activity or join them in their life, it's simply because they want to be friends with you in whatever context is relevant to the two of you. By tending to the grief and love you have for your lost friend, you might find you have more bandwidth for participating with others. The idea here isn't to necessarily recreate what you had with someone else, it's to hold space for a new idea, a different perspective, and expansion into more experience. This is easier when:

- You don't habitually compare others to your friend
- When you do, simply say to yourself something like, "I miss my friend so much, but I know that I can allow myself to see another person for who they are, not who they aren't."
- When you have an automatic "no" response to invitations from others, take heed. Your "no" might be coming from a place of pain and fear rather than from a true wish. Just sit with it. Get in the habit of saying, "Let me get back to you," rather than, "No, thanks," so you can consider where the "no" is coming from. If the "no" is coming from a place that doesn't allow for anyone else to enter your friendship sphere, honor that you have had a protective wall around

your love and loss but know that a "yes" to some things will do nothing to tarnish that—ever! You will simply be allowing yourself to know another person or people, and they you.

As adults, making a new close friend can require effort because we often expect these bonds to form effortlessly like they did when we were younger and spent hours together in school, in the lunchroom, or on the playground. As we get older, although friends may be made at work, many of these organic opportunities begin to dry up. We can no longer just hope that an authentic new friendship will show up on its own without putting in some effort.

Exercise

Put Yourself Out There

Making friends doesn't always happen naturally. It's hard to know where to start when you're out of practice, don't have a lot of opportunity, or are recovering from loss. Remember, it takes time and it's okay if it feels clunky at first. Here are some suggestions of steps you can take to put yourself out there and sow the seeds for new relationships to take root and grow. And know this: new friends add to the texture and richness of your life. They don't detract from it, or take away from the love you've had for someone else.

> Make plans with an acquaintance outside of the place you usually see them. The more sides of yourselves you're willing to reveal to another, the closer your friendships become.

> Invite your acquaintance and a few others to a small group activity. As you get to know this person, it will feel easier to make plans with just the two of you.

> Interact with them regularly. We tend to become closer with consistent exposure to each other.

> Make your acquaintance feel loved and valued by supporting them and letting them know you're there for them. Also, if they're sick or in need, see if you can help— you'll be remembered for your kindness.

> Most importantly, open up to them over time by taking small emotional risks. Being vulnerable means slowly opening up about your fears, struggles, insecurities, or mistakes. It makes the other person feel safe to be vulnerable with you in return and can foster intimacy.

LOSS TO SUICIDE

I don't know how I got over it, really. You don't get over it. I shouldn't put it that way. You get through it, however.

Judy Collins, singer, songwriter, and author of *Sanity and Grace: A Journey of Suicide, Survival, and Strength*

Making peace with a loved one's death by suicide is brutally difficult, creating an emotional and spiritual hurdle tens of thousands of people in the United States alone face year after year.

Very complex factors go into someone choosing to die by suicide. Mental illness, addiction, bullying, chronic pain, terminal illness, and rash decision-making in the face of rage or grief are all possibilities, and there isn't one way to heal from such a loss. There are several complicating factors associated with suicide, making the journey toward healing painfully unique.

The complication for loved ones of someone who dies by suicide is the robust tendency to go back and review what happened in an attempt to sort out what was missed. Unlike other diseases of the body, when someone dies by suicide, those left behind often wonder what they could have done to stop them, how they could have saved them, what the signs were that went unnoticed. Individuals who lost a loved one to suicide also report higher levels of long-term guilt and associated feelings of isolation than those who lose a loved one to natural causes. Stigma is still an issue surrounding suicide, and as discussed earlier in this book, it puts people at a greater risk of suffering from depression, anxiety, and post-traumatic stress symptoms. Anything that remains unprocessed develops its own power and potential for causing harm to the individual griever. Loved ones can be left with a degree of guilt that is difficult to shake.

Phil shared,

Ray and I were extremely close growing up. Like brothers, I felt. We met in middle school, and he was one of the biggest reasons I looked forward to high school. We were never not friends, but in high school other relationships took priority and we drifted apart. In the end, since high school I only remember talking to him once or twice. This was when everyone was reaching out to each other from their past via Facebook because it was so new and exciting. That prompted one phone call. We caught up on life, laughed, talked religion, and promised to be in touch more…but it never happened. I can't remember how long the call was before his death, but I'm so thankful we had that time. When I heard Ray took his life, I wondered if things could have been different. Could I have helped? What if that wasn't our only conversation? What if I had reached out to him afterward. What if we talked about our problems? The what -ifs go on and on…

Gary Roe, writer and chaplain, talks about recovery from loss to suicide as being like "living with a limp." This is true, isn't it? The impact is profound and debilitating for a long time. Roe puts it this way: "We can heal, yes. But we're not good as new. We're not who we were… It reaches into and affects all of life, whether we realize it or not."

Sometimes, just knowing the terrain we are traversing can be enough to lift us out of cycles of blame, judgment, and guilt. Simply knowing that getting back to normal isn't the goal—normal has changed—and a new chapter has begun with devastating and profound insight into human suffering, which might allow you to take the pressure off yourself to get it all figured out.

Question You May Ask Yourself

I feel so guilty about how angry I am about my loved one's death by suicide. I go from feeling such intense grief to guilt to anger. How can I break this cycle that's been so strong for so many years?

Many struggle with anger and resentment, after their loved one made the choice they did, leaving so many behind to make sense of their death. There are some who view the choice to die by suicide as inherently selfish due to the colossal impact it has on them and their families. Ironically, for so many who choose to die by suicide, they see it as a selfless act. One of the top mental health issues related to suicide is a sense of being a burden to the people in their lives, and a belief that friends and family will be better off without them. A deep gulf exists between those who die by suicide and those who are left behind. Those left behind wonder for years to come how they might have created a bridge for each to use, to walk toward the other in hopes of understanding and of surviving.

This anger can extend to others as well and can take the shape of blame and judgment. This is the realm that stigma is born from and lives in. The stigma, or disgrace, becomes the burden of those left living, because so often this blame and judgment silences, suppresses, and steals the right to grieve. You may know the deceased was in the midst of a messy breakup and therefore assume the partner holds some culpability. You may be aware of complex issues in your loved one's family and make associations between stories you may have heard and your loved one's eventual decision.

Or maybe you feel the weight of others' judgment rest upon you as you try to climb out of the quicksand on your path. Maybe you are the one who longed so much for openness, talking, grieving, and processing your loved one's death, but no one could join you because of the stigma attached to their means of death. People are notoriously bad at talking about things that are deeply painful. In fact, we have mechanisms in place that actively support our efforts to deny or repress our pain, and over time they kind of, sort of, work. But there are side effects to this, as you likely know. These side effects impact those who wish to silence the pain through judgment and anger, and those who wish to let light and air into the space where their grief lives. No one wins here. Not in the long run.

While the lines drawn between apparent precipitants and your loved one's death might seem strong and clear, we cannot know for sure what was going on in someone else's mind when they made the ultimate decision. Sometimes there's a note left behind, sometimes not. This may or may not offer clarity and peace of mind. We're not mind readers, and often there is no clear one-way street leading to the choice to die by suicide. Your job is to heal and perhaps support others in their healing. Swimming in the waters of blame, judgment, guilt, and anger can be major roadblocks to this.

Exercise

FORGIVENESS FOR YOUR LOVED ONE AND YOURSELF

First, start with your loved one. When you struggle with metabolizing the anguish you are feeling and are afraid of the anger you might feel toward them, let yourself be. You can have your feelings, and you can wish with all of your might that they chose something else to do with their pain. You can state your anger, your regret, and your pain. Having a special place where you put these feelings can help. Find a box, jar, or bag that can become the container for what you need to get out and use it! Sometimes you might just have a day where you need to get out the pain. Do that. Write down what's hurting you on a piece of paper, and place it inside the container and let it share the load with you. It's okay to articulate. It won't make the feelings suddenly disappear, but it might help you gain enough space from them to be able to consider them from another angle.

Then, offer forgiveness to yourself. If you're having a hard time forgiving yourself for not foreseeing the future, continue to remind yourself that you are not a mind reader, and we cannot foresee the future. Consider putting all of those thoughts in a separate container, one just for you, and allow yourself to put these thoughts away. Pay attention to when they come up, write them down, and put them in their special place.

LOSS OF A PET

> *I had a greyhound, Penny. She was very loving. Her eyes*
> *would pierce right into my soul. I just knew I was loved.*
> *What stands out, Penny died a year to the date of my*
> *mom's passing. The night before she died, I had a dream*
> *about my mom. In the dream, she had her hair in a*
> *ponytail and was cleaning up this tiny house. Sweeping,*
> *cleaning, fixing this tiny weird little house. My mom*
> *said, "Stop telling everybody I'm dead!" The next day*
> *Penny died, and I just knew the little house was for her.*
> *My mom loved that dog. That is what helped me get*
> *through the loss of Penny. I knew my mom had her.*
>
> Amanda

For so many people, pets are the only physical contact or eye contact they regularly receive. The loyalty, love, unconditional affection, and experience of being needed cannot be underestimated for its value in a life. When a person loses the animal companion that participated in their life that way, a gaping wound might remain. Then, on top of that, some are met with little sympathy from others. Not all people understand or appreciate how much an animal can mean to someone. Even those with pets of their own and real animal lovers can discover in themselves a lack of empathy for the long-term suffering of those who continue to ache years past their loss. The grief then goes underground, gets diverted to other things, and in many cases remains unprocessed.

Losing a pet in the midst of other significant life stressors can complicate grief as well. Steven lost both his mother and his beloved dog in the same year. His mother died first, which was devastating. He relied heavily on his dog for comfort at night when he couldn't sleep and for making him leave the house for daily walks. Those walks became somewhat of a ritual for him and an opportunity for him to talk to his mother in nature. When his dog died several months later from natural causes, he was completely undone. Suddenly, aloneness shrouded Steven's life, and he felt like no one could stand to be with him, his grief, and his depression were so great. Enough time had passed that people were not tending to his grief over his mother, and the loss of a pet just doesn't garner the same sympathy from others. It took a long time for him to come back from despair and release the anger he felt.

Questions You May Ask Yourself

How do I stop the feelings of guilt I experience since we euthanized our pet?

Deciding to euthanize a beloved pet family member can, in some cases, cause a lot of guilt and intrusive memories. How this intersects with someone's relationship to guilt can extend the acute feelings of grief. Therapies geared toward helping people find relief from intrusive and repetitive thoughts and memories are important here, as the mind can resemble a broken record playing over the same spot. Interestingly, research has suggested that the long-term care of a sickly pet complicates grief for many people, just as it does for those who are caregivers for sick family members. Tending to a beloved animal as they move toward death is heartbreaking and can leave many feeling powerless and afraid.

You gave your animal companion a good life and wanted to give them a good death, yet you may feel guilty about what you had to do, or perhaps that you didn't do enough. Reaching out to others who have shared similar experiences can truly help. You were in a position of having to make a terrible decision and people who've been there understand better than anyone the weight you carry.

Leaving our family home means leaving our beloved pets who are buried on our property. How can I do that?

While there are a lot of rules unique to wherever you live about the legality and safety of burying animals in your yard, there's no denying that a lot of people do this. Please take the time to research local laws regarding remains, as some don't allow burials of ashes on one's property or in public spaces. Most importantly, take your time to think of a way to memorialize the burial of the ashes. There's no hurry and there needs not to be any guilt associated with your decision. Just go with your heart.

One idea is to take a picture of where your beloved pets are buried and make a little memorial for yourself. You can have a parting ceremony before you leave your home, maybe plant something, or leave behind something meaningful to you. Don't be surprised if grief comes up again for your deceased pets.

Moving can do this on its own, but leaving the place where they are buried can reignite grief that will be part of your journey.

If you choose to dig up your buried pet, this may be a topic worth pursuing with a local pet cemetery, your realtor, or your veterinarian. We can't give legal advice here, but it's important to consider where your pets are buried and to think about the likelihood of them being accidentally exhumed during future owners' renovations or landscaping. There are wonderful organizations and businesses that help people with cremating beloved pets and providing support through the process. We know of at least one occasion where a pet crematory assisted in safely exhuming buried pets, cremating them, and giving the pets' remains to the family. People who work and serve in this way understand and have great compassion for those who love their pets and are extremely attached to them.

My dear pet died and their stuff laying around is a painful reminder of my loss. What do I do with their things?

Animal shelters are grateful for donations. Here are some items you can donate if they're clean and in good shape.

- Unopened food or treats
- Leashes, collars, harnesses
- Sturdy toys
- Metal crates or carriers

How do I help my child through the death of their first pet?
Children might blame themselves, their parents, or the veterinarian for not saving their beloved pet. They might feel guilty, depressed, and frightened that others they love may be taken from them, too. Trying to protect your child by saying the pet ran away could cause your child to expect the pet's return and feel betrayed when they discover the truth. They are looking to you as an example of how to handle this loss, so expressing your own grief may reassure your child that sadness is okay and can help them work through their feelings.

Childhood pet loss is no less important than that of the loss of a family member, because the pet is often considered a member of the family by the child. However, society does not always acknowledge the significance of pet bereavement, which can result in long-term unresolved grief. The intensity of the grief experienced can be magnified by the child's degree of attachment to the pet, the suddenness of the pet's death, history of prior losses, and the role the pet had in the child's life.

Exercise

TIME FOR LAUGHTER

> In the midst of emotional pain, it's difficult to imagine
> ever being happy. It's difficult to see anything positive or
> hopeful… All we want is to have our life our loved one
> back to heal the hurt.
>
> John E. Welshons, author of *Awakening From Grief*

Here is an exercise you might try. It is offered in the spirit of what our animal friends bring to us: love, playfulness, softness, and an opportunity to just be in the moment. Would it surprise you to know that people experiencing long-term grief have forgotten how to laugh or that laughter might be considered disrespectful, given the loss? You might try laughter yoga exercises, which are designed to make you laugh for no reason. Combined with simple yoga breathing techniques, laughter yoga has been known to relieve stress, boost your immunity, help fight depression, and move you into more positive thinking. When you laugh your physiology changes, along with your chance to experience more happiness. Laughter yoga founder Madan Kataria explains that "laughter has two sources, one from the body, one from the mind. Adults tend to laugh from the mind. We use judgments and evaluations about what's funny and what isn't." Children, who laugh much more frequently than adults, laugh from the body. "They laugh all the time they're playing. Laughter yoga is based on cultivating your childlike playfulness. We all have a child inside us wanting to laugh, wanting to play." We invite you to find some fun laughter yoga exercises on YouTube and follow along or find a certified laughter leader in your community.

Epilogue

Let go of your expectations of how you think the loss
of a loved one will affect you. Each experience of loss is
different and there is no map that you can follow. Grief is
not a weakness nor is it your fault. Don't give too much
credit to the difficult days or moments. There will be
darkness, but there will also be light. You can hold
them both.

Sonya

Writing *The Long Grief Journey* was a journey in and of itself, one that we walked together, and one that we are continuing to walk with you, dear reader. There are two things that are absolutely true about all people, no matter where we come from, what we look like, what kind of lives we've led, and what we believe in: we were born and we will die. From beginning to end, we are presented with challenges and hurdles, great and small. Some of those bring us to our knees. The journey of grief and wisdom gained from walking the road of life shapes us and unites us, and we hope you've found stories, ideas, and techniques in this book that will help you on your own long journey. Keep going. And if we pass one another on the road, let's recognize in the other the courage it takes to keep walking.

Life is a savage garden: there are some pretty places here and there, but the garden is mostly full from end to end with scary stuff. In this garden, death is the one and only certainty. I think we are better off to recognize and embrace our mortality because it helps us avoid risk, it helps us care for each other and look out for each other, and, when properly considered, I think it keeps us from wasting time.

So here we are, then, all traveling together on the same dangerous path through this garden. We are born, and we begin walking with the adults who care for us. Some of us walk closer to each other, some farther. Some scoot ahead, and some fall behind. If one of us strays from the path or stumbles, we rush to help them. Later on, they may help us when we fall, and keep us going for another day. From time to time, someone we love more than the others will die and will travel with us no further. We cannot be angry at the garden because it is what it has always been from our first step on its winding paths. We instead should be grateful to those who have helped us as we walk through. This gratitude is central to being

human, because our journey through life is so perilous.
We must be grateful to each other while there is still time,
because eventually we will fall and not get up again, and
our company will keep moving ever onward without us.
In this sense, our gratitude keeps us together, keeps us
safe, makes us feel hope on this long walk to dusty death.
We must be grateful to each other while there is still time.
While there is still time.

Jeff McCullers, teacher

Acknowledgments

We'd like to acknowledge all those who contributed to *The Long Grief Journey*, especially Erin McClary, our editor, who saw the relevance and need for this book, and who helped us bring it to life. To our clients who trusted us with your stories, thank you. And to all of those we interviewed for this book, your generosity of time and thought was profound, and we are grateful. To our colleagues who shared your experiences and insights, it was an honor working with you.

Pam would like to acknowledge her co-author, Bradie Hansen, for joining her in this project, for her many hours of research, and for her patience.

Bradie would like to thank Pamela Blair for asking her to co-write *The Long Grief Journey* and for giving her such an amazing opportunity. Your passion, humor, dedication, and generosity will always be remembered. What an incredible road we are on.

Works Consulted

Allende, Isabel. *The House of the Spirits*. New York: Bantam Books, 1986.

Atwoli, Lukoye, et al. "Posttraumatic Stress Disorder Associated with Unexpected Death of a Loved One: Cross-National Findings from the World Mental Health Surveys." *Depression and Anxiety*, vol. 34(4), 2017, pp. 315–326.

Baker, Barbara. "Art Speaks in Healing Survivors of War." *Journal of Aggression, Maltreatment & Trauma*, vol. 12:1–2, 2006, pp. 183–198.

Bauwens, Jennifer. "Losing a Family Member in an Act of Terror: A Review from the Qualitative Grey Literature on the Long-Term Effects of September 11, 2001." *Clinical Social Work Journal*, vol. 45, 2017, pp. 146–158.

Bellini, S., etal. "Depression, Hopelessness, and Complicated Grief in Survivors of Suicide." *Frontiers in Psychology*, vol. 9, 2018, pp. 1–6.

Boettger, Till. *Threshold Spaces: Transitions in Architecture: Analysis and Design Tools*. Basel: Birkhäuser, 2014.

Boss, Pauline. *Ambiguous Loss: Learning to Live with Unresolved Grief*. Cambridge, MA: Harvard University Press, 2000.

Boss Carnes. "The Myth of Closure." *Family Process* 51(4), 2012, pp. 456–469.

Bozarth, Alisha. December 23, 2018, *Widowhood Is More Than...*, Alisha Bozarth Books, https://alishabozarth.com/2018/12/23 /widowhood-is-more-than/.

Bowen, Murray. *Family Therapy in Clinical Practice.* Lanham, MD: Jason Aronson, Inc., 1993.

Bowlby, J. *Attachment and Loss: Volume III: Loss, Sadness and Depression.* The International Psycho-Analytical Library, v. 109: 1–462. London: The Hogarth Press and the Institute of Psycho-Analysis, 1980.

Bush, Ashley Davis, LICSW, *Transcending Loss*, New York: Berkley Publishing, 1997.

Broderick, Debra J., et al. "Lesbians Grieving the Death of a Partner: Recommendations for Practice." *Journal of Lesbian Studies*, vol. 12, (2–3), 2008, pp. 225–235.

Burke, L. A., and R. A. Neimeyer. "Complicated Spiritual Grief I: Relation to Complicated Grief Symptomatology Following Violent Death Bereavement." *Death Studies*, 38(4), 2014, pp. 259–267.

Cacciatore, Joanne, and John DeFrain. *The World of Bereavement: Cultural Perspectives on Death in Families.* 1st ed. New York: Springer International Publishing, 2015.

Carmassi, C., and M. Menichini, etal., "Panic-Agoraphobic Spectrum and Anxiety Separation Comorbidity in a Sample of Bereaved Individuals with Complicated Grief, PTSD and Healthy Controls." *European Psychiatry*, 29(S1), 2014, p. 1–1.

Carr, D. "Factors That Influence LateLife Bereavement: Considering Data From the Changing Lives of Older Couples Study," in *Handbook of Bereavement Research and Practice: Advances in Theory and*

Intervention. Washington, DC: American Psychological Association, 2008, pp. 417–440.

Cherry, Katie E. Traumatic Stress and Long-Term Recovery Coping with Disasters and Other Negative Life Events. 1st ed., 2015. New York, NY: Springer International Publishing, 2015.

Chödrön, Pema. *When Things Fall Apart.* Boston: Shambala Publications, Inc., 2000.

Chödrön, Pema. *Taking the Leap: Freeing Ourselves from Old Habits and Fears,* Boston: Shambala Publications, Inc., 2009.

Collins, Judy. *Sanity and Grace: A Journey of Suicide, Survival, and Strength.* New York: TarcherPerigee, 2006.

Costello J.., and K. Kendrick. "Grief and Older People: The Making or Breaking of Emotional Bonds following Partner Loss in Later Life." *Journal of Advanced Nursing,* 32(6), 2000.

Corr, Charles A. "Enhancing the Concept of Disenfranchised Grief." *OMEGA—Journal of Death and Dying,* vol. 38(1),1999, pp. 1–20.

Cox, Gerry R., etal, *Complicated Grieving and Bereavement: Understanding and Treating People Experiencing Loss.* Oxfordshire, UK: Taylor & Francis Group, 2000.

Dass, Ram, and Steve Levine. *Grist for the Mill: Awakening to Oneness.* New York: HarperCollins Publishers, 2013.

Didion, Joan. *The Year of Magical Thinking.* New York: Knopf Doubleday Publishing Group, 2007.

Diogenes Laërtius, *The Lives and Opinions of Eminent Philosophers.* Literally translated by C. D. Yonge; Henry G. Bohn, 1853 [Dicta attributed to Aristotle in *The Lives and Opinions of Eminent Philosophers* by Diogenes Laërtius].

Doka, K. J. "Disenfranchised Grief in Historical and Cultural Perspective". In M. S. Stroebe, R. O. Hansson, H. Schut, and W. Stroebe, eds., *Handbook of Bereavement Research and Practice: Advances in Theory and Intervention*, 2008, pp. 223–240. Washington, DC: American Psychological Association.

Eckholdt, Lena, et al. "Prolonged Grief Reactions after Old Age Spousal Loss and Centrality of the Loss in Post Loss Identity." *Journal of Affective Disorders*, vol. 227, 2018, pp. 338–344.

Edelman, Hope. *Motherless Daughters*. Boston: Addison-Wesley Publishing Co., 1994.

Ellard, C. "Look Up: The Surprising Joy of Raising Your Gaze." *Psychology Today*. July 29, 2016. https://www.psychologytoday.com/us/blog/mind-wandering/201607/look-the-surprising-joy-raising-your-gaze.

Essakow, K. L., and M. M. Miller, "Piecing Together the Shattered Heirloom: Parents' Experiences of Relationship Resilience After the Violent Death of a Child." *The American Journal of Family Therapy*, 41(4), 2013, pp. 299–310.

Fletcher, Emily. *Stress Less, Accomplish More: Meditation for Extraordinary Performance*. New York: William Morrow & Company, 2019.

Fogarty, James. *The Magical Thoughts of Grieving Children: Treating Children with Complicated Mourning and Advice for Parents*. Oxfordshire, UK: Taylor & Francis Group, 2000.

Forster, E. M . *A Room with a View*. New York: Penguin Classics, 2012.

Frankl, Viktor E. (Viktor Emil). *Man's Search for Meaning: An Introduction to Logotherapy*. Boston: Beacon Press, 1962.

Goss, R., and D. Klass. "Spiritual Bonds to the Dead in CrossCultural and Historical Perspective: Comparative Religion and Modern

Grief." *Death Studies*, vol. 23(6), 1999, pp. 547–567.

Green, L., and V. Grant. "Gagged Grief and Beleaguered Bereavements? An Analysis of Multidisciplinary Theory and Research Relating to Same Sex Partnership Bereavement." *Sexualities*, 11(3), 2008, pp. 275–300.

Gershman, Nancy, and Jenna Baddeley. "Prescriptive Photomontage: A Process and Product for Meaning-Seekers with Complicated Grief." *Annals*, Fall 2010, pp. 28–34, www.americanpsychotherapy.com.

Graham, Heather L. April 26, 2012, *The Day My Muse Died*. Musings from the Trenches, https://heatherlgraham.wordpress.com/2012/04/26/the-day-my-muse-died/.

Green, Lorraine, and Victoria Grant. "Gagged Grief and Beleaguered Bereavements?" An Analysis of Multidisciplinary Theory and Research Related to Same Sex Partnership Bereavement, *Sexualities*, vol. 11(3), 2008, pp. 275–300.

Guttenberg, Fred. *Find the Helpers: What 9/11 and Parkland Taught Me About Recovery, Purpose, and Hope*, Coral Gables, FL: Mango Publishing, 2020.

Harris, Maxine, PhD. *The Loss That Is Forever: The Lifelong Impact of the Death of a Mother or Father*. New York: Penguin Books, 1995.

Herberman Mash, B. Holly, et al. "Complicated Grief and Bereavement in Young Adults Following Close Friend and Sibling Loss." *Depression and Anxiety*, vol. 30(12), 2013, pp. 1202–1210.

Hood, Ann. *Comfort: A Journey Through Grief*. New York: W.W. Norton & Co., 2008.

Hsu, Albert Y. *Grieving a Suicide: A Loved One's Search for Comfort, Answers, and Hope*. Downers Grove, IL: Intervarsity Press, 2017.

Jancin, Bruce. "Complicated Grief Treatment May Beat Psychotherapy." *Clinical Psychiatry News*, vol. 45, no. 7, July 2017, p. 16. *Gale* com. ezproxy.gc.cuny.edu/apps/doc/A500682332/AONE?u=cuny _gradctr&sid=AONE&xid=095ca827. Accessed 26 May 2020.

Jones-Smith, Elsie, PhD. *Spotlighting the Strengths of Every Single Student: Why U.S. Schools Need a New, Strengths-Based Approach*, ABC-CLIO, LLC, 2011.

Kabat-Zinn, Jon. *Full Catastrophe Living: Using the Wisdom of Your Body and Mind to Face Stress, Pain, and Illness*. New York: Bantam Books, 2013.

Kay, Alan A. *A Jewish Book of Comfort*. Lanham, MD: Jason Aronson, Inc., 1993.

Keller, Helen. *We Bereaved*. London: Forgotten Books, 2017.

Klass, D., "Continuing Bonds, Society, and Human Experience: Family Dead, Hostile Dead, Political Dead." *OMEGA—Journal of Death and Dying*, 70(1), 2014, pp. 99–117.

Klass, D., "The Deceased Child in the Psychic and Social Worlds of Bereaved Parents During the Resolution of Grief." *Death Studies*, 21(2), 1997, pp. 147–175.

Klass, D. "A New Model of Grief from the English-Speaking World." The Institute for Palliative Psychology. April 13, 2022. https://www .academia.edu/1625789/A_New_Model_of_Grief_from_the _English_Speaking_World.

Klass, Dennis. "Sorrow and Solace: Neglected Areas in Bereavement Research." *Death Studies*, vol. 37(7), 2013, pp. 597–616.

Klass, D., and R. Goss, "Spiritual Bonds to the Dead in Cross Cultural and Historical Perspective: Comparative Religion and Modern Grief." *Death Studies*, 23(6), 1999, pp. 547–567.

Kessler, David. *Finding Meaning: The Sixth Stage of Grief.* New York: Scribner, 2019.

Krishnamurti, J. *Commentaries on Living 2.* Wheaton, IL: Quest Books, 1956.

Kubachy, Gretchen. *Moving Through Grief: Proven Techniques for Finding Your Way After Any Loss.* Emeryville, CA: Rockridge Press, 2019.

Kumar, Sameet M. *Grieving Mindfully.* Oakland, CA: New Harbinger Publications Inc., 2005.

Levy, Alexander. *The Orphaned Adult: Understanding and Coping With Grief and Change After the Death of Our Parents.* Lebanon, IN: Da Capo Lifelong Books, 2000.

Lewis, C. S. *A Grief Observed.* New York: HarperCollins Publishers, 2001.

Lighthorse, Pixie. *Prayers of Honoring Grief.* Redmond, OR: Lighthorse Publishing, 2018.

Herberman-Mash, H.B., C. S. Fullerton, and R. J. Ursano, "Complicated Grief and Bereavement in Young Adults Following Close Friend and Sibling Loss." *Depression and Anxiety*, 30, 2013, pp. 1202–1210.

Martin-Matthews, A. "Revisiting Widowhood in Later Life: Changes in Patterns and Profiles, Advances in Research and Understanding." *Canadian Journal on Aging*, 30, 2011, pp. 339–354.

McDevitt-Murphy, M. E., and E. Neimeyer. "The Toll of Traumatic Loss in African Americans Bereaved by Homicide." *Psychological Trauma* 4(3), 2012, pp. 303–311.

Merwin, W. S. *The Second Four Books of Poems.* Port Townsend, WA: Copper Canyon Press, 1993.

Milman, E., and R. A. Neimeyer. "Prolonged Grief Symptomatology Following Violent Loss: The Mediating Role of Meaning." *European*

Journal of Psychotraumatology 8(6), 2018, pp. 1503522–1503522.

Morin, Amy. *Grief Counseling for Children.* Very Well Family. April 20, 2021. https://www.verywellfamily.com/grief-counseling -for-children-4173493.

Morina, N., V. Rudari, G., Bleichhardt, and H. G. Prigerson.. "Prolonged Grief Disorder, Depression, and Posttraumatic Stress Disorder Among Bereaved Kosovar Civilian War Survivors: A Preliminary Investigation." *International Journal of Social Psychiatry,* 56(3), 2010, pp. 288–297.

Morris, Fletcher. "The Grief of Parents After the Death of a Young Child." *Journal of Clinical Psychology in Medical Settings,* vol. 26(3), 2018, pp. 321–338.

Nader, Kathleen, and Alison Salloum. "Complicated Grief Reactions in Children and Adolescents." *Journal of Child & Adolescent Trauma,* vol. 4(3), 2011, pp. 233–257.

Noel, Brook and Pamela D. Blair. *I Wasn't Ready to Say Goodbye: Surviving, Coping and Healing After the Sudden Loss of a Loved One.* Naperville, IL: Sourcebooks, Inc., 2008.

O'Donohue, John. *Eternal Echos: Celtic Reflections on Our Yearning to Belong.* New York: Perennial/HarperCollins, 2002.

O'Neill, Rhonda. *The Other Side of Complicated Grief: Hope in the Midst of Despair.* Wichita, KS: Saudade Publishing, 2016.

Osterweis, M., F. Solomon, and M. Green *Bereavement: Reactions, Consequences, and Care.* Committee for the Study of Health Consequences of the Stress of Bereavement. Institute of Medicine. Washington, DC: National Academy Press, 1992.

Ott, Carol H. "The Impact of Complicated Grief on Mental and Physical Health at Various Points in the Bereavement Process," *Death Studies,*

27(3): 249–272, 2003. https://doi.org/10.1080/07481180302887.

Papa, Anthony, and Nicole Lancaster. "Identity Continuity and Loss after Death, Divorce, and Job Loss." *Self and Identity*, vol. 15, no. 1, 2016, pp. 47–61.

Piatczanyn, Steven A., et al. "'We Were in a Partnership That Wasn't Recognized by Anyone Else': Examining the Effects of Male Gay Partner Bereavement, Masculinity, and Identity." *Men and Masculinities*, vol. 19, no. 2, 2016, pp. 167–191.

Pies, Ronald W. "Depression and the Pitfalls of Causality: Implications for the DSM-V," *Journal of Affective Disorders*, 116, 2009, pp. 1–3.

Prechtel, Martín. *The Smell of Rain on Dust: Grief and Praise*, Berkeley, CA: North Atlantic Books, 2015.

Progoff, Ira. *At a Journal Workshop: Writing to Access the Power of the Unconscious and Evoke Creative Ability*, New York: TarcherPerigee, 1992.

Prokos, Anastasia H., and Jennifer Reid Keene. "The Long-Term Effects of Spousal Care Giving on Survivors' Well-Being in Widowhood." *Social Science Quarterly*, vol. 86(3), 2005, pp. 664–682.

Rajkumar, Anto P, Titus Sp Mohan, and Prathap Tharyan. "Lessons from the 2004 Asian Tsunami: Nature, Prevalence and Determinants of Prolonged Grief Disorder among Tsunami Survivors in South Indian Coastal Villages." International Journal of Social Psychiatry 61(7), 2015, pp. 645–652.

Rando, Therese A. *How to Go on Living When Someone You Love Dies*, New York: Bantam Books, 1991.

Rajkumar, Anto P, Titus SP Mohan, and Prathap Tharyan. "Lessons from the 2004 Asian Tsunami: Nature, Prevalence and Determinants of

Prolonged Grief Disorder Among Tsunami Survivors in South Indian Coastal Villages." *International Journal of Social Psychiatry* 61(7), 2015, pp. 645–652.

Rich, Phil. *The Healing Journey Through Grief: Your Journal for Reflection and Recovery.* Hoboken, NJ: John Wiley and Sons, Inc., 1999.

Robinaugh, D. J., N. J., LeBlanc, H. A. Vuletich, and R. J. McNally. "Network Analysis of Persistent Complex Bereavement Disorder in Conjugally Bereaved Adults." *Journal of Abnormal Psychology,* 123(3), 2014, pp. 510–522.

Roe, Gary. *Aftermath: Picking Up the Pieces After a Suicide.* College Station, TX: Healing Resources Publishing, 2019.

Rossheim, B. N., and C. R. McAdams III. "Addressing the Chronic Sorrow of LongTerm Spousal Caregivers: A Primer for Counselors." *Journal of Counseling and Development,* 88(4), 2010, pp. 477–482.

Rynearson, E. "The Clergy, the Clinician, and the Narrative of Violent Death." *Pastoral Psychology,* 59(2), 2010, pp. 179–189.

Satir, Virginia. Workshop sponsored by the Glendale Humanistic Psychology Center and the California Hispanic Psychological Association at the Ambassador Hotel, Los Angeles, California, February 1986.

Saul, Jack, and Saliha Bava. "Implementing collective approaches to massive trauma/loss in Western contexts: Implications for recovery, peacebuilding and development." *Trauma, Development and Peacebuilding Conference,* New Delhi, India, September 2008.

Saul, Jack. *Collective Trauma, Collective Healing,* New York: Routledge Taylor Francis Group, 2014.

Schulz, Richard, et al. *Caregiving and Bereavement.* American Psychological Association, 2008, pp. 265–285.

Schupp, Linda J, Grief: Normal, Complicated, Traumatic, Eau Claire, WI: PESI, 2007.

Shannon, Ellen Brett D. Wilkinson. "The Ambiguity of Perinatal Loss: A Dual-Process Approach to Grief Counseling," *Journal of Mental Health Counseling*, vol. 42(2), 2020, pp. 140–154.

Shear, Katherine. "Complicated Grief." *The New England Journal of Medicine*, vol. 372(2), 2015, pp. 153–160.

Shear, Katherine, etal. "Optimizing Treatment of Complicated Grief: A Randomized Clinical Trial, *JAMA Psychiatry*, 73(7), 2016, pp. 685–694.

Shear, Katherine, etal. "Treatment of Complicated Grief: A Randomized Controlled Trial," *JAMA*, 293(21), 2005, pp. 2601–2608.

Shear, Katherine, etal. "Treatment of Complicated Grief in Elderly Persons: A Randomized Clinical Trial, *JAMA Psychiatry*, 71(11), 2014, pp. 1287–1295.

Smith, Claire, LCPC. Anxiety: *The Missing Stage of Grief: A Revolutionary Approach to Understanding and Healing the Impact of Loss*, Lebanon, IN: Da Capo Lifelong Books, 2018.

Smolowe, Jill. 2016, August 9. *The Life-Challenging Anguish of Tidying Up*, Next Avenue. https://www.nextavenue.org /possessions-after-loved-ones-death/.

Sparks, Nicholas. *The Choice*, New York: Grand Central Publishing, 2009.

St. Germain, Sheryl. *50 Miles*, Wilkes-Barre, PA: Etruscan Press, 2020.

Steffen, Edith M., and Dennis Klass, "Culture, Contexts and Connections: a Conversation with Dennis Klass About His Life and Work as a Bereavement Counselor," *Mortality*, 23(3), 2018, pp. 203–214.

Stroebe, M. S ., R. O., Hansson, H. Schut, and W. Stroebe, eds. *Handbook of*

Bereavement Research and Practice: Advances in Theory and Intervention, American Psychological Association, 2008.

Supiano, Katherine P., et al. "Sudden-On-Chronic Death and Complicated Grief in Bereaved Dementia Caregivers: Two Case Studies of Complicated Grief Group Therapy." *Journal of Social Work in End-of-Life & Palliative Care,* vol. 11(3–4), 2015, pp. 267–282.

UNODC, Global Study on Homicide, 2019 (Vienna 2019). https://www.unodc.org/unodc/en/data-and-analysis/global-study-on-homicide.html.

Üstündağ-Budak, Larkin. "Mothers' Accounts of Their Stillbirth Experiences and of Their Subsequent Relationships with Their Living Infant: An Interpretative Phenomenological Analysis." *BMC Pregnancy and Childbirth* 15(1), 2015, pp. 263–263.

VanDerKamp, Tim. "Assimilation and Integration of Grief." *Grace Yoga + Pilates.* 2016. https://choosegrace.org/blog_post/assimilation-and-integration/.

Vaudoise, Mallorie. *Honoring Your Ancestors: A Guide to Ancestral Veneration.* Woodbury, MN: Llewellyn Publications, 2020.

Verdery, Ashton M., Emily Smith-Greenawa, Rachel Margolis, and Jonathan Daw. Tracking the reach of COVID-19 kin loss with a bereavement multiplier applied to the United States. https://doi.org/10.1073/pnas.2007476117.

Wall-Wieler, Elizabeth, et al. "Duration of Maternal Mental Health-Related Outcomes after an Infant's Death: A Retrospective Matched Cohort Study Using Linkable Administrative Data." *Depression and Anxiety,* vol. 35(4), 2018, pp. 305–312.

Welshons, John E. *Awaking from Grief.* Maui, HI: Inner Ocean Publishing, 2003.

White, Craig, A. *Living with Complicated Grief*. London: Sheldon Press, 2013.

Wilder, Thorton. *The Bridge of San Luis Rey*. New York: Harper Perennial Modern Classics, 2003.

Willis, Clarissa A. "The Grieving Process in Children: Strategies for Understanding, Educating, and Reconciling Children's Perceptions of Death." *Early Childhood Education Journal*, vol. 29(4), 2002, pp. 221–226.

Williams, Joah L., et al. "Experiential Avoidance Moderates the Association between Motivational Sensitivity and Prolonged Grief but Not Posttraumatic Stress Symptoms." *Psychiatry Research*, vol. 273, 2019, pp. 336–342.

Williams, Joah L., et al. "Prevalence and Correlates of Suicidal Ideation in a Treatment-Seeking Sample of Violent Loss Survivors." *Crisis*, 39(5), 2018, pp. 377–385.

Withrow, R. and V. L. Schwiebert. "Twin Loss: Implications for Counselors Working with Surviving Twins." *Journal of Counseling & Development*, 83(1), 2005, pp. 21–28.

Wolfelt, Alan. *Reframing PTSD as Traumatic Grief: How Caregivers Can Companion Traumatized Grievers through Catch-up Mourning*. Fort Collins, CO: Companion Press, 2015.

Wolfelt, Alan. *The Depression of Grief: Coping with Your Sadness and Knowing When to Get Help*, Fort Collins, CO: Companion Press, 2014.

Wolfelt, Alan. *When Grief Is Complicated: A Model for Therapists to Understand, Identify, and Companion Grievers Lost in the Wilderness of Complicated Grief*. Fort Collins, CO: Companion Press, 2018.

Wong, Brittany. "What Is Toxic Positivity?" Huffington Post. 2020. https://

www.huffpost.com/entry/what-is-toxic-positivity-coronavirus_l_5f0 4bca0c5b67a80bbff7cd3.

Worden, J. William. *Grief Counseling and Grief Therapy: A Handbook for the Mental Health Practitioner.* New York: Springer Publishing Company, 1982.

Wray, T.J. *Surviving the Death of a Sibling: Living Through Grief When an Adult Brother or Sister Dies.* Lagos, Nigeria: Harmony, 2003.

Yalom, Irvin D. *When Nietzsche Wept.* New York: HarperPerennial, 1993.

WEBSITES

US Department of Veteran Affairs: https://www.ptsd.va.gov/understand /what/ptsd_basics.asp

Center for Disease Control: https://www.cdc.gov/nchs /fastats/homicide.htm

The United States Department of Justice: https://www.justice.gov /hatecrimes/hate-crime-statistics

National Endowment for the Arts: Creative Forces: NEA Military Healing Arts Network: https://www.arts.gov/initiatives/creative-forces

National Highway Safety Administration: https://www.nhtsa.gov /traffic-deaths-2018

Appendix

RESOURCES TO CONSIDER

Seeking Medical or Therapeutic Help

When should I go to the doctor?

With long-term grief, it might be hard for you to pinpoint specific things that a doctor can help with, but ask yourself this: "Is how I'm living my life now good for my health?" Further questions might be: "Am I depressed? Am I anxious? Am I drinking too much? Have I gained or lost a lot of weight? Does my body hurt?" As part of a yearly check-up or a singular appointment, these are good things for your doctor to know about and they can talk with you about different options available when it comes to making informed choices about your health care.

Go to your appointment with a list of things that have been of concern to you. In the days or weeks leading up to your appointment, keep track of what you experience. Break this list into three areas: behavioral, emotional, physical. You can also mention to your doctor that you've been reflecting on the impact of grief in your life and would like to take measured steps on regaining (or gaining for the first time) health and balance.

In your list, include things like:

Behavioral

- Sleep patterns: How much each night? Is it restorative?
- Eating habits: Too much? Too little? Balanced?
- Alcohol consumption amounts (and if you have concerns about it)
- Other recreational drug use
- Friendships and social interaction: Do you see people? Too much? Too little?
- Driving habits: Are they safe?
- Hobbies: Do you have any? Do you wish you did?
- Exercise: How much do you exercise in a given week?

Emotional

Which of the following emotions are you feeling?

- Balanced/Neutral
- Tearful
- Worried/Anxious
- Angry
- Cranky or Short-tempered
- Out of character in any way

- Overwhelmed
- Avoidant or wish to isolate
- Flat/disinterested
- Ruminating on things like painful memories, arguments, regrets
- Self-consciousness
- Absent minded, distracted, forgetful

Physical

Are you feeling any of the following physical symptoms?

- Body aches and pains
- Headaches
- Soreness in joints
- General feeling of being unwell
- Run down
- Rashes
- Weight gain or weight loss
- Feeling of racing heart
- Sense of feeling faint

What kind of therapy is right for me?

Therapy is available in many forms. Some are covered by insurance, some are not, so it's important to do your research. Many people do quite well when they've taken the time to consider what type of therapy is the best fit for their situation and personality.

Mental health care and types of therapies

- **Individual**

  Individual therapy is just as it sounds. You will meet with a qualified professional with the idea of talking about what is on your mind. The therapist might be a psychologist, a mental health counselor, a licensed clinical social worker, a pastoral counselor, or a psychoanalyst. Typically, people are drawn to practice in ways that are most congruent with their personality and with their belief system as it relates to how people heal. What you bring to talk about will be held in confidence as a matter of ethics and law, and the space is for you to unpack all of what you want and need to. Sometimes one kind of work is good for some things while another kind of work is good for something else. You don't need to have the idea that everything will get wrapped up in one round of therapy. There's nothing wrong with you if you do it for a while, take a break, then go back to do more work either with the same person or someone else who works differently.

- **Group**

  Group therapy is led by a trained mental health practitioner. There are closed groups and open groups. Closed groups have a set number of members and the same people attend each week (or however often the group meets). When members do leave the group, or new members enter, it is done with care. Open groups are open to any who want to attend. Configurations can change from session to session and therefore, there tends to be less processing of what happens between group members.

Groups usually are formed around a particular issue, like grief and bereavement, relationship issues, addiction, emotional regulation, and parenting. Many find group work to be very helpful because they can be with other people who are struggling with similar issues. Nothing needs explaining because people get it.

- **Family**

In family therapy, typically every member of the immediate family unit meets with a therapist who is trained to work with the complexities of family dynamics. People choose to do this kind of work when they become aware that there are issues playing out between at least two members of a close family system. You can be sure that anything powerful that is playing out between two members of a family is affecting and involving the rest of the family, and sometimes working through the conflicts and learning how to manage oneself can help shift the whole system into greater functioning. Like any therapy, there are different styles of family work. Inquiring with trusted friends, your doctor, or even your hospital chaplain could turn up good referrals.

- **Couples**

  Couples therapy is when just the bonded pair meets with a trained professional to work through issues that prove difficult to sort out on their own. Even the strongest of couples needs support sometimes when the trials, stresses, and traumas of life knock this love relationship about. Couples' therapists are trained to help people get clear on what is taking place, take ownership for themselves and their emotional well-being, and identify ways to move forward. They can also hold space for a couple to fully express their grief and pain and help the couple to see their partner clearly. Couples therapy is often helpful for those who are struggling with parenting issues, as well.

- **Child and Adolescent Therapy**

  There are therapists specifically trained to work with children and adolescents. Often, children need a place where their behaviors can be understood and interpreted so that first, they can understand themselves, and so that parents and schools can respond appropriately. Also, just as it is useful for adults to have a place to say whatever is on their mind, so it is for children and teens. Generally, children's therapists use some form of play therapy and are very skilled at meeting children where they are. They use play as the tool to be with, observe, and interpret what is going on for a child. It might be too difficult or impossible for a child to come in and sit down and say all of what is on their mind, but in play, they might enact a loss, demonstrate frustration and anger, or create images of fear, loneliness and longing. The older a child gets and the more they are able to describe feeling with language, the more they are able to participate in more traditional forms of talk therapy.

How do I pick a style of therapy?

It can be a daunting experience, saddling up to therapy if it has not been a part of your life. First, a few things to know and remember: you are the consumer, and you get to choose who and what feels comfortable. For any type of therapy, you want to ensure that who you are going to is well-trained, or, if in training, is being supervised by someone with experience and oversight. Usually, this will be covered in any initial paperwork. If it isn't, you can ask the given therapist what their experience is, how they work, and what you might expect from the experience. Some therapies lend themselves to long-term, open-ended work, while others are issue - specific and tend to occur either less frequently or over a shorter span of time.

It is also important to know that you don't have to only choose one over the course of a life, and, in fact, some types of therapeutic work can overlap, like acupuncture and psychodynamic therapy. What's most important is that you find someone you feel comfortable with and who is competent. Research has shown time and time again that the single most important aspect of good therapeutic outcome is the therapist–client rapport. If that is solid, a lot of good work can happen.

A note about words: you will see in your search for a therapist different titles such as: psychologist, mental health counselor, licensed clinical social worker, practitioner, master, PhD, analyst, psychotherapist, and coach. All of these names describe a type and level of education and training. In most, if not all, states it is required that anyone providing mental health services be registered with the state and they must follow the rules and regulations that both the state and their profession have.

Helpful Websites

Grief Support

What's Your Grief

This is a robust site that focuses on supporting the griever as well as those who are helping grievers on their long journey. It's filled with resources, training opportunities, a blog, a podcast, and other materials.

> whatsyourgrief.com

Grieving.com

This is a forum filled with conversations surrounding all kinds of grief.

> grieving.com

Suicide Support

Alliance of Hope for Suicide Loss Survivors

This website is dedicated to those suffering from grief due to a loved one dying by suicide. Resources include support groups, readings, information of professionals on how to better help their clients who are grieving, help for those who have lost loved ones in the military, and personal reflections from survivors.

> allianceofhope.org

Natural Disaster Support

Substance Abuse and Mental Health Services Administration (SAMSA)

This organization is part of the US Department of Health and Human Services and is replete with information on how to access mental health and/or substance use support. They share resources for both practitioners serving their community as well as survivors of natural disasters, among other things.

> samhsa.gov

American Red Cross

The American Red Cross is an agency that responds to all kind of emergency situations and has an incredible amount of information for people seeking support, including mental health support, following natural disasters.

> redcross.org

Addiction Support

Alcoholics Anonymous

Useful for anyone concerned about their own drinking or looking toward sobriety and would like to pursue the twelve-step program.

> aa.org

Al-Anon

Geared toward those who are in a relationship with someone who struggles with addiction or abusive use of substances. It has resources that help people find local meetings as well as online.

> al-anon.org

Narcotics Anonymous

For anyone looking for help with an addiction to any narcotic. There are guides for finding meetings, readings, and information for family and friends as well as professionals looking to better support their clients.

> na.org

Gray Area Drinking

Supportive and informational site for anyone who is thinking about their drinking and might be concerned about their alcohol use.

> grayareadrinkers.com

Tempest

This site is devoted to helping people explore their relationship with alcohol.

> jointempest.com

Specific Therapies

Ambiguous Loss

"Ambiguous loss" is a term coined by Pauline Boss, who has developed and now teaches, lectures, and writes about therapy geared toward this specific kind of grieving. While this site does not have a list of therapists specializing in ambiguous loss, it has resources listed that might be useful for grievers and practitioners.

> ambiguousloss.com

The Columbia Center for Complicated Grief

M. Katherine Shear, MD, is the director of the Columbia Center for Complicated Grief. She has researched extensively in the field of prolonged grief and the center is devoted to helping the public and practitioners identify and treat long-term grief.

> complicatedgrief.columbia.edu

Organic Intelligence

For anyone looking to tend to their nervous systems and heal from trauma, this site will be incredibly helpful. Steve Hoskinson developed Organic Intelligence to help people find within themselves their own healing potential. There are ways to interact with and learn from the site as well as opportunities to participate in online workshops, classes, and ongoing trainings.

> organicintelligence.org

Psychology Today

This site is a great way for people to find therapists in their area. Every therapist on this site lists their bio, particular specialties, and insurance/payment information. People can reach out directly to therapists through this site, making it easier to connect with someone to check on availability. The site has other useful information to do with self-care and mental health as well.

> psychologytoday.com

Loss of a Child

The Compassionate Friends

For anyone in a family who has lost a child, including parents, siblings, and grandparents. With chapters all over the world, their dedication to healing in community and with support is clear.

> compassionatefriends.org

Miss Foundation: A Community of Compassion and Hope for Grieving Families

This site has online and face-to-face support, education,

resources for researchers, and support people. Their programming includes help for all bereaved, including parents, siblings, and grandparents. They also have Selah Care Farm with a special focus on the healing benefits of connecting with animals.

> missfoundation.org

Accidental Death

Accidental Impacts

This site is for people who have caused accidental death or injury and are struggling in the aftermath of this unique kind of grief. Access to peer support, opportunities to write, links to helpful sites to find therapists, and other support, as well as the language that is unique to this kind of grieving.

> accidentalimpacts.org

PTSD Support

EMDR International Association

Eye Movement Desensitization and Reprocessing (EMDR) is a therapy designed to help people who suffer from trauma and post-traumatic stress disorder (PTSD) as well as other mental health disorders and struggles. This website is geared toward helping people find therapists who are trained to practice EMDR.

> emdria.org

Daily Strength—Posttraumatic Stress Disorder Support Group

A place where people can find support for their struggles with post-traumatic stress and engage in dialogue with a community that understands the complexities of living with trauma.

> dailystrength.org

Disenfranchised Grief

Online Grief Support—A Social Community

This is a robust online grief support page that has a specific group just for disenfranchised grief. This is a peer-support rather than a therapist-supported page.

> onlinegriefsupport.com

Loss of a Pet

The Pet Loss Support Page

This site is filled with information about pet loss and grief as well as links to services state by state for local support. Much of the information is geared toward recent pet loss, but you'll also find good advice and wisdom.

> pet-loss.net

Mental Health Information and Support

Asian Mental Health Project (AMHP)
This site is devoted to reducing stigma around mental health struggles in Asian communities. Readers will find educational information, support, and clear information on finding a therapist as well as links that help with that process.

> asianmentalhealthproject.com

National Alliance on Mental Illness (NAMI)
NAMI is an advocacy organization that works to support, educate, and raise awareness about mental health issues to elevate the quality of life for those struggling with mental illness.

> nami.org

Inclusive Therapists—A Safer, Simpler Way to Find Care
This site is dedicated to helping marginalized people find therapeutic care in a way that is safe, supportive, and informed. Central are black, indigenous, and people of color and people anywhere on the spectrum of gender and sexual identity. Also served are neurodiverse individuals.

> inclusivetherapists.com

Index

B

C

D

E

H

R

S

W

Y

About the Authors

Pamela D. Blair, PhD, (pamblair-books.com) was a psychotherapist for thirty years. She is the co-author of *I Wasn't Ready to Say Goodbye* (Sourcebooks) now considered a classic in bereavement literature. She is also the author of *The Next Fifty Years: A Guide for Women at Midlife and Beyond* (Hampton Roads/Red Wheel) and *Getting Older, Better* (Hampton Roads/Red Wheel). She has appeared on national television, been a guest on dozens of radio shows, and has spoken at the Virginia Festival of the Book, the Vermont Women's Expo, Women's Images Conferences, *Menopause The Musical*, The Transition Network, the 92nd Street Y, Full Circle Conference and various institutions around the country including the NY Open Center, Wainwright

House and the Interface Institute in Massachusetts, and will appear in a television special entitled "Widowsville" (in production). Although she is currently retired from private practice, she is active in the community where she speaks to various organizations, facilitates a group for women writers and meta-physicians, mentors in the school system, and has completed her first novel. She lives in Shelburne, Vermont with her husband and two mischievous cats.

Bradie McCabe Hansen, M.A., is a clinical psychologist in private practice who has been working with children, adolescents, and adults for over twenty years. Bradie is also a fiber artist and crafter and teaches children and adults about the wonderful world of handcrafting, both for its creative and healing possibilities. She is certified as an archetypal pattern analyst through the Assisi Institute and is a *Weaving a Life*™ leader. Fiber art has become an integral way that she works with people who are interested in visually expressing their lived experience. She lives in Shelburne, Vermont with her husband, two children, one dog, and two cats.